DS63.2.U5 C28 2012
The Gulf :
33663005292087
EVC

 **W9-AUY-114**

# DATE DUE

# The Gulf

# THE GULF

## The Bush Presidencies and the Middle East

MICHAEL F. CAIRO

UNIVERSITY PRESS OF KENTUCKY

Copyright © 2012 by The University Press of Kentucky

Scholarly publisher for the Commonwealth,
serving Bellarmine University, Berea College, Centre College of Kentucky,
Eastern Kentucky University, The Filson Historical Society, Georgetown
College, Kentucky Historical Society, Kentucky State University, Morehead
State University, Murray State University, Northern Kentucky University,
Transylvania University, University of Kentucky, University of Louisville,
and Western Kentucky University.
All rights reserved.

*Editorial and Sales Offices:* The University Press of Kentucky
663 South Limestone Street, Lexington, Kentucky 40508–4008
www.kentuckypress.com

16  15  14  13  12      5  4  3  2  1

Maps by Dick Gilbreath, University of Kentucky Cartography Lab.

Library of Congress Cataloging-in-Publication Data

Cairo, Michael F., 1970-
The Gulf : the Bush presidencies and the Middle East / Michael F. Cairo.
   p. cm.
Includes bibliographical references and index.
ISBN 978-0-8131-3672-1 (hardcover : alk. paper) —
ISBN 978-0-8131-3673-8 (pdf) — ISBN 978-0-8131-4074-2 (epub)
   1. Middle East—Foreign relations—United States. 2. United States—Foreign
relations—Middle East. 3. United States—Foreign relations—1989-1993.
4. United States—Foreign relations—2001-2009. 5. Bush, George, 1924-
6. Bush, George W. (George Walker), 1946-  7. Arab-Israeli conflict. 8. Persian
Gulf War, 1991. 9. Iraq War, 2003-2011. I. Title.
   DS63.2.U5C28 2012
   327.7305609'049—dc23                                    2012029586

This book is printed on acid-free paper meeting the requirements of the
American National Standard for Permanence in Paper for Printed Library
Materials.

♾

Manufactured in the United States of America.

Member of the Association of
American University Presses

For Carey, Maxwell, and Sophia

This is an historic moment. . . . We have before us the opportunity to forge for ourselves and for future generations a new world order— a world where the rule of law, not the law of the jungle, governs the conduct of nations. When we are successful, and we will be, we have a real chance at this new world order, an order in which a credible United Nations can use its peacekeeping role to fulfill the promise and vision of the U.N.'s founders.

—George H. W. Bush, January 16, 1991

This young century will be liberty's century. By promoting liberty abroad, we will build a safer world. By encouraging liberty at home, we will build a more hopeful America. Like generations before us, we have a calling from beyond the stars to stand for freedom. This is the everlasting dream of America.

—George W. Bush, September 2, 2004

# Contents

# Maps

# Preface

Arguably, the Middle East is the most important region in the world. Its history is ancient and since ancient times, the Middle East has been at the center of world affairs. It is located at the juncture of Eurasia and Africa, connecting societies and cultures. It is the birthplace of the world's earliest civilizations. It is also the origin of the world's three major monotheistic religions—Judaism, Christianity, and Islam. All of this has combined to make the region politically, economically, strategically, culturally, and religiously significant.

The American entrance onto the world stage after World War I meant that the Middle East would become a high priority for American policy makers as the United States thrust itself into the great power struggles of the region. It wasn't until after World War II, however, that American foreign policy was permanently wedded to events in the Middle East. World War II demonstrated the region's geopolitical significance, and policy makers aimed to ensure that the territory and its resources remained available to the United States and its allies. With the emergence of the cold war and the creation of Israel, American policy makers raised the significance of the Middle East to new heights. Ever since that time, the Middle East has been at the center of American foreign policy, and American interests have been intertwined with the politics of the region in times of war and peace.

Like previous presidents, George H. W. Bush and George W. Bush found that the Middle East played an important role in their foreign policies. Both presidents engaged in the politics of war and peace in the region, discovering that the Middle East could determine the success or failure of an American presidency and its historical legacy; in fact, both presidencies revealed the ways in which the region could define a presidency.

The research for this book began with these two premises: the significance of the Middle East to world affairs and the significance of the

Middle East to the defining legacies of the presidencies of George H. W. Bush and George W. Bush. It began many years ago at the University of Virginia, where my dissertation focused on the role of the George H. W. Bush administration at the end of the cold war; significantly, that dissertation focused only one chapter on the events in the Middle East. However, hindsight is twenty-twenty, and as events unfolded in the early part of the twenty-first century, it became increasingly clear that reviving my earlier research on the George H. W. Bush administration was warranted. More important, the comparisons and contrasts being drawn between the George H. W. Bush and George W. Bush administrations by scholars, journalists, and laypeople raised important questions that were receiving only superficial discussion.

I undertook this endeavor to investigate both general and specific questions surrounding these debates and discussions. First, was the George W. Bush administration merely "Act II" of the George H. W. Bush administration? In what ways was it a continuation, if at all? In what ways was it new? No place stood out as more significant in answering these questions than the Middle East. George H. W. Bush and George W. Bush both engaged in war in the region; more notably, both engaged in war with Iraq. In addition, both undertook attempts at peace in the region.

Second, what can we learn from the comparison of the George H. W. Bush and George W. Bush administrations' policies in the Middle East? Were these two administrations anomalies? In examining these two administrations, and more specifically these two presidents, we are given a window into presidential decision making. Studying presidential decision making in foreign policy crises provides lessons for wider understandings of presidential decision making and leadership. Ultimately, this book is about more than the George H. W. Bush and George W. Bush policies in the Middle East; it is about their decision-making styles and worldviews, and the significance of decision-making styles and worldviews to presidential actions in any administration.

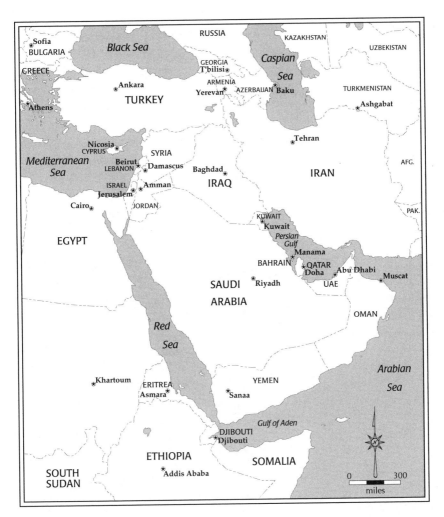

The contemporary Middle East

# Introduction

Prior to 2000, the casual observer of politics might have named the Kennedys as the most important contemporary American political dynasty. However, with the election of George W. Bush to the presidency, eight years after his father had held the office, no one could deny the power and influence of the Bush family on the American political scene. Both Bushes left a significant foreign policy legacy; both led the country into wars that would come to define the post–cold war era. And yet, these presidencies were very different, particularly in their conduct of foreign policy; the idea that George W. Bush's presidency was a continuation of George H. W. Bush's was quickly dispelled. What, then, are we to make of these two presidents, particularly in foreign policy, the area in which, arguably, each left an indelible mark?

The twelve years of the George H. W. Bush and George W. Bush presidencies brought monumental changes to the world stage and highlighted important differences in policy, warranting a comparison. The changes that took place from 1989 to 1993 and from 2001 to 2009, and the Bush presidencies' responses to them, were dramatic and consequential. Their effects did and will continue to impact international relations for some time. A complex combination of factors shaped American foreign policy during these periods. Among them are the personalities, beliefs, and values of George H. W. Bush and George W. Bush; the foreign policy leadership style of each president; and the traumatic global events that dictated action. While the trajectory of world events in each of these presidencies is significant, this volume focuses on the personalities and leadership styles of the two presidents as the most important factors in determining the foreign policies of their administrations.

The thesis of this book is that personal beliefs and character in the presidency matter in the determination of foreign policy. The way both Bush administrations responded to the global changes taking place was a result of how each President Bush, and a small number of his advisors, defined those events. With the election of George W. Bush to the presidency in 2000, much was made of the return of familiar faces to the White House, including many foreign policy advisors who had been present in the first Bush administration, notably Richard B. Cheney, Colin Powell, and Condoleezza Rice. This prompted the question of whether the younger Bush intended a regeneration of the foreign policy of the George H. W. Bush administration. This idea was quickly rejected, as the George W. Bush administration pursued policies that were in stark contrast to the earlier Bush administration. Ultimately, the differences between these two presidencies were more significant than their similarities, and this book suggests that the most important difference lay in the personalities of the men at the top, George H. W. and George W. Bush, especially regarding their conduct of foreign policy and their definition of American interests in the world. The title of this book, *The Gulf,* alludes to this difference; while the Gulf denotes an important region of the Middle East, it also denotes the differences between these two presidents.

Both presidents held office at a time when the power to define the international scene was facilitated by rapid changes and crises, which gave their administrations exceptional ability to shape circumstances and guide American foreign policy. Occupying the presidency as the cold war came to an end, George H. W. Bush had the opportunity to guide American foreign policy into a new era. The political transition taking place throughout Western and Eastern Europe, and in American relations with the Soviet Union, gave the president an ability to define the "new world order" that was emerging and the American approach to that new order. Likewise, George W. Bush's response to the terrorist attacks on September 11, 2001, led to the adoption of his vision for American foreign policy. Much can be said of the success and effectiveness of George H. W. Bush's approach at the end of the cold war, but there is heated debate over the impact of George W. Bush's policy. I side with those who suggest that negative consequences emerged as a result of American actions during the latter period, and George W. Bush's success in accomplishing his goals must be measured against the effects of his policies.

In particular, George H. W. Bush's and George W. Bush's disparate character and personalities were of utmost significance in their decisions to pursue war and peace. As Stanley Renshon has written, "By examining the range of choices available to the president, as well as those he selects, both within and across circumstances, one can begin to discern the underlying patterns . . . that [shape] his behavior. . . . Character shapes beliefs, information processing, and, ultimately, styles of behavior."[1] Too often, scholars overlook the individual personalities and beliefs of a president, instead favoring institutional factors as the primary shapers of policy outcomes.[2] However, the individual occupying the Oval Office is vastly more important than many conventional views portray. Presidents are endowed with different assets and liabilities, strengths and weaknesses. Understanding the worldview of a president, thus, is highly significant.

In the case of the two George Bushes, their beliefs and personalities mattered to the extent that they had a significant impact on the foreign policy decisions of their administrations. Their beliefs ultimately established the path of their administrations and guided foreign policy. As Alexander George explains, "It is important for scholars who are interested in developing policy-relevant knowledge not to over-intellectualize policy-making by assuming that it is or should be devoted exclusively to identifying and choosing high-quality policy options based on the criterion of analytic rationality."[3] In investigating the two George Bushes, one is left with an interesting contrast that demonstrates the significance of George's statement.

## "Enlightened" Realism vs. "Cowboy" Liberalism

In his book *Logics of American Foreign Policy: Theories of America's World Role,* Patrick Callahan argues that "clashes of interpretation are foundational to all important debates over foreign policy."[4] He goes on to explain that foreign policy logics, "stripped down ideolog[ies] or worldview[s]," determine foreign policy purposes, national interests, the nature and use of power in the international system, and the role of morality in American foreign policy. Callahan constructs six "logics" of American foreign policy: hegemonism, realism, isolationism, liberalism, liberal internationalism, and radical anti-imperialism. While these "logics" are useful to our understanding of the foreign policy of the two George Bushes, both Bushes remain difficult to categorize according to Callahan's six types.

George H. W. Bush most closely fits the logic of realism; however, his pursuit of multilateral solutions to problems and his desire to work through international institutions more closely reflects Callahan's description of liberal internationalism. As a result, I compound the categories and categorize George H. W. Bush as an "enlightened" realist, borrowing the phrase from his national security advisor, Brent Scowcroft. Likewise, George W. Bush fails to adequately fit into one of Callahan's categories. While he most closely resembles a hegemonist, his desire to expand American democracy and its values and his presumption that the United States has a moral obligation to fulfill this goal fit more succinctly into Callahan's liberal logic. Thus, I suggest that George W. Bush is a "cowboy" liberal; this label also fits well with his self-identification with the values of Midland, Texas (see chapter 1). This characterization of George W. Bush might come as a surprise, since he was identified as a conservative and his advisors as neoconservatives. However, neither the conservative nor neoconservative label accurately describes the entirety of George W. Bush's thinking. Since the conservative position often includes isolationism, the conservative label is particularly problematic in this instance. George W. Bush's emphasis on democracy as a source of peace is more aptly characterized as liberal thinking. Furthermore, the neoconservative label is problematic since it was developed during the late 1960s, and in the 1970s its adherents exhibited skepticism toward democracy promotion; as a result, much of the neoconservative ideology fails to explain George W. Bush's views and actions. The characterization of George W. Bush as a cowboy liberal, thus, illustrates the difficulty of neat categorizations and highlights the nuances of George W. Bush's worldview.

The fact that the two men do not adequately fit into theoretical categories is not surprising. As Senator John Kerry argued during the 2004 presidential campaign, American "foreign policy has achieved greatness . . . only when it has combined realism and idealism."[5] Kerry's observation gets to the heart of the problem—politicians rarely fit into simple categories, nor are these categories adequate for explaining every aspect of their foreign policy. They, like all of us, are complex and multifaceted individuals. As a result, the vast majority of our presidents have combined elements of different categorical labels in the practice of foreign policy. Most significant, while many presidents have contained elements of liberal and realist approaches, it is the different emphases within these approaches that can produce and help to explain vastly different results. Therefore, while both George Bushes can be categorized as realists, they also can be categorized as liberals; however, the differences within each approach explain the different outcomes in their policies.

### Bush vs. Bush

To begin to understand the approaches of these two presidents, we must first understand the approaches of the realist and the liberal. Realism is the dominant paradigm of international relations. According to the realist approach, the nature of international politics has remained rather constant throughout the millennia. The realist policy maker stresses the virtues of diplomacy over moralism, political flexibility over ideological rigidity. Like George Kennan, a leading authority and diplomat of the early cold war, the realist policy maker is "alive to the possibilities of diplomatic maneuver while at the same time aware of the limitations imposed by history and the national interest."[6] Henry Kissinger, another prominent realist policy maker, argued for a greater appreciation and application of American power on the global stage. Most significant, Kissinger suggested that the United States possessed a naïve attitude toward power, a naïveté demonstrated by its continued belief in reforming the international system. Rather, Kissinger suggested, the United States must act prudently, with great attention given to the national interest.[7]

For the realist, one of the most significant issues is the distribution of power among states in the international system. As a result, realists define the national interest quite narrowly, believing that the United States will be safer by seeking to avoid unnecessary conflicts in the world. Thus, George Kennan argued that "the most serious fault" of American foreign policy is "the legalistic-moralistic approach to international problems. . . . It is the belief that it should be possible to suppress the chaotic and dangerous aspirations of governments . . . by the acceptance of some system of legal rules and restraints."[8] Realists argue that self-interested states compete for power and security, and no amount of legal rules will alter that fact. At its core, realism suggests that states behave similarly, regardless of their governmental structure; thus, there exists only one consideration of state motivations: relative power. A state must constantly be vigilant and ultimately must assume the worst of its adversaries and be suspicious of its friends. Failure to do so may leave the state unguarded and open to attack.

Therefore, states must focus attention on their military power and its diplomatic and political uses. Perhaps the best illustration of this is the realist emphasis on the balance of power. According to Hedley Bull, the balance of power is designed to ensure the continued existence of the state system by preventing any one power from dominating. The balance of power is essential to maintaining order in international politics as well as to maintaining the state system itself. States engaged in the balance of power are concerned, first and foremost, with their security and survival.[9] Further, it is significant that the balance of power is about preserving not peace but the state system; in fact, peace may be violated in order to preserve the system. Thus, the traditional realist policy maker is defensive in nature and wary of risky policies that might threaten the state's interests.

This does not, however, remove the applicability of force from the policy maker's equation. In fact, force is essential to maintaining the security of the state and protecting the state's interests. The realist policy maker sees military force as a guarantor of peace and stability. While not willing to pursue risky policies, the realist policy maker understands that the world is an uncertain and unstable place. Keeping the state secure requires constant vigilance, and the policy maker who chooses not to prepare for the worst will be left unable to defend and protect the state's interests. The realist policy maker views the world with suspicion and this, in turn, entails a readiness to defend state interests.

The traditional realist policy maker's defensive position has been modified by some contemporary realists who argue for a more offensive approach. These newer realists, agreeing with the old that the world is a dangerous place whose uncertainty requires a military posture, reject a reactive, defensive approach as failing to adequately protect state interests. These "offensive" realists argue that in order for a state to obtain security, it must seek to increase its power and dominate those around it. Security, thus, is obtained by expanding military power rather than constraining it. John Mearsheimer argues that anarchy in the international system provides strong incentives for states to use their force in order to expand their values and interests. Rather than protecting and defending their interests, states are inclined to promote and spread their interests through their military power. According to Mearsheimer, "Given the difficulty of determining how much power is enough for today and tomorrow, great powers recognize that the best way to ensure their security is to achieve hegemony now, thus eliminating any possibility of a challenge. . . . Only a misguided state would pass up an opportunity to become a hegemon in the system because it thought it already had sufficient power to survive."[10]

The first necessity confronting any analysis of the two Bush presidencies is to understand that each president approached the world with a different set of realist prescriptions in mind. While both were realists, George H. W. Bush can best be described as a defensive realist, preferring a risk-averse approach to world politics, and George W. Bush's worldview fits well with the offensive realist perspective, because of his willingness to take risks to expand American power with the intention of creating a more stable world within which America could operate.

George H. W. and George W. Bush also embraced different liberal models. At their core, liberals argue that the spread of democracy, global economic ties, and international organizations strengthen peace. Since liberalism is a divided house, policy makers often pick and choose variants of liberalism to emphasize. Traditional liberals suggest that states are inherently different types of actors and that differences in behavior can be attributed to differences in regime type. A democracy does not act like a dictatorship. While realists often "black-box" the state and pay less attention to domestic political consequences, liberals argue that domestic politics has significant consequences for international relations. According to Michael Doyle, "Modern liberalism carries with it two legacies. . . . The first . . . is the pacification of . . . relations among liberal states. . . . Second . . . peaceful restraint only seems to work in liberals' relations with other liberals."[11] Liberals' development of the democratic peace argument has its roots in Immanuel Kant's essay "Perpetual Peace." According to the democratic peace argument, there is no historical case of two democratic states fighting each other because democratic states are cautious about initiating conflicts, respect each other in their relations, and have a high degree of interdependence that makes war against the states' interests.

However, while democracies do not fight each other, they are prone to launch crusading struggles against authoritarian regimes in order to create democracies, and in the process, they argue, a more stable and peaceful world.[12] Furthermore, liberals argue that the motivations of states go beyond mere security and survival to the promotion of individual rights and global justice. Therefore, in contrast to the realist view, in the liberal formulation, the domestic structure of a state has a significant impact on international relations.

In addition, liberals believe that states are not alone in the international system, as the realists posit. Rather, states act alongside international institutions, commercial interest groups, and other nonstate actors to preserve peace and promote cooperation. Robert Keohane and Joseph Nye explain that in contemporary international politics, states are constrained from acting; there are mutual costs involved in their behavior, making it difficult for states to do anything they like and forcing them to work together to achieve common interests.[13] As a result, the anarchic system that realists posit as inherently dominated by conflict can be moderated by the development of international law, international organizations, and the global market. At the same time, these actors, particularly nonstate actors, can constrain states negatively. The rise of terrorist groups or drug cartels, for example, forces states to alter their foreign policy to meet new challenges.

The idea of mutual costs suggests a wider range of cooperation between states than realists are willing to concede. Keohane and Nye call this phenomenon "complex interdependence." Accordingly, where "reciprocal . . . costly effects [exist], there is interdependence." For example, the United States and the Soviet Union experienced interdependence in nuclear weapons since the security and survival of one was tied to the security and survival of the other. Keohane and Nye take interdependence a step further, arguing that there are "multiple channels" of influence that "connect societies"; again, actors beyond the state, including international institutions, nongovernmental organizations, and multinational corporations, can influence the behavior of states and, ultimately, encourage cooperation. In addition, liberals suggest an absence of hierarchy among issues, meaning that military force becomes less significant in solving problems between states. Where there exist "intense relationships of mutual influence . . . force is irrelevant or unimportant as an instrument of policy."[14] In other words, mutual dependence reduces the significance of force in international relations.

In a liberal world, relationships become more complex as issues are linked. Furthermore, international institutions can increase in significance since they provide contexts for resolving disputes among states. In a realist world, states are dominant and the struggle for security and survival creeps into all aspects of international politics. In the liberal world, however, governments can organize to cope with international problems and challenges. Thus, international organizations are involved in agenda setting and induce coalition building among states.[15] Neoliberal institutionalism, an important variant of liberalism, suggests that international institutions build cooperation between states. When states enter into international institutions, their interests become tied to the interests of other states. The mutual dependence thus created serves all states involved by enhancing security and protecting interests.

The variants within the liberal approaches present the second problem with any analysis of the Bush presidencies' foreign policies. Since policy makers can choose to emphasize various liberal assumptions, George H. W. Bush and George W. Bush diverge in their liberalism as well as their realism. While George H. W. Bush emphasized the importance of international institutions and multilateral processes in the pursuit of American foreign policy goals, George W. Bush stressed the democratic peace argument. In particular, the latter believed in the importance of democracy in building peace and viewed it as America's mission to promote and spread democracy to authoritarian regimes in order to secure peace and stability in the world, and thus protect and promote American interests.

Therefore, one can see that neither President Bush fits neatly into the realist or liberal category. Rather, the worldviews of both presidents borrow heavily from each approach. While the older Bush emphasized defensive realism and neoliberal institutionalism, the younger stressed the offensive variant of realism and the democratic peace argument. These combinations are particularly significant in the context of their policies in the Middle East. George H. W. Bush's response to Iraq's invasion of Kuwait and his approach to Middle East peace reflected his particular combination of realism and liberalism. His immediate concern and response to the Iraqi invasion was to protect Saudi Arabia and American petroleum interests, a defensive realist position. As it became increasingly clear that Saddam Hussein would not voluntarily leave Kuwait, Bush built an international coalition to evict Iraq, a defensive realist position using neoliberal institutionalist means. Most significant, Bush's decision to use force emphasized limited goals and demonstrated his unwillingness to engage in risky policy action, particularly in the war's conclusion; while the United States encouraged revolution against Saddam Hussein, it did not directly engage in toppling him because of the uncertainties and risks involved.

Likewise, throughout the Middle East peace process George H. W. Bush's actions reflected his risk aversion and multilateral approach to world problems. He was unwilling to expend too much of his political capital on the peace process, but when an opportunity emerged, he took measured steps, and only once he was able to secure the support of world leaders. Significantly, Bush did not want Middle East peace to be an "American" responsibility; he insisted on Soviet cosponsorship of a peace conference, in part to guarantee that the United States would not be solely responsible for the potential failure of the conference.

His son's approach to the Middle East was significantly different. George W. Bush's actions reflected his combination of offensive realism and the liberal democratic peace. With regard to Iraq, the younger Bush pursued a more aggressive approach, emphasizing preventive prescriptions that called for the eradication of the Iraqi "threat" and an end to the Saddam Hussein regime; George W. Bush's prescription for the anarchic world was to eradicate threats through force. In addition, he emphasized replacing Saddam Hussein with a democratic regime. This, in turn, would be the first step toward bringing peace and stability to the Middle East. His approach to Middle East peace also reflected these two theoretical strands. Throughout his tenure in office, he tolerated the actions of the "only democratic" regime, Israel, against Palestinians, seeing the situation as part of the larger struggle in the war on terrorism. Further, he refused to deal with the Palestinian Authority's leadership until it pursued democracy through democratic elections, a policy that backfired with the election of Hamas.

## A Brief Overview

The remainder of this book will sketch the life and worldviews of both George Bushes and examine their approaches to the wars in Iraq and the Israeli-Palestinian conflict. One of the difficulties in writing a book on the two Bush presidencies is ensuring clarity. Thus, rather than referring to each man as President Bush, I will refer to George H. W. or George W. It is also important to note that the research materials for the policies of George H. W. are more extensive. Not only is a vast public record, including memoirs, available, but the George Bush Presidential Library at Texas A&M University provides access to numerous important documents and materials related to the Persian Gulf War and the Israeli-Palestinian conflict. The research materials for George W. are less extensive but have increased recently. There are a number of accounts in the public record, including memoirs, but there are also government documents specifically relating to the war in Iraq available from the National Security Archive at George Washington University.[16] This online resource has been particularly helpful in writing this book. The Palestine Papers, available from Al Jazeera, also offer a glimpse into the policy of George W.'s presidency, since they provide access to internal documents related to the Israeli-Palestinian conflict. In both cases, however, I cannot nor will I try to claim a completely unbiased presentation. I believe that the policy of enlightened realism espoused by the George H. W. Bush administration served this country better than the policies of the George W. Bush administration. However, I try to offer sound reasoning for this opinion and hope that this will satisfy the reader.

In chapter 1, I will discuss and examine the background experiences of George H. W. and George W. The formative experiences of a leader are important for understanding that leader's beliefs and style. We are all, in a sense, a product of our experiences; therefore, understanding those experiences and gaining a sense of background is important to comprehending each president's worldview. One must understand, however, that worldviews are neither developed nor acted upon in a vacuum—the circumstances in which they operate are also prominent.

In chapter 2, I establish and compare the beliefs of George H. W. and George W. I emphasize four important issues that help to construct the enlightened realist and cowboy liberal approaches. Enlightened realism is characterized by George H. W.'s pragmatism and experience, his flexibility and willingness to compromise. This is contrasted with George W.'s cowboy liberalism and its reliance on ideology and gut instinct, his certainty, and an emphasis on competition. In addition, the two men offered very different approaches to diplomacy and negotiation. And although their views on America's role in the world share some similarities, the enlightened realist and cowboy liberal approaches significantly differed on the importance of multilateralism vs. unilateralism and the meaning of American leadership.

In chapters 3, 4, and 5, I examine how these beliefs were applied in the specific cases chosen here. Chapter 3 focuses on the decisions for war in Iraq in 1990–91 and 2001–3. I compare and contrast each president's approach to policy, emphasizing the role of his worldview throughout. Chapter 4 examines the decisions that took place during the wars and in their immediate aftermath. The decision to go to war does not represent an end to the policy process. Rather, presidents continue to be engaged in policy making, and they often reassess and reevaluate the war policy over time. Most significant, this chapter analyzes George H. W.'s decision not to march on Baghdad and remove Saddam Hussein from power with American force against George W.'s decision to do just that. The final case chapter, chapter 5, analyzes how each president approached the Israeli-Palestinian peace process. In each of these chapters, I apply each president's beliefs as laid out in chapter 2 as a part of the analysis of the cases.

In the final chapter I offer general and specific conclusions. I will assess the relative successes of each presidency, providing my reasoning for favoring the enlightened realist approach over the cowboy liberal strategy. Finally, I will provide lessons from the examination of these two presidents. What can we learn from this examination? Does our understanding of George H. W. and George W. lead us to more general conclusions about American foreign policy and the presidency? Is George W. an anomaly? That is to say, is the cowboy liberal approach unique to his personality and administration? While these issues are not exhaustive, I hope that the book will raise important questions about these two presidents.

# 1

# Formative Experiences

Forty-four men have served as president of the United States of America. They have led in times of war and peace, of economic hardship and plenty. For both George Bushes, serving as commander in chief epitomized their roles in the presidency. Both men faced crises and both men used the armed forces in dealing with those crises. One of the premises of this book is that the formative experiences of a president provide a context for greater understanding of a president's approach to the challenges the world presents. Thus, we must begin with an examination of the formative years of George H. W. and George W.

## GROWING UP BUSH

### Obliged to Serve

George Herbert Walker Bush was born on June 12, 1924, in Milton, Massachusetts, to Prescott and Dorothy Walker Bush. His father was raised in Columbus, Ohio, graduated from Yale University, and served in World War I. His mother was born in Kennebunkport, Maine, and attended private schools in St. Louis and Connecticut. Prescott and Dorothy Bush were married in 1921 and moved to New York, where Prescott accepted a lucrative partnership in the investment firm of Brown Brothers Harriman.

As a result of his family background, it was easy for George H. W.'s political opponents to charge him with being an elitist and out of touch with the people. To illuminate this point, and the fact that George H. W. was not the most eloquent speaker, Texas governor Ann Richards stated in an address at the 1988 Democratic Presidential Convention, "Poor George. He can't help it. He was born with a silver foot in his mouth."[1]

While George H. W. certainly lived a privileged life, his father stressed self-reliance and encouraged active service, refusing to allow his children to live as "spoiled rich kids." For the Bush family, wealth was a "safety net." However, the Bush children "were expected to go out, earn their own wealth, and do the same."[2] According to Randall Rothenberg, Prescott Bush "personified noblesse oblige serving on sundry political boards and committees"; he later became a U.S. senator, representing Connecticut from 1952 to 1963.[3]

Even before his election to the Senate, Prescott Bush was active in political and social issues, serving as treasurer of the first national campaign of Planned Parenthood and as an early supporter of the United Negro College Fund. From 1947 to 1950, he served as the Connecticut Republican finance chairman and was the Republican candidate for the Senate in 1950. As a senator, Prescott Bush staunchly supported President Eisenhower. He was a key congressional ally in the passage of the Interstate Highway System and the establishment of the Peace Corps. Prescott Bush encouraged these values of service in his son.

George H. W.'s mother, Dorothy Walker Bush, added competitiveness to the sense of service and responsibility instilled by his father. Upon her death, Hugh Sidey wrote, "George Bush was shaped and tempered by his mother's nature. His was a soul formed by strata of love and discipline relentlessly laid down."[4] Dorothy Bush insisted that her children excel and work hard. Yet, in winning, they were expected to be gracious—their mother did not approve of bragging or self-aggrandizement. As George H. W. explains, his parents "embodied the Puritan ethic. . . . Whatever we wanted, we'd have to earn. . . . Dad entered his first political race. . . . He'd made his mark in the business world. Now he felt he had a debt to pay. . . . [He] had an old-fashioned idea that the more advantage a man has, the greater his obligation to do public service."[5] In many ways, George H. W. was expected to follow his father's path, achieve success, and then give back by providing service to the community.

Despite the "Puritan ethic" instilled in him by his parents, there can be no doubt that George H. W. still lived a rather privileged life. He attended the Greenwich Country Day School until he completed the eighth grade. Beginning in 1936, he attended Phillips Academy in Andover, Massachusetts. There he held a large number of leadership positions, including president of the senior class, secretary of the student council, president of the community fund-raising board, member of the editorial board of the school newspaper, and captain of both the varsity baseball team and the soccer team. While attending Phillips, he also met his future wife, Barbara Pierce; the only thing that had a greater impact on his life at the time was the Japanese bombing of Pearl Harbor. He describes his reaction upon hearing about the Japanese attack as something he'd never forget. "I was walking across campus . . . near the chapel . . . with a friend. . . . And somebody yelled across at us, and it just made a profound impact at that very moment."[6] He was due to graduate at the end of the year and, in keeping with his belief in service, George H. W. enlisted in the navy. As he explains, "My thoughts immediately turned to naval aviation. College was coming up the following fall, but that would have to wait. The sooner I could enlist, the better."[7]

That dedication to service would define his career. During World War II, he served as a navy pilot and squadron leader, collecting aerial surveillance as a part of the navy's Fifth Fleet on the aircraft carrier USS *San Jacinto*. On September 2, 1944, George H. W. and his crew were sent to bomb a Japanese radio site at Chichi Jima. On that day, he almost lost his life, but instead became a hero: "Coming in, I was aware of black splotches of gunfire all around. Suddenly there was a jolt. . . . Smoke poured into the cockpit, and I could see flames ripping across the crease of the wing, edging towards the fuel tanks. I stayed with the dive, homed in on the target, unloaded our four 500-pound bombs, and pulled away. . . . Once over water, I leveled off and told [the crew] to bail out. . . . Alone in my raft . . . I was slowly drifting toward Chichi Jima."[8]

After several hours in shark-infested waters, he was rescued by a submarine, the USS *Finback*. Following his recovery, he was eligible for leave and used it to get married. He had also earned enough time to be discharged, but chose instead to return to the Pacific, arguing, "It was different then; 'we gotta go back and do our duty.'"[9] However, Japan surrendered before he could be shipped back into conflict. During his time in the navy, George H. W. had flown fifty-eight missions, accrued 1,228 hours of flying time, and earned a Distinguished Flying Cross.[10]

After the war, he enrolled in an accelerated program at Yale University that allowed him to graduate with his BA in economics in two years. He distinguished himself at Yale, graduating as a member of Phi Beta Kappa and the Skull and Bones Club, a secret fraternal society. He was also a member of the Delta Kappa Epsilon fraternity and was elected its president. As the captain of the Yale baseball team, George H. W. played in the first two College World Series games. After his 1948 graduation, Prescott Bush's connections proved useful, getting him a job at Dresser Industries, a subsidiary of Brown Brothers Harriman, as a sales clerk. He moved his family to Midland, Texas, and within three years, he ventured off on his own; along with John Overby, a friend, he started the Bush-Overby Oil Development Company in 1951. Later, they cofounded Zapata Petroleum Corporation when they merged their firm with another run by William and Hugh Liedke. Zapata proved successful and, in 1959, George H. W. became the president of a Zapata subsidiary, Zapata Offshore, and moved to Houston.

### Midland's Son

George W. Bush was born in New Haven, Connecticut, on July 6, 1946, but spent most of his childhood in the world George H. W. made for him in Texas. As a result, Midland, Texas, values became, in many senses, the values of George W. During the 2000 presidential campaign, he told Tony Carnes, "I don't know what percentage of me is Midland, but I would say people—if they want to understand me—need to understand Midland and the attitude of Midland."[11] Midland was a community of traditional values. In 1923, Midland experienced a boom when the Santa Rita No. 1 oil well blew. The introduction of the oil industry into the region clashed with the traditional culture of cattle ranching. However, Midland welcomed all kinds of newcomers into the region: wealthy and not-so-wealthy investors, highly educated engineers and geologists, blue-collar workers, bankers, truckers, and new service employees, like hoteliers. The new industry also brought prostitution and dance halls to Midland. Traditional Midland did not approve; it was a place of hardworking, religious people. Thus, the oil industry made Midland a bundle of contradictions, a reflection of old and new. Midland's traditional values were being challenged.

While George H. W. and Barbara Bush were transplants to the region, George W. viewed Midland as home. Emphasizing these feelings, George W. once told a colleague, "If I died today, I'd like to be buried in Midland."[12] Despite not having been born in Texas, George W. became the "most Texan" of the Bush children, and many of his values are a consequence of his Midland upbringing. Midland's values were conservative, and they encouraged his respect for tradition and religion. Nicholas Kristof puts it best, arguing that Midland gave George W. "an anchor in real America. . . . Midland was a world of clear rights and wrongs, long on absolutes and devoid of ethical gray shades."[13] Throughout George W.'s presidency, these values would play an important part in defining his worldview and his approach to decision making.

Midland also brought personal tragedy to the Bushes. The 1953 death of Robin, George H. W. and Barbara's three-year-old daughter and George W.'s sister, from leukemia proved to be a defining moment for the seven-year-old George W. He found himself surrounded by grief. He later wrote, "I guess I learned in a harsh way . . . never to take life for granted. But rather than making me fearful, the close reach of death made me determined to enjoy whatever life might bring."[14] In fact, Robin's death was pivotal in encouraging George W.'s ebullient personality. He used extraversion and his sense of humor to deal with the pain of losing his sister. In addition, Robin's death helped establish George W.'s life philosophy. According to George Lardner and Lois Romano, many close to the Bushes suggest that Robin's death was a "singular event in George W.'s childhood. . . . Life would be full of humor and driven by chance . . . it would be something approached with a certain fatalism."[15]

As George W. got older, it was clear that he was expected to follow his father's path. Like George H. W., he attended Phillips Academy in Andover. Academically, he was nothing like his father, performing poorly and receiving a zero on his first English assignment. In contrast to his struggles in the classroom, however, he was a social success. Within months, he had created an extensive network of friends. His desire to live life to its fullest was reflected in his extracurricular involvements. He was the head football cheerleader, a member of a rock-and-roll band, and the organizer of a stickball league. He "almost instinctively managed to be the center of the action." Stickball was a tradition at Andover, but Bush organized campus teams into a league and deemed himself the "High Commissioner."[16]

Andover gave George W. a great deal of confidence. He later explained that his time there taught him "independence" and it convinced him that he "could make friends, and make my way, no matter where I found myself in life."[17]

After graduating from Andover, George W. continued to follow his father's path, heading for Yale University in 1964. His years at Yale coincided with the tumultuous events of the 1960s and helped shape his conservative views. He resented the "liberal orthodoxy that pervaded" the campus and later criticized Yale's "self-righteousness" and "intellectual superiority."[18] At a time when the youth of America was challenging authority and questioning the direction of the country, George W. was praising tradition and the values of the past. Nicholas Kristof explains that during the great upheavals of the 1960s, George W. remained largely a "noncombatant." When he was forced to take sides, "he ultimately retreated to the values and ideals of his parents' generation. . . . Unlike others of his generation [he] never wore his hair long, agonized over Vietnam, wrestled with existentialism or cranked up Rolling Stones songs to annoy his parents."[19] To George W., Yale was the embodiment of the liberal East. One event in particular confirmed his misgivings. Soon after his father's 1964 Senate loss to Ralph Yarborough, George W. ran into a family friend, Reverend William Sloane Coffin. Coffin had turned his back on his conservative upbringing, become a radical, and encouraged students to resist the draft. Upon meeting Coffin, George W. bitterly recalled, Coffin told him that his father had "lost to a better man."[20] For George W., this only solidified his beliefs that the liberal notions of the 1960s were misguided.

At the same time, Yale continued to develop his extraversion. He emphasized extracurricular activities over academic experiences. He was a member of Delta Kappa Epsilon fraternity, the Skull and Bones secret society, and he played rugby and baseball. In 1968, Bush graduated from Yale, eager to return to Texas and escape the "snobs" and "intellectual arrogance" of the university.[21] All along, George W. perceived himself as being outside the Yale establishment. His support for the Vietnam War demonstrated this well. In discussing Vietnam and the draft, he wrote, "I knew I would serve. Leaving the country to avoid the draft was not an option for me; I was too conservative and too traditional. My inclination was to support the government and the war until proven wrong.[22] As graduation at Yale approached, many students were caught up in how to avoid Vietnam. As one of George W.'s classmates explained, "Everybody did something: medical school, Naval Officer Candidate School. You either got drafted or flunked your physical." Another classmate added, "The Army was not the spot to end up. . . . The general opinion was to get into a branch of the service that if you'd be sent to Vietnam you had to volunteer to get there rather than just be sent."[23] George W. registered for the selective service, knowing that he would be unable to avoid some kind of military service, since his father was in politics. Like the sons of many powerful men, including sons of the Connallys and Bentsens, he pursued a precious slot in the Texas National Air Guard as a way to escape going to Vietnam. He later explained that he "was not prepared to shoot my eardrum out . . . in order to get a deferment. Nor was I willing to go to Canada."[24] George W. graduated Combat Crew Training School on June 23, 1970, fulfilling his two years of active duty. Unlike his father after World War II, George W. did not emerge from Vietnam as a war hero.

## LIFE BEFORE THE PRESIDENCY

### Living Up to Expectations

During the time George W. was at Yale and then serving in the National Guard, George H. W. was beginning his political career. However, he faced the challenge of being a Republican in a state controlled by the Democratic Party. His first attempt at political office came in 1964 when he ran for the U.S. Senate seat held by Democrat Ralph Yarborough. The conservative leanings of the state gave George H. W. an early edge, but the Texas state Democratic Party regrouped after the assassination of President John F. Kennedy, changing the political landscape and ending George H. W.'s quest for the Senate. George H. W. did not let this loss deter him. In 1966, he sold his interest in Zapata and tried for the congressional seat in Texas's Seventh District. He made a point of running on a platform of moderate Republicanism, supporting a pro-choice stance on abortion, for example. Unopposed in the primary, George H. W. handily defeated his opponent and served two terms in the House of Representatives.[25]

In 1970, he decided to run for the U.S. Senate once again. He assumed

that he would be running against Yarborough, but Yarborough's liberalism made him ripe for defeat and he unexpectedly lost the Democratic
primary to Lloyd Bentsen. Bentsen was a more conservative Democrat
than Yarborough and, despite the fact that President Richard Nixon campaigned on George H. W.'s behalf, Bush lost the general election. Nixon's
support in the election proved useful, however. After his defeat, George
H. W. was nominated and later confirmed as the U.S. ambassador to the
United Nations. This post began a long career dedicated to international
relations and foreign policy in which he cultivated numerous friendships
and earned a positive reputation, both personally and for American diplomacy as a whole, among his colleagues. Unlike some of his predecessors at the United Nations, George H. W. made a special effort to call on
and get to know the representatives of all countries—including those in
Africa—a policy that was mainly unheard of before his arrival.

His career took another turn in 1972, at the beginnings of the Watergate scandal. After his reelection, President Nixon asked George H. W. to
chair the Republican National Committee (RNC). George H. W. was reluctant to leave his post at the United Nations, but his loyalty to the administration pulled stronger than his desire to remain a diplomat. Throughout
Nixon's second term, George H. W. defended the president amid the
Watergate allegations. He finally conceded the president's guilt when the
final tapes, clearly demonstrating that Nixon was guilty of obstruction
of justice, were released to the public. Notably during this time, George
H. W. turned down a request from Nixon aide John McLaughlin for RNC
mailing lists so that the White House could organize additional support.[26]
Finally, on August 7, 1974, two days before Nixon's resignation, George
H. W. sent a letter to the president urging him to resign. "Dear Mr. President," he wrote, "Resignation is best for the country, best for this President.
. . . If you do leave office, history will properly record your achievements
with lasting respect."[27] His actions during Watergate earned him a great
deal of respect on both sides of the aisle, and he quickly emerged as the
front-runner to become the new vice president under Gerald Ford. However, revelations that George H. W.'s 1970 Senate campaign had received
illegal contributions from a Nixon slush fund ended his chance, and he
was offered ambassadorships in the United Kingdom and France instead.
He turned both of those offers down and requested a post in China.[28]

George H. W.'s time in China proved his abilities as a spokesman for American foreign policy. In requesting and accepting the position, he demonstrated how he valued international relations, noting, "A new China was emerging, and the relationship between the United States and the People's Republic would be crucial in the years to come, not just in terms of Asian but of worldwide American policy." Most important, his post in China proved his impeccable diplomatic skills and his reliance on personal diplomacy and relations. He wrote, "If diplomacy means anything at all, it's establishing contacts." His style did not receive support in Washington, particularly from Henry Kissinger, but George H. W. insisted on cultivating personal relationships: "My purpose wasn't to win popularity contests . . . but to get to know the Chinese people—and to get them to know Americans—at a personal level."[29] To facilitate this, he made a point of attending national celebrations at various embassies, something his predecessor, David Bruce, believed was a waste of time. Initially, George H. W.'s appearance at these events was met with surprise but eventually it was considered routine.

After a little over a year in China, he was ready to return to the United States. His desire to do so coincided with allegations against the Central Intelligence Agency that it was underestimating Soviet military power and misinterpreting Soviet strategic objectives. The administration was determined to address the problem. George H. W. had already proven his ability to clean up messes as the chairman of the RNC during Watergate and his name was quickly circulated as the leading candidate for the position of the new director of the CIA. President Ford offered him the job and he accepted. George H. W. was surprised at the offer, and somewhat apprehensive about the position, writing Henry Kissinger, "In all candor I would not have selected this controversial position if the decision had been mine, but I serve at the pleasure of the President and I do not believe in complicating his already enormously difficult job."[30]

As the director of the CIA, George H. W. "drew a careful line between protecting secrets and accountability, discreetly acceding to the possibility of greater congressional oversight." He used his contacts and personal relationships to inform Congress and took congressional oversight seriously, making fifty-one appearances on Capitol Hill during his directorship.[31] In addition, he continued to enhance his reputation in

Washington, DC, as a competent politician, and emerged as the CIA's "most popular director since Dulles"; so much so that, during his presidential campaign, Jimmy Carter spoke highly of him: "I happen to think a lot of George Bush. I would not include [him] among those who were appointed without qualifications."[32] Nevertheless, and despite George H. W.'s request to remain at the CIA in the Carter administration, he became the first director of Central Intelligence (DCI) in history to be dismissed by an incoming administration.

For the next couple of years, George H. W. was in a holding pattern, serving on numerous corporate boards but continuing to eye political office. In 1978, he began to explore a run for the presidency. On May 1, 1979, he announced his candidacy for the Republican nomination. While Ronald Reagan courted the conservative wing of the Republican Party, Bush staked himself out as a moderate. That, coupled with the fact that his campaign was no match for the Reagan campaign's political machine, led to his eventual withdrawal from the race. His political fortunes changed, however, when Reagan asked him to join the Republican ticket as the vice presidential nominee.

As he had with so many previous political offerings, George H. W. accepted his role dutifully. Throughout the campaign, he demonstrated his loyalty to Reagan and Reagan's policies, despite disagreements during the primary. In fact, he repressed some of his policy beliefs, including his moderate pro-choice stance, and supported a much more conservative policy agenda. Despite gaining credibility with Reagan himself, however, Reagan's staff and wife, Nancy, did not trust him. After Reagan and Bush won the 1980 election handily, George H. W. served two terms as vice president. Throughout the eight years, he chaired most National Security Council (NSC) meetings and exercised significant influence on foreign policy issues. He used the personal relationships he had cultivated to facilitate outcomes, personally negotiating with the Chinese on arms sales to Taiwan, for example. And he continued to demonstrate his loyalty throughout the Iran-Contra scandal, supporting Reagan and his administration's policies with, according to some, alarming consistency. By 1988, George H. W. had developed the necessary political support to become the next president of the United States.

*If at First . . . Try, Try Again*

While George H. W. was rising through the ranks of the Republican Party, George W. was drifting, unsure of his future direction. He later referred to this period in his life as his nomadic years, as he held short-lived jobs, continued to fly for the Air National Guard, and worked on a number of election campaigns.[33] At the same time, he had a rambunctious social life filled with wild parties, drinking, and numerous girlfriends. All of George W.'s carousing came to a head one night when he took his fifteen-year-old brother, Marvin, out drinking with him. Upon returning home, he ran over the neighbor's garbage cans. His father confronted him, demanding an explanation, and George W. responded by challenging his father to go "mano a mano right there." His brother Jeb lightened the moment by announcing that George W. had secretly applied and been accepted to Harvard Business School.[34] It finally appeared that George W. might gain some direction in his life.

At Harvard, George W.'s Texas identity was reinforced. Much like his experience at Yale, he found Harvard pretentious and continued to exhibit an anti-intellectual attitude. Unlike his classmates who wore suits and ties to class, George W. wore his bomber jacket and cowboy boots, and spit tobacco into a Styrofoam cup.[35] By 1975, he had completed his MBA and headed back to Midland. With $13,000 he set out in the oil business with his friends Joe O'Neill and Don Evans in an attempt to replicate his father's success. However, following his father's path brought little success as George W. faced numerous challenges. By 1986, he was facing a serious crisis. Spectrum 7, his oil exploration and development company, reported a net loss of $1.6 million due to the quickly deteriorating value of its holdings. As oil prices plummeted from $25 to $9 per barrel, his firm was on its way to losing significantly more. At the same time, his company owed $3 million and his investors had all but disappeared. George W. decided to use his family name and find a bigger company to rescue him. Harken Oil and Gas, a Dallas-based firm, was willing to take the company over, assuming its debts. According to Paul Rea, a geologist with Spectrum 7, "One of the reasons Harken was so interested in merging was because of George. . . . They believed having George's name there would be a big help to them. They wanted him on their board."[36]

The buyout rescued him financially and gave him enough money to eventually pursue a new venture, the Texas Rangers baseball team; finally, George W. would make it on his own and become a millionaire. With his failed attempts at the oil business behind him, and his success in baseball, George W. caught the political bug and turned to help his father's 1988 presidential campaign. This would not be his first political campaign, however. In 1977, he announced that he was running for Congress in Texas. Throughout his campaign, George W. emphasized conservative themes, such as wanting to halt the "bureaucratic spread of federal government that is encroaching more and more on our lives."[37] This helped him convincingly win the Republican primary, but he lost the general election by a wide margin. Despite this, it was clear that he was a natural at campaigning. Unlike his father, George W. loved the campaign contest and his 1977 failure provided a basis for his role during his father's 1988 presidential campaign.

Before he could assist with his father's campaign, however, he had to deal with his own demons. George W. had been fighting a drinking problem for some time. His social carousing as a teen had never really stopped. In 1986, following his fortieth birthday bash, George W. had a personal awakening, telling his wife, Laura, that he was going to quit drinking altogether. "He just said, 'I'm going to quit,' and he did," remembers Laura Bush. According to some friends, "He didn't want to do anything under the influence that might embarrass" his father and hurt his presidential campaign.[38] At the same time that he decided to quit drinking, George W. experienced a religious awakening: "Drawing from the spiritual lives of those around him, he oriented to simple truths, personal experiences, and stories. It serves him well and had its benefits. Friends have noted that he is uncharacteristically teachable in spiritual matters . . . these years . . . are critical to an understanding of how Bush's faith was changing him and inspiring him to achieve. The discerning can find in these years an unleashing of his energies, and impartation of some force that infused the former nomad with drive, with an intense hunger to make his mark."[39] George W. himself explained, "My faith frees me. Frees me to put the problem of the moment in proper perspective. Frees me to make decisions that others might not like. Frees me to try to do the right thing, even though it may not poll well. Frees me to enjoy life and not worry about what comes next."[40] Perhaps more than anything, George W.'s guiding faith helps to explain his approach to decision making.

By 1988, his awakening helped him to become a full-fledged member of his father's presidential campaign. "Junior," as he was known in the campaign, was energetic and worked closely with Lee Atwater, the campaign manager. Atwater understood that George W. could convince his father on a variety of things and George W. acted as a conduit between the two. He also served as the "loyalty thermometer" of the campaign, "coming down hard on leakers, loose cannons and snarky reporters, [and] mediating staff disputes."[41] According to Jim Pinkerton, an advisor to George H. W.'s 1988 campaign, George W. was an asset. George W. was there as a "resource" to the campaign and he did "more than his fair share of . . . listening."[42] More important than his political skills, however, were the lessons that he would take from his father's 1988 and 1992 presidential campaigns (see chapter 2).

After his father's successful bid for the presidency in 1988, George W. returned to Dallas and Texas Rangers baseball. His association with the Rangers was his first business success. His time at the Rangers allowed him to hone his managerial and political skills as well. As Tom Grieve, the general manager of the Texas Rangers, explained, "He was the spokesperson. He dealt with the media, he dealt with the fans, and it was obvious to us . . . that that's what he was made for . . . when there were tough decisions to be made he accepted responsibility for them." Grieve went on to say that he believed these "human qualities" would make George W. a "spectacular president."[43]

After his father's loss to Bill Clinton in the 1992 presidential race, George W. was freed to run for political office himself. He decided to take on Texas's popular Democratic governor, Ann Richards, in 1994. During the campaign, Richards tried to bait George W. into self-destruction, referring to him as "shrub" and "jerk," but the newly refined George W. demonstrated a great deal of self-control, never straying from his campaign themes and refusing to take the bait Richards was offering. On Election Day he won. As governor, he demonstrated extraordinary political skills, but also illustrated his strong anti-intellectualism. His strength was strategy while policy was left for others. Paul Sadler, a Texas Democrat, argued, "His strength is not policy, not details. . . . His strength is that you like him and you want him to succeed."[44] This would become a defining trait of George W.'s politics, and it would make him a much more success-ful politician, as illustrated by his meteoric rise to the presidency in 2000, than his father, but it also would be a source of weakness as a president.

## 2

# Beliefs and Style

While foreign policy is invariably the result of numerous factors, the president occupies a central place in the foreign policy process. As Rahm Emanuel, former chief of staff to President Barack Obama, has explained, "Every president is different and presidents define their presidency."[1] The personality of a president is unique and has a significant impact on decision making in the White House. The international challenges faced by the United States from 1989 to 1993 and from 2001 to 2009 made the president's personality of particular importance. Both eras were marked by a high degree of crisis, insulating White House decision making and placing the president at the center of the action. For George H. W., crises came in the form of the end of the cold war coupled with the Iraqi invasion of Kuwait, while for George W., the terrorist attacks of September 11, 2001, served to put the White House on a constant state of alert.

Despite other factors that impede the impact of personality on decision making—such as bureaucratic politics—during each of these periods, the president's personality appears to have had a substantial impact. One important factor in elevating the significance of each president's personality was that the United States faced fundamental changes in the international political system during both administrations. For George H. W., the end of the cold war left the United States without a clear purpose, unsure of what the future might hold. For George W., the United States faced a situation similar to the formative period of the cold war. Such transitions require direct presidential involvement, allowing for a greater impact by the president and other personalities in the White House. Thus, this chapter will examine the beliefs and styles of George H. W. Bush and George W. Bush. In doing so, the characteristics of enlightened realism and cowboy liberalism will be enunciated further, as we compare the two men to gain a better understanding of them. I will discuss the four main characteristics of George H. W.'s enlightened realist approach: pragmatism and experience; flexibility and compromise; negotiation; and multilateral internationalism. Together, these attributes helped to produce the caution and risk aversion characteristic of the man. On the other hand, George W.'s cowboy liberal approach is characterized by an emphasis on ideology and gut instinct; certainty and competition; messianic universalism; and unilateral nationalism. These characteristics combined to emphasize a risk-acceptant approach to American foreign policy. Subsequent chapters will demonstrate how these beliefs impacted the decisions the two Bushes made in the Middle East.

## Pragmatism and Experience vs. Ideology and Gut Instinct

Few presidents have been as prepared and experienced as George H. W. Bush when they were elected into office. George H. W.'s experiences proved significant to his decision making, as he relied considerably on his own ideas and was essentially his own chief foreign policy advisor. In addition, he had knowledge about, interest in, and understanding of foreign policy and the foreign policy process. In contrast, George W. had a lack of knowledge about and interest in the field of foreign policy. In responding to questions about his competence in foreign policy, George W. openly "admitted that he had much to learn about world affairs."[2] The contrast could not have been starker.

George H. W. shunned the politics of ideology, preferring to rely on his experience and knowledge when making decisions. Rather than digging in and holding fast to ideological principles, George H. W. preferred cautious examination and finding pragmatic solutions to problems. When he served as the director of the CIA, for example, the agency faced a credibility crisis. A number of critical external investigations, most significant President Ford's Foreign Intelligence Advisory Board (PFIAB), claimed major flaws in the CIA's annual reports on Soviet strategic capabilities. The PFIAB report suggested that the CIA was vastly underestimating Soviet capabilities and called upon President Ford to allow an external review of the CIA's estimates. George H. W. put his own politics aside, sought a "safe" route, and supported the idea of an external review. Team B, the external review team, took a hawkish view of Soviet capabilities—one far to the right of his personal position—while the internal estimates of Team A suggested a more moderate Soviet adversary. Despite his personal disagreements with the Team B analysis, George H. W. accepted it, signing National Intelligence Estimate (NIE) 11-3/8, ending any further criticism of the CIA, particularly from Congress. He could have fought the Team B presentation, but instead chose a more pragmatic route that would benefit the organization in the long run.

Examples of George H. W.'s pragmatism influencing his foreign policy choices abound. As vice president, he neither wholeheartedly accepted Reagan's conservative ideology, nor did he accept Reagan's sudden turn to embrace Mikhail Gorbachev. In the first case, he believed that moderation in rhetoric and policy would be better. In the second, he was suspicious of Gorbachev's motives. During his 1988 presidential campaign, George H. W. stated that the United States must view Soviet reforms and policy with a "prudent skepticism," adding that the proper approach to the Soviet Union ought to be to "keep your guard up."[3] In his campaign autobiography, he added that "experience tells us that in dealing with the Soviets optimism is best tempered with realism."[4]

This pragmatic and cautious approach carried into his administration's policies. Preferring to rely on past experiences, George H. W. was reluctant to fully embrace the changes taking place throughout Eastern Europe and in the Soviet Union. He also refused to claim an ideological victory, fearing that this might cause greater instability in an already insecure situation. Throughout 1989 and 1990, while Eastern Europe was embroiled in revolution, he refused to grandstand, taking criticisms from all sides for his silence. In responding to the changes in the world, George H. W. relied heavily on his experiences. Recalling the era of détente, he feared that the reforms going on throughout Eastern Europe and the Soviet Union could be reversed.

Even as the Berlin Wall fell and German reunification became a reality, he remained cautious and unwilling to push the process forward too rapidly. As George H. W. and Brent Scowcroft, his national security advisor, wrote, the White House preferred a quiet approach to reunification, one that would support the Germans but would not "aggravate the situation." Significantly, George H. W. was concerned about the reaction from Moscow. Suspecting difficulties from Moscow, in turn, increased his suspicions about Soviet motivations and policies.[5] This led the administration to structure a policy that would "avoid alarming the Soviets."[6] George H. W. illustrated his pragmatic and cautious approach, arguing, "I wanted to send a signal by not jumping up and down on the Berlin Wall."[7] In contrast to his son, George H. W. did not believe that ideological grandstanding could advance the process. Perhaps more than anything else, this assessment was the result of his experience. He did not need to rely on a strict ideology to guide him. His experiences served him well.

George W., on the other hand, preferred ideological mantras and gut instinct. Scott McClellan explains, George W. was "always . . . an instinctive leader. . . . He is not one to delve deeply into all the possible policy options . . . before making a choice. Rather, he chooses based on his gut and his most deeply held convictions."[8] Most important to that gut instinct was his faith. Dan McAdams argues that George W.'s "religious faith was more than a mere 'influence' in [his life story]; it was instead the very essence of his moral steadfastness."[9] In addition, he had a Manichean view of the world; George W.'s "decisions and actions are clearly informed by a need to order his world into good and bad. . . . He denies his fallibility, vulnerability, and responsibility."[10] This led to an exaggerated degree of rigidity in his thinking, illustrated by his well-documented reliance on daily routines such as eating the same bowl of fruit for breakfast every morning. These rigid routines go hand in hand with rigid thought processes; religion not only offered a sense of purpose, it also created the image of order out of chaos. Justin Frank suggests that faith gives George W. a "pervasive sense of unreality. . . . Religion doesn't just replace doubt with certainty; it replaces ambiguity with dualism . . . a perspective divided into good and evil. . . . He cloaks himself in the certainty of being good, absolving the self of responsibility . . . disregarding the possibility that he could make a mistake."[11]

George W.'s ideological beliefs and gut instincts were coupled with a lack of experience, interest, and knowledge in foreign policy, which facilitated his reliance on ideology when making decisions. The fact that George W. lacked the experience of his father made comparisons unavoidable. To respond to critics arguing that he lacked the necessary experience and knowledge to be president, George W. emphasized his intention to rely on advisors who did possess experience and knowledge in foreign affairs. In addition, he relied on his gut instinct and ideological values, as noted above. However, while he may have been surrounded by competent advisors, George W. lacked the ability to discern between good and bad advice, and was easily swayed by policies that reflected his values. During the 2000 presidential campaign, Zbigniew Brzezinski argued that he "betrayed a basic ignorance of world affairs" and lacked preparation for the presidency.[12]

His inexperience and reliance on ideology and gut instinct in foreign policy was evident throughout his presidency. One example involves the Middle East peace process. During a meeting with a congressional delegation, it was suggested that Sweden might provide a viable peacekeeping force in the West Bank and Gaza Strip. George W. responded by insisting that Sweden was neutral and lacked an army, confusing Sweden with Switzerland. Later, he admitted his mistake.[13] In addition to lacking knowledge of foreign affairs, George W. displayed a lack of interest in the subject. Robert Jervis has explained that he "did not have deeply rooted views about foreign policy."[14] In fact, George W.'s lack of knowledge contributed to his suspicion of intellectuals and his general attitude of anti-intellectualism. He purposely projected himself as a man who acted on the basis of instincts and morality (framed by religion and his conservative ideology). This combination meant that in the George W. White House there would be little debate; his morality gave him a certainty in his decision making that would not allow for flexibility or challenging discussions. Typifying this, he tended to gravitate toward ideas and books that confirmed what he already believed; he ultimately sought confirmation of his values and ideology in making policy. Thus his gravitation toward Natan Sharansky's *A Case for Democracy,* which argued in favor of spreading democracy and against appeasing dictators and tyrants.[15]

While George H. W. relied on his experience and understood that different situations often require different responses, George W. relied on his ideological values when making decisions. Unlike George H. W., George W. made the facts fit his value system. The experience, or lack thereof, of each man also contributed to the problem-solving capacity of each administration. George W. was less willing to listen to alternatives, especially once his mind was made up. As Bob Woodward has suggested, George W. often dismissed attempts to alter his policy decision after he had chosen the administration's course.[16] In addition, Ron Suskind explained that George W.'s sublime confidence infiltrated his decision making, contributing to an overall sense of certainty throughout the administration. According to Suskind, the George W. administration did not promote "open dialogue, based on facts . . . as something of inherent value"; this could "create doubt, which undercuts faith. It could result in a loss of confidence in the decision-maker and, just as important, by the decision-maker."[17]

## Flexibility and Compromise vs. Certainty and Competition

George H. W.'s experience and pragmatism meant that he was more willing to examine a problem without closing off options. On the other hand, George W.'s ideological rigidity led him to believe in the certainty of his decisions. When confronted with facts that contradicted his beliefs, George W. often refused to back down. Much of George W.'s certainty came from his religious convictions, while George H. W. tended to shy away from ideological and moral politics and rhetoric.

Charles Kegley described George H. W. as a president who "back[s] away from . . . confrontation and seeks compromises."[18] His personal leadership emphasized cooperation and negotiation. As a child, George H. W. was encouraged not to be selfish and to seek solutions that would benefit everyone.[19] As vice president during the Reagan administration, George H. W. willingly subordinated his views to those of the administration. This illustrated his flexibility and loyalty as well as his willingness to compromise. During the 1980 presidential campaign, for example, he "preferred not to make waves or distract from the importance of getting Reagan to the White House." He aimed at the "very avoidance of extremism."[20] Vice President Bush had a reputation for flexibility. Bill Casey, the director of the CIA, was "surprised" by his accessibility, describing George H. W. as "easy to get along with, probably more flexible than anybody" in the administration. Howard Teicher, the NSC Middle East expert, added that George H. W. was "good at conducting diplomatic dialogue. He knew the style."[21]

George H. W.'s penchant for flexibility and compromise was illustrated throughout the foreign policy of his administration. In 1989 and 1990, as changes occurred in Eastern Europe, he, as noted earlier, remained cautious. Yet, as the changes became clearer and as the international landscape changed, George H. W. was willing to adapt and examine the new realities that were emerging. A good example of his flexibility and willingness to compromise can be seen in his administration's handling of conventional arms control in Europe. Conventional arms control in Europe had always been a thorny problem in Soviet-American relations, dating back to the 1970s. Throughout the negotiations, Western and Soviet purposes remained at odds. The West, especially the United States, was particularly concerned about the military threat posed by Soviet forces in the East and wanted to ensure a large-scale American presence in Europe by tying that presence into the arms control negotiations. The Soviets, on the other hand, sought political legitimacy for the postwar European system; essentially, the Soviets wanted the West to sanction their annexation of territory and presence in Eastern Europe after World War II.

By the time George H. W. entered the presidency, negotiations had stalled. Throughout 1989 and 1990, however, George H. W. demonstrated his willingness to compromise. By May 1989, he decided to seize the initiative and push the process forward, despite arguments to the contrary, particularly from Defense Secretary Richard Cheney and the Joint Chiefs of Staff (JCS). He proposed a 25 percent cut in U.S. troops in NATO forces, with a Soviet decrease to an equal number. He believed that this was large enough to demonstrate a "serious" commitment to the "positive changes" throughout Eastern Europe and the Soviet Union. The JCS was unhappy, suggesting a much more modest proposal. George H. W., demonstrating his flexibility, writes, "I was reluctant to ignore [their] advice. . . . I was determined not to bulldoze the military . . . or drag them into agreement. . . . I . . . sternly prodded. . . . This allowed us . . . to claim a more respectable 20 percent reduction."[22] His willingness to compromise, both within the American government and with the Soviets, ended with the successful signing of the Conventional Forces in Europe Agreement.

In stark contrast, George W.'s ideological rigidity meant he often refused to compromise or change course even when the facts contradicted the policy. A self-described born-again Christian, he viewed the world as one of absolutes and approached policy decisions with a degree of certainty that few presidents have possessed. His beliefs reflected a radical evangelicalism that divided the world into good and evil forces, and he tended to view the world as a clash between good and evil, right and wrong; in this clash, the forces of good not only would but also must prevail. In his 2000 presidential campaign, when asked who was the philosopher or thinker that he most identified with, without hesitation, Bush responded, "Christ, because he changed my heart."[23] Speaking privately to a Pennsylvania Amish group, Bush stated, "I trust that God speaks through me."[24] As a result, he viewed decisions simplistically and with alarming decisiveness and certainty. In Stephen Rubenzer and Thomas Faschingbauer's analysis of presidential personality and character, George W. ranked last on openness to experience. According to Rubenzer and Faschingbauer, this translated to his certainty in decision making and his being uncomfortable with change.[25] On a visit to an elementary school in Crawford, Texas, George W. stated, "Is it hard to make a decision . . . ? Not really. If you know what you believe, decisions come pretty easy. If you're one of these types of people that are always trying to figure out which way the wind is blowing, decision making can be difficult. But I find that I know who I am. I know what I believe in, and I know where I want to lead the country. And most decisions come pretty easily for me."[26] His certainty about decision making could be seen in the "stubborn, almost obsessive way in which he [held] on to ideas and plans after they [had] been discredited." George W. has an "inability to tolerate complexity" and "is anxious to limit new input, because any new information that challenges his beliefs can make him anxious about the choices he has already made."[27]

His certainty was coupled with a view of the world as one of competition in which the forces of good were destined to prevail. If God is on your side, an analysis of facts and alternatives is almost entirely unnecessary in policy making. A true believer has no place in his mind for an examination of contrary ideas, and George W. had an intolerance of doubters. Unlike George H. W., George W. possessed an air of arrogance and infallibility that guided his decision making. Even prior to 9/11, this was evident. Throughout 2001, "a cluster of particularly vivid qualities was shaping George W. Bush's White House . . . a disdain for contemplation or deliberation, an embrace of decisiveness, a retreat from empiricism, a . . . bullying impatience with doubters and even friendly questioners."[28] George W. relied on moral justifications over facts, and, most significant, his messianic, evangelical vision coincided politically with the views of many of his advisors. Richard Shweder referred to the president's view as "missionary moral progressivism," stressing that George W. had non-negotiable demands grounded in his view of universal moral truths.[29] For example, he renounced the Kyoto Protocol in March 2001, arguing that the treaty was flawed because it "exempt[ed] 80 percent of the world . . . from compliance" and would impose too heavy a burden on the American economy.[30] Despite evidence to the contrary from a variety of sources, George W. refused to alter his course on this issue. Once his mind was made up, there was no turning back.

Again, George H. W. and George W. Bush demonstrated very different approaches to decision making. While George H. W. examined each situation as unique and was flexible in his approach to decision making, George W. operated with a dead certainty about his decisions. George H. W. behaved like a diplomat on the world stage, cajoling and compromising with others. George W., on the other hand, was a crusader; despite promising to exercise a humble American foreign policy during the 2000 presidential campaign, his policy became one of the most ambitious in American history.

## NEGOTIATION VS. MESSIANIC UNIVERSALISM

George H. W. was a master of personal relations and diplomacy. He cultivated and relied on personal contacts, or Rolodex diplomacy, to facilitate policy. While most presidents rely on some form of personal diplomacy, George H. W. raised it to a new art form, using it to enhance his reputation and garner support for his policies. As ambassador to the United Nations, for example, he was "informal, his manner casual." On one occasion, he invited the Economic and Social Council to Shea Stadium for a baseball game; for George H. W., the personal touch was extremely important.[31] By the time he reached the Oval Office, he had a Rolodex of over twenty thousand names for sending out Christmas cards. And he took the time to get to know the various politicians, ambassadors, and staffers that he came into contact with, also knowing their families and interests. Unlike his predecessor, Ronald Reagan, George H. W. did not rely on index cards for this information; he understood the importance of knowing and remembering people.

His skill at personal diplomacy proved important throughout his presidency. George H. W. understood the significance of building alliances and preferred to proceed with multilateral support. This was evident during the end of the cold war but most clear after the Iraqi invasion of Kuwait, when he arranged a coalition of forces to evict Saddam Hussein's military. George H. W. comprehended the importance of allied support and the nuances of the use of force in the Middle East; further, he listened to allies and consulted with them on policy. He knew, for example, that introducing forces into Saudi Arabia would require delicate maneuvering and, as a result, he worked hard to cultivate and maintain the support of Arab regimes in the region.

In contrast, George W.'s approach in many ways reflected a form of messianic universalism. He believed that the United States had a universal message with unlimited global application. As Ivo Daalder and James Lindsay explain, many officials in the George W. Bush White House "argued that the United States should actively deploy its overwhelming military, economic, and political might to remake the world in its image, and that doing so would serve the interests of other countries as well as the United States."[32] George W.'s January 2005 inaugural address reflected his belief in the imperial mission of the United States. He explained, "The survival of liberty in our land increasingly depends on the success of liberty in other lands. The best hope for peace in our world is the expansion of freedom in all the world."[33] In addition, George W. argued, "I believe the United States is the beacon for freedom in the world. And I believe we have a responsibility to promote freedom that is as solemn as the responsibility is to protecting the American people. . . . I say that freedom is not America's gift to the world. Freedom is God's gift to everybody in the world. . . . And I believe that we have a duty to free people."[34]

The intensity of George W.'s adoption of this messianic vision was something of an innovation. But most significant, the adoption of this vision left little room for diplomacy. If peace could only be achieved with the establishment of the American model throughout the world, diplomacy was hardly necessary. Diplomacy would not work with dictatorships or, more generally, nondemocracies. Further, George W.'s vision was coupled with vast military power and the belief that military force would be required to fulfill that vision. Lastly, his vision included little, if any, place for international law and organizations. In contrast, George H. W. resisted the calls to enact American universalism, instead promoting American power through international law and organizations.

## Multilateral Internationalism vs. Unilateral Nationalism

Both George H. W. Bush and George W. Bush saw an important role for the United States on the global stage. However, while George H. W. emphasized the importance of multilateral internationalism as the basis for that role, George W. stressed American nationalism in pursuing a place for the United States in the world. Ultimately, this meant that George W. pursued a more ardent nationalism, using military force with the aim of establishing American hegemony, as the "carrier" of American ideals, while George H. W. saw the United States as "one among many"—a leader among followers.

As the cold war came to an end, George H. W. argued that international peace and security required an active American presence on the global stage. Shouldering this task was not only America's duty, but in its vital interest as well. He believed in the "idea of America as a beacon of hope throughout the world, and of freedom, justice, and opportunity for all its citizens." It is important to understand, however, that George H. W. believed allies were a significant part of this American ideal, arguing, "Overseas that translates into honoring our commitments to our friends and allies."[35] His view was reflected in the 1990 *National Security Strategy:* "In the aftermath of World War II, the United States took on an unaccustomed burden—the responsibility to lead and help defend the world's free nations. . . . The challenge of an aggressive, repressive Soviet Union was contained by a system of alliances, which we helped create, and led. In this historic endeavor, America has succeeded . . . new conditions created by this success . . . call for a new kind of American leadership. . . . We will not let that opportunity pass, nor will we shrink from the challenges created by new conditions." While the United States was "inescapably the leader . . . pivotal . . . for ensuring the stability of the international balance," George H. W. made clear that the first priority of his foreign policy would be "solidarity with . . . friends and allies." According to the 1990 *National Security Strategy,* the United States had "never been able to 'go it alone,' even in the early days of the Cold War." Further, "to attempt to do so would alter [the American] way of life . . . and jeopardize the very values [the United States is] seeking to protect." The report went on to argue that other democratic centers of power were welcome and consistent with American interests. Ultimately, the George H. W. Bush administration recognized the importance of alliances and demonstrated a willingness to "share the responsibilities of global leadership."[36]

As noted earlier, this was evident throughout the end of the cold war. Rather than imposing an American vision on post–cold war Europe, the George H. W. Bush administration ensured that the interests of the various parties were secured, using consultation and dialogue to facilitate support for policies. On German reunification, George H. W. understood the complexities of the process as well as the historical animosities and concerns raised by the British, French, and Soviets. His administration worked to build coalitions of support and, most significant, listened to the concerns of other states, addressing those concerns as the policy proceeded.

George H. W.'s internationalism contrasted with George W.'s brand of American nationalism, which downplayed the significance of alliances and, at times, willingly ignored allies in favor of American interests. There were three important aspects of George W.'s vision in this arena; all three contributed to a virulent nationalism that promoted American hegemony. First, George W. and his advisors believed that democratizing the world would provide the best security guarantee for the United States. Second, the instruments of American power were mainly military. George W. and his team relied on power politics to achieve their goals. And finally, George W.'s religious values contributed to his nationalist fervor; he combined his religious faith and the interests of the United States in a way that few presidents had ever done before.

All three ideas contributed to an imperialistic worldview, as noted earlier, that had little room for divisive voices. George W.'s post-9/11 "You are either with us or against us" rhetoric was not limited to the war on terrorism. Ultimately, American power would be used to establish a "benevolent" American hegemony. The United States would be not only the leader on the global stage but also the predominant player, establishing and enforcing the rules. As noted earlier, one reflection of his combative personality was a view of the world as a place of constant conflict. The main vehicle for resolving conflict, in his view, was American power; this meant that American action would often be required to achieve peace and security.

In the George W. Bush administration, faith and nationalism were linked. His fundamental beliefs gave George W. an unquestioned confidence in the United States' abilities. Faith meant that he viewed the United States as good and any opposition to the United States as evil. Dividing the world in such a way preordained conflict and gave way to an arrogant American nationalism that suggested a "My way or the highway" approach. George W.'s brand of American nationalism was often referred to as "cowboy diplomacy," a brash, risk-taking approach relying on intimidation and American military might. Thus, unlike his father, George W. pursued a policy of domination rather than cooperation and coordination. According to Justin Frank, George W. possessed a "sense of omnipotence." Frank adds, "His Iraq war 'coalition' was an affront to [George H. W.'s] internationalist policies. Even his pursuit of Saddam Hussein can be seen as a contemptuous repudiation of the first Bush presidency's military moderation."[37]

This brings to light George H. W.'s and George W.'s different views of American power and strategy. George H. W. preferred multilateral solutions, understanding that such a strategy could accrue benefits to the United States. While multilateral strategies often involve costs, many American interests cannot be achieved without the assistance of allies and coalitions. George H. W.'s pursuit of multilateralism, particularly after the Iraqi invasion of Kuwait, allowed him to secure American interests and influence world powers. George W., on the other hand, pursued a unilateral strategy from the start of his administration, pulling the United States out of various treaties, including the Kyoto and the Anti-Ballistic

Missile treaties. This only weakened American power and influence. As we shall see, these different approaches were significant to the outcomes of American foreign policy.

## CONCLUSION

Lloyd Gardner has argued, "What men think about the 'system' and what it needs to function well at a given time is often as important as its supposed determinants. Indeed, what men think about helps to determine the 'system.'"[38] Many scholars reject such a claim, suggesting instead that the international system generates inevitable outcomes.[39] However, these certainties often evaporate when one examines the historical record. Often, the unforeseen contingencies, like personality factors, became the bases of causation. Even Louis J. Halle, who argued that the cold war was an inevitable "historical necessity," concedes, "When we see what actually happens in operational terms . . . the whole situation appears to offer a range of possibilities incompatible with the rigidity of physical laws. Accidents seem to play their part. The mistakes of individual statesmen are seen to be significant. . . . Unusual human weakness or unusual human virtue appears to alter what might otherwise have been the course of events. . . . We must beware of the absoluteness of the great abstractions represented by the metaphor of the power vacuum. We must assume a range of choice in the actual play of events."[40] Ultimately, a systemic explanation is insufficient and does not discriminate between the possible options that could have emerged within the international system. The system, for example, cannot explain policy makers' internalization of their own rhetoric, and why they accepted and acted on certain premises and choices. Thus, we turn to an examination of these two presidents and the world each faced; both were complex, multifaceted individuals, with personality needs and political goals, trying to cope with monumental challenges in the international environment and the constraints and opportunities it posed.

In the case of George H. W. and George W., the enlightened realist and cowboy liberal worldviews produced vastly different results. George H. W.'s enlightened realist approach was much more cautious and preferred strategies that fostered cooperation and burden sharing. George W.'s cowboy liberal approach, on the other hand, was much more accepting of risks and sought ways to expand American power. In Iraq, both presidents faced challenges and opportunities, and the manner in which they confronted the issue reflected each president's beliefs and style.

## 3

# Boots on the Ground

Since the founding of the United States, American presidents have engaged in over three hundred separate uses of force. However, one could
argue that the United States' use of force against Saddam Hussein and
Iraq constituted one of the longest periods of hostility against another
country. The hostilities began with Iraq's invasion of Kuwait and the subsequent Persian Gulf War in 1990–91 and continued well into the first
part of the twenty-first century with the end of operations in December
2011. Thirteen years separated George H. W.'s eviction of Iraq from Kuwait, aided by the United Nations, and George W.'s eviction of the Saddam
Hussein regime from power. In both cases, the president established the
strategy, determined the policy choices, and guided the country from his
convictions.

### CRISIS

*1990: The Iraqi Invasion of Kuwait*

On August 1, 1990, President George H. W. Bush learned of Iraq's invasion of Kuwait. American officials, although concerned about Iraq's pos-
turing against Kuwait in previous months, were caught off guard. The
shock rippled through the administration and concerns began to arise
that Saudi Arabia might be Iraq's next target. George H. W's response to
the crisis would serve to define his administration. Additionally, it presented an opportunity for the administration to establish a new era of
peace and stability in world politics.

The Bush administration's Iraqi policy was inherited from the Reagan
administration, and initially George H. W. did not offer any significant

Iraq and surrounding countries

changes. Throughout the previous decade, the United States had cultivated a relationship with Iraq based on the shared interest of limiting
Iranian influence in the region. This policy was the result of the Iranian
revolution of 1978–79, which brought a radical Islamic fundamental-
ism, led by Ayatollah Khomeini, into power in Iran. Further, Khomeini's

staunch anti-Western rhetoric and actions threatened American interests and moderate Arab regimes throughout the Middle East. The humiliation of the overthrow of the pro-American government of the shah was furthered when revolutionaries seized the American embassy in Tehran in November 1979, holding fifty American hostages for 444 days.

During the crisis, Saddam Hussein seized the opportunity to attack Iran. Following a long history of border disputes, and fears related to the aggressive and expansive nature of the Iranian revolution, Iraq invaded Iran on September 22, 1980. While Iraq took early advantage of the chaos of the Iranian revolution, Iran had regained all lost territory by 1982 and went on the offensive. For the next six years, the two countries were at war, despite multiple cease-fire urgings by the UN Security Council. Throughout the crisis, the Reagan administration supported Iraq, deciding that Iran and its revolution were antithetical to American interests and policy. As a result, the United States provided technological aid, intelligence, and military equipment and weapons to Saddam Hussein's regime. As Howard Teicher, a former NSC official, explained, "President Reagan decided that the United States would do whatever was necessary . . . to prevent Iraq from losing the war with Iran . . . the United States actively supported the Iraqi war effort by supplying the Iraqis with billions of dollars of credits, by providing U.S. military intelligence and advice to the Iraqis, and by closely monitoring third country arms sales to Iraq to make sure that Iraq had the military weaponry it required. The United States also provided strategic operational advice."[1] In addition, the United States provided tactical battlefield assistance to the Iraqi Army. American intelligence officers helped interpret satellite information and promoted vast intelligence sharing. In some cases, American troops were actually crossing the border into Iran alongside Iraqi troops.[2]

When George H. W. arrived in the Oval Office, he inherited a policy that clearly supported Iraq and was aiming to make it a key ally in the Middle East. The Bush administration decided to continue and extend Reagan's policy. Domestic considerations weighed heavily in this decision. The Department of Agriculture's Commodity Credit Corporation had dramatically expanded its grain credit guarantees to Iraq; this benefited American farmers since Iraq used those credits to purchase American agricultural products. By 1989, Iraq was the ninth-largest purchaser of American agricultural products. In fall 1989, President Bush signed National Security Directive 26 (NSD-26), concluding that normal relations between the United States and Iraq would serve long-term American interests. However, as was also apparent in George H. W.'s prudent attitude toward the Soviet Union, the directive remained cautious, reserving the option of force if the relationship proved unsuccessful. Thus, while American policy aimed to cultivate Iraq as an ally in the region, George H. W. remained reactive to changes on the ground, a reflection of his enlightened realist approach, and was not willing to move forward without clear signs of progress from Iraq. As explained in NSD-26, U.S. policy was to "propose economic and political incentives for Iraq to moderate its behavior. . . . At the same time . . . any illegal use of chemical and/ or biological weapons will lead to economic and political sanctions."[3]

Early efforts at engaging Iraq, however, were questionable. Saddam Hussein was highly critical of American policy and threatened America's longtime ally in the region, Israel. As Brent Scowcroft, national security advisor from 1989 to 1993, explained, "The relative moderation [Saddam] had adopted . . . was abandoned."[4] A reflection of this shift came on July 25, 1990, when Hussein met with the American ambassador to Iraq, April Glaspie, and noted a rift in American-Iraqi relations. According to an Iraqi transcript of that meeting, Hussein told Glaspie, "We had hoped for . . . cooperation. . . . But . . . relations have suffered . . . we want pride, liberty and our right to choose. . . . I do not believe that anyone would lose by making friends with Iraq." Hussein continued, arguing that the American media had orchestrated a campaign against him and hinting at the worsening relations between Iraq and Kuwait. "Kuwait and the U.A.E. were at the front of [a] policy aimed at lowering Iraq's position and depriving its people of higher economic standards. . . . It is not reasonable to ask our people to bleed rivers of blood . . . then to tell them, 'Now you have to accept aggression from Kuwait, the U.A.E. or from the U.S. or from Israel.'" As the discussion continued, Hussein became more belligerent and hinted at his upcoming actions against Kuwait. He told Glaspie that Iraq would not act against Kuwait unless negotiations failed, but he went on to explain that "Iraq will not accept death."[5]

After the meeting, Ambassador Glaspie sent a wire to Secretary of State James Baker. Glaspie noted that Hussein went to great lengths to "assure President Bush that his intentions are peaceful." At the same time, she explained that Hussein warned that "if publicly humiliated . . . he would have to 'respond.'"[6] Glaspie's response cautioned Hussein, according to her testimony before the Senate Foreign Relations Committee in March 1991, emphasizing the need to solve the dispute "through negotiation without violence."[7] She added that the United States was "committed to ensure the free flow of oil from the gulf and to support the sovereignty and integrity of the gulf states . . . [and] strongly committed to supporting the individual and collective self-defense of our friends in the gulf."[8]

On August 2, almost one week after the Hussein-Glaspie meeting, Iraq invaded and annexed Kuwait, seizing its vast oil reserves and liquidating billions of dollars of loans provided by Kuwait to Iraq during the Iran-Iraq War. The Bush administration was surprised by the invasion, despite the presence of one hundred thousand Iraqi troops along the Kuwaiti border. At the time, General H. Norman Schwarzkopf, commander of U.S. Central Command, wrote to the chairman of the Joint Chiefs of Staff, General Colin Powell, emphasizing that "at most . . . Iraq was poised to launch a punitive but limited strike at Kuwait." Neither Powell nor Secretary of Defense Richard B. Cheney disagreed. As late as August 1, Powell's chief of operations, General Thomas Kelly, did not believe an invasion was imminent. Once again, Cheney agreed, arguing that there was no way to distinguish between a bluff and the real thing.[9] In addition, analysis by the American embassy in Baghdad and Richard Haass suggested that Iraq's intentions remained uncertain and gave no clear understanding for American officials to act on. On July 26, Glaspie noted that the "central issue for Iraq is revenue, not the border"; she added that Saddam Hussein was interested in debt forgiveness, for example. On the same day, Haass argued that "there is yet no clear indication of what is truly behind [Saddam Hussein's] behavior." However, Haass suggested an "eerie parallel between Iraq's actions [in] the Iran-Iraq War. . . . Saddam has been careful to build a case that Iraq has tried all reasonable diplomatic means."[10]

George H. W., characteristically prudent and cautious, did not want to risk potential progress in U.S.-Iraqi relations; this meant that the administration was left unprepared for the Iraqi invasion, able to react to Iraqi actions only after the invasion. As a result, George H. W.'s beliefs and experiences played a large role. The surprise nature of the crisis increased the importance of the main players, particularly the president.

At first, George H. W. was reluctant to act too aggressively, reflecting his characteristic caution and realist worldview. The administration's initial focus was on the deterrence of further aggression and the defense of Saudi Arabia and its vast oil reserves. In one of his first post-invasion contacts with a world leader, President Bush called King Fahd to make clear that Saudi Arabian "security is important to us and [the United States] want[s] to do everything possible to deter any Iraqi aggression against the Kingdom." At the same time, he nudged the Arab League to take the lead in the crisis, proceeding toward a possible solution, arguing that "collective Arab action would be good."[11] Ultimately, the administration was concerned that Saddam Hussein would push farther than Kuwait, threatening world oil supplies and the international economy. The August 4 National Security Council meeting best illustrates George H. W.'s realist approach. After a discussion of various options, George H. W. expressed interest in using a small ground force with air cover to protect Saudi Arabia. "Our first objective," he argued, "is to keep Saddam out of Saudi Arabia. Our second objective is to protect the Saudis against retaliation when we shut down Iraq's export capability."[12]

Ultimately, this meant pressuring the Saudis to accept American troops on their soil and moving troops there as quickly as possible. In another phone call to King Fahd, President Bush stressed the necessity of getting forces to Saudi Arabia, explaining, "We need to get those forces there soon or Saddam . . . might grab the oil fields. . . . The security of Saudi Arabia is vital."[13] In addition, he wanted to pursue action through the United Nations. On August 5, he told the National Security Council, "What we have got to do is get Chapter 7 sanctions and convince Saudi Arabia and Turkey to close the pipelines while we cut off the Gulf."[14] But George H. W.'s push for Chapter 7 action, referring to the UN Charter and the chapter that sets out the powers of the United Nations Security Council to maintain peace, proved controversial.

British prime minister Margaret Thatcher, America's staunchest ally, later explained that George H. W. initially urged calm and emphasized an Arab solution to the situation. According to Thatcher, it was only after numerous meetings and discussions that George H. W. made clear his desire to use force, if necessary, to evict Iraq from Kuwait. More important, Thatcher explains that President Bush was determined to seek UN support throughout the process. She disagreed with his approach: "The Security Council Resolution [661] which had already been passed, combined with our ability to invoke Article 51 of the UN Charter on self-defence, was sufficient" for action. In fact, Thatcher remained critical of Bush's approach after she left office, arguing, "I committed myself . . . to [throwing] some cold water on the ambitious internationalism which the Gulf War spawned. . . . . I . . . urged caution. . . . Multilateralism . . . became almost an obsession in the years that followed."[15]

George H. W., however, felt strongly about receiving UN approval.[16] He explained in his own recollections that his experience cautioned against an approach that failed to build multilateral support. In particular, he wanted a coalition of states, including the Soviet Union, to condemn and respond to Iraqi actions. "I was keenly aware that this would be the first post-Cold War test of the Security Council in crisis. . . . Soviet help in particular was key, first because they had veto power in the Security Council, but also because they could complete Iraq's political isolation."[17] In a press conference on the day of the invasion, George H. W. stressed his belief in the importance of international law and a multilateral solution to the crisis, arguing that Iraq's actions constituted "naked aggression that violates the United Nations Charter."[18] Throughout the crisis, the administration pushed for a multilateral solution that would demonstrate that it had "explored fully our . . . options and . . . given sanctions a fair chance to work."[19]

Further, drawing on his World War II and cold war experiences, he stressed the importance of American leadership in the world: "When it comes to . . . security, America can never afford to fail or fall short. . . . . It's good versus evil . . . nothing like this since World War II; nothing of this moral importance."[20] Emphasizing his personal understanding of history, George H. W. equated Hussein with Adolf Hitler, and later warned against a policy of appeasement, arguing that the failure of leaders to stand up to Hitler's aggressive ambitions had only "[encouraged] those regimes."[21] It is important to note that this was not simply a rhetorical device. He also equated Hussein with Hitler in private conversations with world leaders.[22]

Furthermore, the administration viewed the response to the crisis as linked to the significant international changes taking place. The change in the relationship between the United States and the Soviet Union meant that this crisis could be handled differently than it would have been in the past. The administration hoped that the United States and the Soviet Union could cooperate to find a resolution. Accordingly, this would signal a new international system, one in which the United Nations might be able to serve its original purposes. In a conversation between Baker and Soviet foreign minister Eduard Shevardnadze, Baker stressed that "nothing . . . would better symbolize the change in US-USSR relations than our joint participation in protecting the vulnerable states of the Gulf."[23]

Within days of the invasion, other aspects of George H. W.'s worldview were emerging and influencing policy. World War II had demonstrated the importance of American resolve against aggression; the cold war had illustrated the value of patience and firmness in dealing with an adversary; and the Vietnam War had shown the failures of committing military forces halfheartedly and micromanaging crises. After an initial reluctance, George H. W. was prepared to use force, but he focused on an approach that stressed acting within a multilateral coalition and was unwilling to proceed without exercising all of his other options first.[24] Relying on his extensive personal contacts with foreign leaders and diplomats, George H. W. began organizing an international coalition to evict Iraq from Kuwait. While the Bush administration acknowledged it could unilaterally solve the problem, George H. W. understood the importance of diplomacy and recognized the need for a multilateral solution. As Secretary of State Baker explained, evicting Iraq from Kuwait "could have been a unilateral American initiative. . . . As a practical matter, the United States [pursued] a coalition approach. . . . Otherwise we'd never attract the breadth of support to convince Saddam he was confronting the entire . . . world, not just a single superpower he might be able to demonize."[25]

Relying on multilateralism proved significant. In an unprecedented move, and at George H. W.'s request, Cheney received permission from Saudi Arabia's monarchy to move American troops onto Saudi soil. Further, George H. W. maintained frequent contact with numerous leaders throughout the region, including President Hosni Mubarak of Egypt, Prince Bandar, the Saudi ambassador to the United States, and King

Fahd of Saudi Arabia. He also engaged in a flurry of negotiations with NATO allies and allies at the United Nations. Most notably, George H. W. reached out to the Soviet Union, engaging America's former adversary as an ally in the crisis. Mikhail Gorbachev, Soviet premier at the time, later explained the significance of George H. W.'s multilateral approach, emphasizing the "mutual understanding and trust" that he and the American president had for each other and the importance this played in establishing a "responsible and open dialogue" between the United States and the Soviet Union. Further, Gorbachev stressed George H. W.'s acknowledgment that the United States could not lead alone and the significance of the emerging Soviet-American partnership: "We played a fundamental role in shaping the world community's common reaction to the aggression and its reversal, and we helped consolidate the United Nations' role. We were able . . . in conjunction with the leadership of the United States, not just to preserve but also to reinforce Soviet-American mutual understanding, trust, and partnership, sustaining them throughout this acute conflict—the first such test since the Cold War's end."[26] In another significant move, George H. W. demonstrated his willingness to reach out to President Assad of Syria. George H. W. personally contacted Assad and cajoled him into the coalition despite criticism. Furthermore, the administration understood that this would have significant ramifications for its overall policy. According to an internal memo, "The principal reason for going to Syria is what [the United States] gain[s] in the region from the symbolism of our ability to work with Assad."[27] This approach was very different from the one that George W. would take over a decade later.

### 2001: The Attacks of 9/11 and Iraq

Throughout the 1990s the United States opted for a policy of containing Iraq. That policy was based on post–Persian Gulf War UN Security Council resolutions. Ultimately, containing Iraq meant that Saddam Hussein and his regime remained in power and could potentially complicate American actions in the Middle East. As a result, in 1998, Congress passed the Iraq Liberation Act stating, "It should be the policy of the United States to support efforts to remove the regime headed by Saddam Hussein from power in Iraq and to promote the emergence of a democratic government to replace that regime."[28] It left it up to the president to determine how to achieve these goals. At the same time, a number of then governor George W. Bush's future presidential advisors were urging President Bill Clinton to overthrow Saddam Hussein's regime in Iraq.

For his part, George W. suggested that he was not interested in nation building during his 2000 presidential campaign. During one of the presidential debates with his rival Al Gore, then vice president, George W. criticized the Clinton administration's foreign policy, explaining, "I would take the use of force seriously. . . . I don't think we can be all things to all people in the world. I think we've got to be careful when we commit our troops. The vice president . . . believes in nation building. I would be very careful about using our troops as nation builders."[29] However, at the same time, he argued that he would be in favor of stronger opposition to the Iraqi regime and Saddam Hussein, stating that he would "take him out if he continued to develop weapons of mass destruction."[30] The latter view proved more prescient of the future George W. Bush administration's policy toward Iraq.

Paul O'Neill, George W.'s first secretary of the treasury, revealed that Iraq was a major item on the first National Security Council meeting agenda on January 20, 2001.[31] In fact, three days after the inauguration in January 2001, Secretary of State Colin Powell requested an analysis of America's Iraq regime change policy.[32] Early on, the administration appeared to be obsessed with Saddam Hussein. Almost immediately, the administration established an interagency policy review on how to deal with Iraq; specifically, George W. directed the Pentagon to examine various military options.[33] As Scott McClellan, White House press secretary from 2003 to 2006 and principal deputy White House press secretary from 2001 to 2003, explains, "Bush . . . made clear that we were determined to pursue a tougher approach for dealing with Saddam Hussein and his rogue regime. . . . Bush and his advisors were sending clear signals that more robust military action . . . was likely."[34] The interagency review, chaired by Richard Haass, the director of policy planning in the Department of State, never reached the president's desk. Nor did its counterpart report on Al Qaeda and international terrorism. The events of September 11, 2001, intervened. However, in the months prior to the attacks, the administration's focus was on Iraq.

State Department documents from June and July 2001 indicate a high degree of interest in aluminum tubes purchased by Iraq. What is striking about these documents is that the government had not yet made a determination about the intended uses of the aluminum tubes; yet, the information made its way to the president and was used to "[get] the right story out."[35] In addition, the documents emphasize reporting the analysis to the United Nations "even if it concludes that the tubes do not meet specifications for nuclear end use."[36] By the end of July, Iraq's possible weapons program was of the utmost concern to the principal policy makers. In a memo to National Security Advisor Condoleezza Rice, Secretary of Defense Donald Rumsfeld argued, "Within a few years the U.S. will undoubtedly have to confront a Saddam armed with nuclear weapons. . . . If Saddam's regime were ousted, we would have a much-improved position in the region and elsewhere."[37]

Then, on September 11, 2001, the unthinkable happened as terrorists struck the World Trade Center and other targets in an attack on American soil. Throughout the summer, Secretary of State Powell had been given considerable leeway to negotiate new "smart" sanctions that aimed to limit Iraq's access to dual-use technologies, like nuclear energy, while reducing food-related sanctions. Essentially, this reflected a continuation of the Clinton administration's approach, using air strikes to maintain the Iraqi regime's compliance. However, at the same time, it became clear that many in the administration believed that "smart" sanctions and air strikes would not solve the "Iraq problem." McClellan explains that "as concern grew . . . that the sanctions of the previous decade were continuing to weaken, Russia prevented the new smart sanctions approach . . . from getting through the Security Council."[38] Russia's actions only served to confirm what many in the administration already believed with regard to Iraq—diplomacy was no longer an option. As a result, a diplomatic approach was unraveling before 9/11.

The terrorist attacks of 9/11 thrust the Iraqi challenge to the top of the policy agenda. In the wake of the attacks, Deputy Secretary of Defense Paul Wolfowitz analogized 9/11 to Pearl Harbor and pushed the issue of Iraq, urging the necessity of developing a new strategic vision to deal with terrorism and advance American interests in the world. He insisted that "to win against terrorism, the United States must go after the leaders of

Iraq, Iran and Syria."[39] Rumsfeld and Cheney supported Wolfowitz's view, arguing that 9/11 offered an opportunity to put a grand strategic vision in place, establishing American political and military predominance on the global stage in the wake of the drift that had occurred after the end of the cold war. A Defense Department document indicates that hours after the 9/11 attacks, Rumsfeld wanted to attack Iraq and Osama Bin Laden, and directed Jim Hayes, a Defense Department lawyer, to get "support" for a link between Iraq and Al Qaeda.[40] And on the evening of September 11, Rumsfeld argued, "You know, we've got to do Iraq—there just aren't enough targets in Afghanistan."[41]

Cheney, Rumsfeld, and Wolfowitz all espoused similar views and saw in the wake of 9/11 an opportunity to fulfill American interests and goals. Cheney believed that Saddam Hussein was in league with Osama Bin Laden, despite evidence to the contrary, and clung to the conviction that Hussein would eventually provide weapons of mass destruction (WMD) to Al Qaeda. Like Wolfowitz, Cheney had urged George H. W. to push on to Baghdad during Operation Desert Storm, believing it was a terrible error not to remove the regime. Later, referring to the elder Bush's decision not to pursue that action in 1991, Cheney would state, "Very seldom in life do you get a chance to fix something that went wrong."[42]

Wolfowitz was perhaps the most invested in the war in Iraq. When he was the U.S. ambassador to Indonesia, Wolfowitz became interested in the Islamic reform movement and he envisioned an Iraq that could become like Indonesia under President Suharto—a secular, pro-Western regime promoting American interests in the Middle East. Prior to 9/11, therefore, many in the administration espoused a transformative vision for American foreign policy in the Middle East. However, it took the events of 9/11 to allow them to implement that vision. Often referred to as neoconservatism, this vision was revisionist and opposed the status quo. Similar to offensive realism, it promoted the maximal use of American power to foster not only American interests but also what it believed to be good for the world as a whole. Neoconservatives wished to establish a "benevolent American hegemony" in the world, with American ideals established worldwide as a way to secure peace and prosperity for the United States.[43] Ultimately, 9/11 fortified the thinking of these neoconservatives and offered an opportunity for the implementation of this vision.

During the 1990s, Cheney, Rumsfeld, Wolfowitz, and others who became members of the George W. Bush administration had developed a reputation as members of the Project for the New American Century (PNAC), which espoused the establishment of a neoconservative world order. In June 1997, PNAC issued a statement of principles outlining its vision and arguing for a "Reaganite policy of military strength and moral clarity." Further, it encouraged increasing defense spending, strengthening democracies, and challenging "regimes hostile to [American] interests [by promoting] political and economic freedom abroad."[44] In a letter to President Clinton in January 1998, PNAC made Iraq the centerpiece of this strategy: "[The] policy of 'containment' of Saddam Hussein has been steadily eroding. . . . Given the magnitude of the threat, the current policy . . . is dangerously inadequate. The only acceptable strategy is one that eliminates the possibility that Iraq will be able to use or threaten to use weapons of mass destruction. . . . In the long term, it means removing Saddam Hussein and his regime from power."[45] These ideas fit well with George W.'s faith and his views regarding America's place in the world. Furthermore, it reinforced his view, expressed in 1998, that George H. W. had "made a mistake not going into Iraq, when he had an approval rating in the nineties." George W. added, "If I'm ever in that situation, I'll use it—I'll spend my political capital."[46] On September 12, George W. made clear to his advisors the significance of Iraq to his larger vision: "I want you, as soon as you can, to go back over everything, everything. See if Saddam did this. See if he's linked in any way. . . . Look into Iraq, Saddam."[47] By September 15, George W.'s intentions were clear; referring to Saddam Hussein, he said, "We will get this guy but at a time and place of our choosing."[48] Therefore, in the days following 9/11, the administration began building its case for a new strategic vision—one that included Iraq as a prime target.

Driving and sustaining the administration's policies was its concern about another wave of terrorist attacks. On October 4, word reached the White House that a Florida man had contracted a lethal dose of anthrax. Soon afterward, the man died and letters containing anthrax began turning up in New York and Washington, DC, including one sent to the office of Senate Majority leader Tom Daschle. Meanwhile, reports of possible letters containing anthrax began to emerge throughout the country, although most turned out to be false alarms. However, the anthrax attacks served to heighten the fears of the American public and provided the necessary basis for the administration to build its case for a global war on terror aimed at eradicating more dangerous threats.[49] As a White House insider explained, "I think the seminal event of the Bush administration was the anthrax attacks. It was the thing that changed everything. It was the hard stare into the abyss."[50]

Thus, by the end of 2001, George W. was actively promoting his global vision. Using the war in Afghanistan, he began to advance a wider claim of a global war on terrorism with Iraq as the next target. Again, early in September 2001, George W. had laid out the claims for more extensive action against terrorism, arguing, "These guys are like rattlesnakes; they strike and go back in their holes; we're not only going to go after the holes; we're going to go after the ranchers."[51] His own sense of right and wrong—his Manichean view of the world—and his sense of purpose defined by God marked out a course for him.

George W. moved quickly to advance his strategic vision. By December 2001, the administration had developed an Iraq war plan;[52] now, George W. was ready to make his case. In January 2002, George W. stressed that there was no difference between the terrorists themselves and the states that harbored or assisted them. In addition, he began to link the issues of terrorism and WMD. In his January 29 State of the Union address, he explained,

> My hope is that all nations will heed our call, and eliminate the terrorist parasites who threaten their countries and our own. . . . But some governments will be timid in the face of terror. And make no mistake about it: If they do not act, America will. [We must also] prevent regimes that sponsor terror from threatening America or our friends and allies with weapons of mass destruction. . . . States like [North Korea, Iran, and Iraq], and their terrorist allies, constitute an axis of evil, arming to threaten the peace of the world . . . these regimes pose a grave and growing danger. . . . And all nations should know: America will do what is necessary to ensure our . . . security. . . . I will not wait on events, while dangers gather. I will not stand by as peril draws closer and

closer. . . . Our war on terror is well begun, but it is only begun.
. . . I know we can overcome evil with greater good.[53]

With this speech, George W. made an unmistakable commitment to the
expansion of America's strategic presence throughout the globe, particularly in the Middle East. This was, in many senses, radical; with the end
of the cold war, the United States had begun to pull back, but George W.
was reversing that trend, aiming to establish American dominance. Thus,
9/11 and its aftermath provided George W. with a unique opportunity to
implement his strategic vision: to expand American power and influence
throughout the world.

Throughout 2002, the administration continued to make its case for
expanded American power and influence. That case focused on Iraq; it
appeared that there was no turning back. In March, Cheney told a group
of Senate Republicans who were sworn to secrecy, "The question was no
longer if the U.S. would attack Iraq, the only question was when."[54] In the
same month, George W. was more blunt, stating, "Fuck Saddam. We're
taking him out."[55] Throughout the spring, the administration was honing
its arguments. On June 1, George W. spoke at the U.S. Military Academy
in West Point, New York, emphasizing that "new threats require[d] new
thinking."

In defending the peace, we face a threat with no precedent. . . .
The gravest danger to freedom lies at the perilous crossroads
of radicalism and technology. . . . For much of the last century,
America's defense relied on the Cold War doctrines of deterrence
and containment. . . . Deterrence . . . means nothing against shad-
owy terrorist networks. . . . Containment is not possible when
unbalanced dictators with weapons of mass destruction can deliver those weapons on missiles or secretly provide them to terrorist allies. We cannot defend America . . . by hoping for the
best. . . . If we wait for threats to fully materialize, we will have
waited too long . . . the war on terror will not be won on the defensive. We must take the battle to the enemy. . . . In the world
we have entered, the only path to safety is the path of action. And
this nation will act.[56]

Reflecting his view of the world as one of absolutes, good vs. evil, black vs. white, this speech laid out what eventually would become known as the Bush Doctrine, a doctrine justifying the use of force in the face of potential future threats. Further, George W. would stress the need for American hegemony to establish peace and order throughout the world. By mid-2002, it was clear that the United States was on a path toward war with Iraq. The only question was when.

## PREPARING FOR WAR

### 1990: Operation Desert Shield

Over a decade earlier, George H. W. was on his own path to war with Iraq. George H. W. worked to build international and domestic support for a possible war to evict Iraq from Kuwait. Scowcroft explained that as the crisis wore on, the president was prepared to use force.[57] The president's decision to confront Iraq was reinforced by others in his administration. Secretary of Defense Cheney made clear his dislike of Iraq's growing power in the Gulf and saw this as an opportunity to eliminate the growing Iraqi threat in the region once and for all. He also believed that taking the time to let economic sanctions work was a mistake, allowing Iraq to expand its power.[58] His concerns led him to direct Paul Wolfowitz to work secretly on an alternative plan for action against Iraq.[59] Scowcroft and Deputy Secretary of State Lawrence Eagleburger agreed that military action was necessary, arguing that the United States must stand firm to resist Iraqi aggression. Baker agreed that force might be necessary, but emphasized the importance of building international support and maintaining international cooperation as a prerequisite of evicting Iraq from Kuwait.[60]

The strategy that quickly unfolded, therefore, stressed relying on multilateral support against Iraq in the event that the administration needed to use force. George H. W. and Baker both saw the significance of a multilateral solution and urged the UN Security Council to resist Iraqi aggression. As Baker explains, "First and foremost . . . Desert Shield was a global confrontation. . . . The decision to go to the United Nations from the beginning clearly underscored the global nature of the crisis."[61] Others in the administration disagreed, but George H. W. insisted on pursuing a response through the United Nations.[62] The key to this strategy was getting Soviet support; the Soviets, however, were reluctant to follow the American lead and were searching for a way to end the crisis on their own. Constant diplomacy was necessary, therefore, to get the Soviets on board and maintain their support.[63]

To build and maintain an international coalition, George H. W. emphasized personal diplomacy, encouraging and pressuring other foreign leaders, particularly those with influence in the United Nations, to oppose Iraqi actions. As a result, and at the United States' request, the UN Security Council passed Resolution 660 by a vote of 14 to 0, condemning the Iraqi invasion and demanding the complete and unconditional withdrawal of Iraq from Kuwait; only Yemen abstained. This was historically significant, since the Soviet Union voted against its previous ally and with the coalition led by the United States. George H. W. and Baker's extensive diplomacy, coupled with the Soviet Union's decreasing power and Mikhail Gorbachev's "new thinking," combined to produce a joint American-Soviet effort in the Gulf.

George H. W.'s multilateral strategy had significant benefits. In addition to demonstrating that the administration had the support of world opinion, it put pressure on Congress and the American public to support the administration's policy.[64] Throughout the fall, the administration focused on expanding the international coalition against Iraq, while pursuing diplomatic solutions to the crisis. By the end of September, the United States had succeeded in getting ten UN Security Council resolutions dealing with the situation in the Persian Gulf passed. Resolution 661 continued to stress Iraqi noncompliance with the Security Council and the demands in Resolution 660, but, most important, imposed the first set of economic sanctions on Iraq.[65]

George H. W.'s pursuit of multilateralism in dealing with the crisis was not surprising. The policy was a general reflection of his worldview of enlightened realism. In addition to his multilateralism, as noted earlier, he stressed his past experiences and linked Saddam Hussein to Adolf Hitler, enunciating the importance of avoiding appeasement. This reflected his traditional realist approach and desire to contain the threat. On August 8, for example, George H. W. addressed the nation, emphasizing Iraqi aggression and linking it to past atrocities and the cold war. "There is no justification . . . for this outrageous and brutal act of aggression. . . . No one . . . should doubt our desire for peace; and . . . our determination to confront aggression. . . . If history teaches us anything, it is that we must resist aggression. . . . Appeasement does not work. As was the case in the 1930's, we see in Saddam Hussein an aggressive dictator threatening his neighbors." In addition, his speech stressed his emphasis on multilateralism; he wanted collective pressure on Saddam Hussein:

> This is not an American problem or a European problem or a Middle East problem: It is the world's problem. And that's why . . . the United Nations Security Council, without dissent, condemned Iraq. . . . The Arab world . . . courageously announced its opposition to Iraqi aggression. Japan, the United Kingdom, and France, and other governments around the world have imposed severe sanctions. The Soviet Union and China ended all arms sales to Iraq. And . . . the United Nations Security Council approved for the first time in 23 years mandatory sanctions under chapter VII of the United Nations Charter.[66]

George H. W. made this crisis a test of American leadership in a post–cold war world, but it was also a test for the world itself; while the administration was prepared to "go it alone," it would only do so once a multilateral option had been exhausted, and only if no other option emerged.

Continuing to build support, George H. W. pursued multiple channels of diplomacy. Throughout the fall, the administration moved to tighten economic pressure on Iraq, allowing time to build international and domestic support for military intervention. The world was not ready for war and George H. W. understood the risks of unsupported military action. The vast majority of countries around the world voluntarily halted economic relations with Iraq. However, in the Middle East, Jordan, Iraq's neighbor, remained a major obstacle to sealing off trade completely. Fearing retaliation from Iraq, Jordan continued to allow economic interactions across its borders. George H. W. wanted to halt this trade, publicly declaring that the United States could unilaterally act under Article 51 of the United Nations Charter,[67] but he realized that unilateral action might threaten the unity of the growing international coalition against Iraq. Despite mounting pressure, especially from within the administration, to intervene and cut off all trade to Iraq, George H. W. moved cautiously, focusing instead on the importance of building an international coalition to evict Iraq from Kuwait, and privately expressing disagreement but understanding for Jordan's position.[68]

Meeting on August 22 with advisors at his home in Kennebunkport, Maine, George H. W. insisted on obtaining UN authorization to evict Iraq from Kuwait, over the objections of Scowcroft and British prime minister Margaret Thatcher. Thatcher feared that George H. W. might "go wobbly" on the use of force.[69] She later explained that she "did not like unnecessary resort to the UN, because it suggested that sovereign states lacked the moral authority to act on their own behalf." However, Thatcher eventually supported pursuing UN Security Council Resolution 665, understanding its significance to George H. W.'s policy.[70] Resolution 665 moved the international coalition beyond diplomatic and economic pressure and toward the use of force. It specifically authorized member states "deploying maritime forces to the area to use such measures . . . as may be necessary . . . to halt all . . . maritime shipping, in order to inspect and verify their cargoes and their destinations and to ensure strict implementation of . . . resolution 661(1990)."[71] Essentially, the United States was able to get Security Council approval to enforce compliance with earlier resolutions. To get full support, George H. W. called Gorbachev personally. Gorbachev agreed to the resolution but only after the Soviet Union made diplomatic overtures to Saddam Hussein. The United States supported Gorbachev's actions, and, after receiving a defiant response from the Iraqi leader, the Soviets were ready to support American policy; thus, supporting Soviet diplomatic maneuvering served to strengthen the coalition and American policy.

By September, there was an increasing sense of urgency. Satellite photos revealed that Iraq had amassed a sizeable army in Kuwait and an elaborate line of defense along the border with Saudi Arabia. George H. W. now became convinced that force would be necessary to reverse Iraqi aggression. Writing in his diary, he explained, "A day of churning. . . . I think we can draw a line in the sand."[72] George H. W. may have been ready to use force, but neither America nor the world was ready.

The Soviet Union remained the greatest external challenge for the American-led coalition of force. On September 9, in Helsinki, Gorbachev told George H. W. that Saddam Hussein had been effectively contained and suggested a face-saving plan linking his retreat from Kuwait to Middle East peace. George H. W. refused to link the issues and, when pushed, Gorbachev reaffirmed his commitment to removing Iraq from Kuwait.[73] George H. W. argued that if Iraq was not removed from Kuwait with force, his military would remain intact and could threaten the region in the future. Further, he was not convinced that Saddam Hussein could be trusted; the linkages between his retreat and Middle East peace could not be guaranteed. The discussion demonstrated the crux of George H. W.'s problem, however. Maintaining an international coalition proved to be extremely difficult and often left American policy makers with few choices.

The president faced similar challenges at home. In early October, both houses of Congress passed resolutions supporting George H. W.'s actions but encouraged continued diplomatic efforts to reach a solution to the crisis.[74] George H. W. also faced challenges to the use of force within the military. In October 1990, General H. Norman Schwarzkopf, commander in chief of U.S. Central Command, stated, "Now we are starting to see evidence that the sanctions are pinching." He added that going to war made no sense.[75] Powell agreed, arguing that the administration should slow the pace of war.[76] However, George H. W. pushed for a war plan and the military reluctantly presented one to him on October 11. Scowcroft described the plan as "unenthusiastic, delivered by people who didn't want to do the job."[77] George H. W. added that the military was not ready to move forward.[78] He then instructed the military to develop a new plan.

Meanwhile, the administration continued its diplomatic initiatives. George H. W. understood that diplomatic overtures toward Saddam Hussein could risk an unacceptable compromise, but he also understood coalition politics. Maintaining the coalition required diplomacy and George H. W. did not want to give the appearance of a rush to war. In addition, diplomacy gave allies an opportunity to prepare their publics for war. In the end, diplomacy strengthened George H. W.'s arguments since Saddam Hussein proved to be his own worst enemy, appearing on television with Western hostages, using anti-Western rhetoric, and refusing various diplomatic initiatives dealing with the status of Kuwait.

By the end of October, George H. W. was pressing congressional leaders to support military action in Iraq. However, congressional leaders were pushing back, urging that diplomacy be given more time. Representative Thomas Foley, a Democrat and the Speaker of the House, told George H .W., "The country and Congress are not prepared for offensive action." George H. W. argued, however, "The time has come to determine whether we continue to place most of our eggs in the sanction basket . . . or whether we raise the pressure on Saddam by pressing ahead on both the military and diplomatic tracks. . . . Indeed it may be necessary to push things to the brink of war if we are to convince Saddam to compromise."[79]

The lessons of the cold war were present in George H. W.'s thinking. In his view, containment worked only because it was backed by sufficient strength. Achieving successful diplomacy, therefore, required military strength, pressuring the opponent to choose compromise over certain defeat. The United States had already amassed 250,000 troops in its defense of Saudi Arabia and the wider Persian Gulf. Now, George H. W. wanted to increase the number of American forces in the region, nearly doubling them. On November 9, he informed congressional leaders of his decision. It came one day after congressional elections; the administration did not want to make the troop increases a part of the campaign debate. Known as the "November surprise," the move angered congressional leaders who criticized George H. W. for failing to seek their consultation and not giving sanctions a chance.[80] Senator Daniel Patrick Moynihan, a New York Democrat who had served in the Nixon administration, was particularly angered, arguing that George H. W. had put the country on "war footing without proper consultation."[81]

It was clear from his actions that George H. W. was convinced that military force was likely, and, like most of his predecessors in the Oval Office, he believed that he did not require congressional authorization or additional UN resolutions to proceed. However, he also understood that proceeding without additional authorization could be politically and diplomatically costly. Thus, he continued to concentrate on building additional support. He hoped as well that international support could increase domestic support for his actions. As Scowcroft explains, "By and large there was no appetite for forceful action . . . a U.N. resolution would bolster our case."[82] The administration continued its diplomacy and, more significant, used these skills to build the case for war. It was important that the administration demonstrate it had investigated all of its options and given sanctions an opportunity to work.[83]

The administration pursued additional UN backing. Baker and the State Department drafted a new resolution that would authorize the use of "all necessary means," including the use of force, to evict Iraq from Kuwait. Timing was key in the negotiations for this resolution. The administration wanted to secure the resolution by the end of November, while the United States held the presidency of the Security Council. In December, Yemen would hold the presidency and would surely slow the process, opposing action against Iraq, making it difficult for the United States to place the resolution on the agenda.

On November 3, Baker began meeting with the heads of state of all the Security Council members.[84] He met the greatest resistance to a new resolution in China and the Soviet Union. The leadership in both countries pushed to give sanctions more time to work. While China was concerned about the use of force, Baker persuaded Foreign Minister Qian to agree to support multinational action.[85] Gorbachev, however, was particularly obstinate. Still, he was willing to support the resolution, seeing in it another opportunity for diplomacy: "While for some this resolution opened the way for the decision to apply military force, for [the Soviet Union] its significance consisted above all in providing the last chance to avert war."[86]

Baker also received challenges from allies, including Thatcher in the United Kingdom. She continued to be troubled by the pursuit of another resolution, fearing that it would establish a dangerous precedent. According to Thatcher, "If it became accepted that force could only be used . . . when the United Nations approved, neither Britain's interests nor those of international justice and order would be served. The UN was a useful . . . forum. But it was hardly the nucleus of a new world order."[87] President François Mitterand of France agreed, arguing that there was "no difference between what [was] going on in Kuwait and what [was] going on in Lebanon. . . . If I had asked [the United Nations] to help in Lebanon, no one would have shown up."[88]

George H. W. was determined to produce another Security Council resolution, however, believing it would bolster Arab support for the use of force against Iraq. The language of the final resolution would set a deadline for Iraq to withdraw from Kuwait—January 15, 1991—and allow for the use of force by member states thereafter. On the day before the vote, Baker made final but ultimately frustrating efforts to gain the support of Cuba, Yemen, and China. On the afternoon of November 29, with Baker presiding, the Security Council embarked on a historic vote. Referring to the ill-fated decision by the League of Nations not to evict Italy from Ethiopia in the interwar period, Baker opened the meeting explaining, "History now has given us another chance. . . . We now have the chance to build the world envisioned by the founders of the United Nations. . . . We must not let the United Nations go the way of the League of Nations. . . . We must meet the threat to international peace. . . . If Iraq does not reverse its course peacefully, then other necessary measures—including the use of force—should be authorized."[89] The meeting lasted two hours. In the end, Resolution 678 passed by a vote of 12 in favor, 2 opposed (Cuba and Yemen), with China abstaining. China's abstention was significant since its opposition to the resolution would have prevented its passing. Diplomacy had paid off.

Resolution 678 demanded that Iraq "fully comply" with all UN resolutions pertaining to the crisis and gave the Iraqi government "one final opportunity, as a pause of goodwill." It authorized member states to "use all necessary means . . . to restore international peace and security in the area" if Iraq failed to comply by January 15, 1991.[90] In order to secure the successful passing of the resolution, the administration had to remove the words "including the use of force"; however, George H. W. made clear that "all necessary means" implied that force was an option. Confident that he had gained international support to use force if Iraq did not reverse its actions, George H. W. now turned to cultivating domestic support for the use of force.

In many ways, this would prove more difficult. Ironically, many prominent officials criticized the administration for rushing into war. Admiral William J. Crowe, former chairman of the Joint Chiefs of Staff, was one of the most outspoken critics, arguing before a Senate committee on November 29, "Our dislike for Hussein seems to have crowded out many other considerations. . . . I would argue that we should give sanctions a fair chance before we discard them. I personally believe they will bring him to his knees."[91]

Responding to these criticisms, George H. W. argued, "No one is more determined than I am to see Saddam's aggression reversed . . . people caution patience. . . . I will . . . be patient. But . . . time is running out." He then suggested he would "go the extra mile for peace" and issued an invitation to Iraqi foreign minister Tariq Aziz to meet and discuss "all aspects of the Gulf crisis."[92] However, George H. W. made clear that his willingness to continue to pursue diplomacy did not mean he would accept anything less than an unconditional Iraqi withdrawal from Kuwait.

His conciliatory gestures attracted a great deal of attention. In December, he decided to send Secretary Baker to Baghdad and invited Iraqi foreign minister Tariq Aziz to Washington. George H. W. argued that collaboration with the Soviet Union had been "crucial . . . in cementing the . . . coalition. . . . I thought this an essential step to take to highlight that the choice of peace or war is Saddam's to make."[93] But these gestures failed to convince Saddam Hussein to change course. In fact, Iraqi actions were helping to make the case for war. Hussein became increasingly bellicose, and he publicly "postponed indefinitely" any high-level talks with the United States that could have avoided war.[94] On New Year's Eve, George H. W. wrote a letter to his children: "I have the peace of mind that comes from knowing that we have tried hard for peace. . . . We have waited to give sanctions a chance . . . sometimes in life you have to act as you think best—you can't compromise, you can't give in."[95]

On the following day, George H. W. met with Scowcroft, Cheney, Powell, and CIA director Robert Gates. Despite believing that the time for peace may have passed, and in spite of objections from numerous advisors, George H. W. decided to give diplomacy one more chance. For the president, this was the final opportunity to convince Saddam Hussein of the seriousness of the coalition—and at the same time, convince the coalition as well as his domestic critics that force was only a last resort. On January 5, 1991, he wrote to Hussein, pleading the case for peace: "We stand at the brink of war. . . . This is a war that began with your invasion of Kuwait; this is a war that can be ended . . . by Iraq's full and unconditional compliance with U.N. Security Council Resolution 678. I am writing you now . . . because what is at stake demands that no opportunity be lost to avoid what would be a certain calamity for the people of Iraq. . . . The international community is united. . . . This is not simply the policy of the

United States. . . . We prefer a peaceful outcome. However . . . principle cannot be compromised." George H. W. continued, explaining that the January 15 deadline marked a "pause of good will" and he hoped that the crisis could end "without further violence."[96] On January 9, Secretary of State Baker hand delivered the letter to Iraqi foreign minister Aziz. The two then met in an attempt to resolve the dispute peacefully, but the meeting ended without agreement.[97] For the administration, this meeting represented the last opportunity to end the dispute without the use of force.

George H. W. now turned to Congress to garner its support. Once again, numerous advisors objected, but George H. W. was convinced that successful and effective action required Congress's backing. This was a risky policy, since many in Congress had been strong critics of his Iraq policy to date. However, he also knew that gaining congressional support would increase the legitimacy of the use of force. In a January 8 letter to House Speaker Foley, George H. W. wrote, "The current situation in the Persian Gulf . . . threatens vital U.S. interests. . . . It would . . . enhance the chance for peace if Congress were now to go on record supporting the position adopted by the UN Security Council on twelve separate occasions. Such an action would underline that the United States stands with the international community. . . . I therefore request that the House of Representatives and the Senate adopt a Resolution" stating that Congress supports the use of all necessary means to implement UN Security Council Resolution 678."[98] It is important to note that George H. W. did not ask for a declaration of war. Like his predecessors in the office, he did not believe he needed such a declaration to pursue the use of force against Iraq. Rather, the congressional resolution was aimed at increasing the legitimacy of American actions and gaining public support for them.

On January 12, with numerous congressional Democrats in opposition, and only a 52-47 vote in favor in the Senate and a 250-183 vote in favor in the House of Representatives, Congress passed a resolution in support of the president's use of force against Iraq. Specifically, the joint resolution authorized "the use of United States Armed Forces pursuant to United Nations Security Council Resolution 678."[99] George H. W. had gotten what he wanted. He had built an international coalition in support of American actions; now, he had domestic support for those actions. Within days, the United States would launch its forces to evict Iraq from Kuwait. Over a decade later, George W. would follow a very different course in making his case for war.

### 2002: The Case for Regime Change

Throughout 2002, George W. was building the case for a new strategic doctrine, one based on a strategy of prevention—removing a threat before it materialized. This meant that the United States would be prepared to actively use military force; the United States would not wait to be attacked but would place itself on a wartime footing, going on the offense. This was a radical departure from the reactive policies of the past; generally, the United States did not attack first. With the dangerous combination of terrorism and weapons of mass destruction, George W. was arguing that the United States *must* attack first. The first test of this strategy would be Iraq.

Throughout the year, George W. made the case for attacking Iraq; ultimately, he relied on the links between terrorism and weapons of mass destruction as the basis for an attack. He and his advisors went even further, attempting to connect Saddam Hussein to the terrorist attacks of 9/11, Osama Bin Laden, and Al Qaeda. Events had served to reinforce this view. In October 2001, American intelligence identified a plan to use a "dirty bomb" in a major city. This was coupled with the anthrax attacks in the wake of the attacks on 9/11. In addition, as American troops battled the Taliban and Al Qaeda in Afghanistan, they found rudimentary drawings and information regarding weapons of mass destruction.

As events progressed, administration officials seized upon the intense fear throughout the country in order to build a case for George W.'s new strategic vision, which soon was referred to as the Bush Doctrine. Vice President Cheney was put in charge of reviewing what went wrong prior to the 9/11 attacks and determining how to prevent any future terrorist attacks. Cheney appeared more concerned than anyone in the administration about the potential for attacks by terrorists possessing weapons of mass destruction. The vice president's view reinforced the president's, increasing the intensity of the administration's strategic vision. Faced with what appeared to be overwhelming evidence of future terrorist attacks, George W. was convinced that preventive war was the only credible option. As a result, the administration began to push hard for a forward-leaning policy.

What sealed the deal for many in the administration was the belief that Saddam Hussein's *intentions* were evil. The administration disregarded critics who argued that Iraq was not connected to 9/11, suggesting instead that a Saddam Hussein with links to terrorism would be more dangerous than 9/11 and posed a grave threat to future peace and security. Further, administration officials believed that not acting would be worse than acting prematurely or incorrectly. Testifying before Congress in September 2002, Secretary of Defense Rumsfeld argued,

> As we meet, state sponsors of terror . . . are working to develop and acquire weapons of mass destruction. . . . We have entered a new security environment . . . we are in an age of little or no warning, when threats can emerge suddenly. . . . Let there be no doubt: an attack will be attempted . . . the one thing that is not an option is doing nothing. There are a number of terrorist states. . . . But no terrorist state poses a greater and more immediate threat . . . than the regime of Saddam Hussein in Iraq. [Saddam Hussein] has shown the murderous combination of intent and capability. . . . The world has acquiesced in [his] aggression, abuses and defiance. . . . Iraq is a part of the Global War on Terror—stopping terrorist regimes from acquiring weapons of mass destruction is a key objective of that war. . . . We must decide whether the risks of acting are greater than the risks of not acting.[100]

Rumsfeld's public assessments were coupled with internal Department of Defense assessments. By April 2002, the Department of Defense had put together a "decision package" of materials, with specific details for military support of the Iraqi opposition. Furthermore, Rumsfeld made clear his disdain for continuing inspections under UN auspices.[101] In an interview with Margaret Warner from PBS, Condoleezza Rice buttressed the administration's case: "The United States has always reserved the right to try and diminish or to try to eliminate a threat before it is attacked. It simply wouldn't make sense to sit and wait to be attacked if you thought that you could eliminate the threat."[102]

Throughout the administration, therefore, there was a consensus of thinking on Iraq. By March 2002, it was clear that the administration planned to attack Iraq. According to British officials, the British government had come to the conclusion that "the U.S. administration has lost faith in containment and is now considering regime change."[103] George W.'s limited experience in national security and foreign policy meant that he relied heavily on his advisors and on his own personal instincts—and the two reinforced one another. After the September 11th attacks, his inclination to view the world in absolutes, in terms of good and evil, made an attack on Iraq a priority. As Michael Duffy and Massimo Calabresi explain, "There are moments in history when ideology stops being a parlor game for academics and actually shapes the future of the world. . . . No one can say this Bush lacks the vision thing. . . . In just over two years in office, the President has displayed a preference for the bold stroke."[104] Furthermore, by his own admission, George W. suspected Iraq of involvement in 9/11 almost immediately after the attacks, despite the fact that the counterterrorism unit reported that there was no compelling supporting evidence.[105] By the end of 2002, the only member of the administration expressing any reluctance on war with Iraq was Secretary of State Colin Powell; while Powell agreed that Saddam Hussein posed challenges for American foreign policy, he did not believe launching an invasion was the best option for the United States.

From his first day at the State Department, Powell found himself an outsider in the administration. Foggy Bottom, the nickname for the State Department, was essentially sidelined in the policy-making process. Fred Kaplan explains, "From the start . . . Powell found himself almost consistently muzzled, outflanked, and humiliated by the true powers . . . Cheney and . . . Rumsfeld. . . . Powell suffered the . . . indignity of swatting off continuous rear-guard assaults from his own undersecretary of state, John Bolton, an aggressive hard-liner."[106] It was no accident that it was at Cheney's request that John Bolton had been placed at the State Department, where he served to divert and counter arguments in favor of international organizations and multilateralism.

Powell was in a difficult situation—an "old-guard conservative" among the neoconservative, hard-line activists. His voice was often drowned out by Cheney, Rumsfeld, and Wolfowitz. Furthermore, George

W.'s own inclinations often prevented Powell from making his case and presenting alternative options. In particular, George W. claimed he was on a mission from God to destroy Saddam Hussein and liberate Iraq.[107] Events helped George W. and other administration officials solidify their position further. Following the attacks of 9/11, Powell was treated like a pariah within the administration. The main problem he faced was philosophical. He had a pragmatic outlook and was rarely motivated by ideology in an administration filled with ideologues and led by a president who saw the world in terms of absolute ideas. But worst of all, at least from the point of view of many within the administration, Powell preferred multilateral, international solutions to problems; while many in the administration saw little use for the United Nations and other international organizations, Powell believed they were central to American foreign policy. In addition, Powell believed in the usefulness of methods short of force to produce desirable international outcomes. In his 1995 biography, for example, he wrote, "I . . . believe that sanctions are a useful weapon in the armory of nations. They helped . . . to hasten the meltdown of apartheid in South Africa."[108] This also was contrary to the general impatience with and disdain for sanctions demonstrated by others within the administration, including the president. In essence, the rift between Powell and others in the George W. administration mirrored the rift between the enlightened realist and cowboy liberal points of view.

Powell had little influence before 9/11, as the administration's decision to cut off funds for the UN Population Fund demonstrated. George W. argued that the fund supported abortions in China and therefore ran contrary to American foreign policy. A State Department fact-finding team found no evidence supporting this claim, so Powell tried to preserve the funding. However, he was never given a chance to state his case, since the decision was made without his input.[109] After 9/11, the situation worsened.

On the issue of Iraq, Powell was alone. Soon after 9/11, Cheney and Rumsfeld agreed that the terrorist attacks provided the United States with an opportunity to launch an attack on Iraq, eliminating the Iraqi problem for good. Powell, however, "adamantly opposed" attacking Iraq, arguing that countries in the "rapidly forming international coalition [in support of American actions against terrorism and Al Qaeda] would jump off

the bandwagon." But September 11th was a seminal event, reinforcing
George W.'s worldview. George W. argued, "Clinton was risk-averse. . . .
September the 11th obviously changed my thinking a lot about my responsibility . . . [and] Saddam Hussein's capacity to harm." Powell increasingly "found himself frozen out by the White House—in the 'icebox' or
the 'refrigerator.'"[110]

Throughout 2002, it became less and less likely that Powell could effectively prevent action against Iraq as Cheney, Rumsfeld, and George W.
were prohibiting a change of course. In an interview with Tim Russert
on *Meet the Press* in March 2002, Cheney "outflanked" Powell's position
when he responded to questions about Saddam Hussein and Iraq; in doing so, he essentially announced the administration's policy. He made it
clear that George W. had decided to pursue war with Iraq. Further, he explained that any action would be a part of a wider global war on terror that
aimed to prevent future attacks on the United States. Echoing earlier statements by George W., he argued that September 11, 2001, "demonstrated
[American] vulnerability. . . . We're worried about the possible marriage
. . . between terrorist organizations and . . . weapons of mass destruction
capability, the kind of devastating materials that Saddam used against his
own people . . . the evidence is overwhelming. . . . [We will do] whatever
is necessary to make certain that the United States and our friends and
allies are not threatened by a nuclear-armed Saddam Hussein."[111] With
that, Powell's arguments were muzzled. The administration was clearly
preparing to remove Saddam Hussein from power. As the "loyal soldier,"
Powell now found himself supporting a policy he didn't entirely embrace.
In April 2002, the State Department provided an intelligence assessment
on west European public support for action against Iraq. The assessment
suggested a high degree of support throughout the region; however, no
future assessments were conducted and the administration continued to
rely on this assessment's conclusions: fear of WMD.[112] Cheney continued
to be the "point man" on Iraq, making the case for action. In the summer,
he spoke to the National VFW Convention, explaining,

> The President and I never for a moment forget our number one
> responsibility: to protect the American people against further at-
> tack, and to win the war that began last September 11th. The dan-

ger to America requires action on many fronts . . . wars are never won on the defensive. We must take the battle to the enemy. . . . The President has made clear that there is no neutral ground in the fight against terror. Those who harbor terrorists share guilt for the acts they commit . . . a regime that harbors or supports terrorists will be regarded as hostile to the United States. . . . As we face this prospect, old doctrines of security do not apply. . . . Saddam Hussein . . . has systematically broken agreements. The Iraqi regime has . . . been very busy enhancing its [WMD] capabilities. . . . Simply stated, there is no doubt that Saddam Hussein now has weapons of mass destruction. . . . The risks of inaction are far greater than the risk of action.[113]

Rumsfeld supported this view, further isolating Powell. He went further than Cheney, however, making a clear case for a policy of prevention whereby possible future threats would be eliminated before they emerged. Speaking at the U.S. Air Force Academy commencement, Rumsfeld stated, "Prevention and preemption are the best, and indeed in most cases the only defense against terrorism. Our task is to find and destroy the enemy before they strike us."[114]

Throughout the summer, the administration's case gained momentum. In the fall, George W. was scheduled to address the UN General Assembly. He decided to give the world an ultimatum, making it clear that the United States was prepared to take action alone or as the leader of a coalition. It was clear that his mind was made up, and there would be no change of course; George W. was determined to remove Saddam Hussein from Iraq, despite objections from others. Using a cowboy analogy out of the plains of Midland, he stated,

Our principles and our security are challenged . . . by outlaw groups and regimes that accept no law of morality and have no limit on their violent ambitions. . . . In one place—in one regime—we find all these dangers, in their most lethal and aggressive forms, exactly the kind of aggressive threat the United Nations was born to confront. . . . The conduct of the Iraqi regime is a threat to the authority of the United Nations, and a threat to peace. Iraq has answered a decade of U.N. demands with a decade of defiance. All the world now faces a test, and the United Nations a difficult and defining moment. . . . My nation will work with the U.N. Security Council to meet our common challenge. . . . But the purposes of the United States should not be doubted.[115]

Thus, with or without UN support, the United States was preparing to use force against Iraq. His willingness to go it alone, if necessary, in responding to Iraq's defiance stood in contrast to George H. W.'s multilateral, coalition-building approach over a decade earlier.

This speech sidelined Powell. John Bolton, Undersecretary of State for Arms Control and International Security, added to his challenge in convincing the president about the necessity of an international coalition in confronting Iraq. Bolton clearly agreed with Cheney, Rumsfeld, and George W. Speaking at the Hudson Institute in November, Bolton argued, "The greatest threat to international peace and stability comes from rogue states and transnational terrorist groups that are unrestrained in their choice of weapon and undeterred by conventional means." He went on to explain that the administration was resolute in its aim to prevent rogue states from protecting terrorists; this would mean directing "international condemnation" toward these states.[116] In an earlier speech, Bolton had supported a preventive strategy, stating, "the Bush administration believes that the Cold War concepts . . . are no longer appropriate. . . . The international security system has changed and we must adapt our defenses and resources to it."[117]

As 2002 drew to a close, the decision to go to war with Iraq was final. The new national security strategy report had been released in September, and it clearly stated the administration's intentions. According to Condoleezza Rice, the *National Security Strategy of the United States of America* was based on three pillars: first, defending the peace "by opposing and preventing violence by terrorists and outlaw regimes"; second, preserving the peace "by fostering an era of good relations among the world's great powers"; and third, extending the peace "by seeking to extend the benefits of freedom and prosperity across the globe."[118] The Bush Doctrine, as this strategy came to be known, reflected George W.'s cowboy liberal approach, combining four elements: the promotion of democracy throughout the world; a preventive strategy; unilateralism; and American dominance in the world.

First, the *National Security Strategy* emphasized the importance of freedom and the history of its success throughout the world. Taking a liberal tone, it began, "The great struggles of the twentieth century . . . ended with a decisive victory for the forces of freedom—and a single sustainable model for national success: freedom, democracy, and free enterprise."[119] Echoing President Woodrow Wilson's ideals, it went on to argue that "these values are right and true" and "make the world not just safer but better."[120] Reflecting George W.'s belief in the destiny of the United States and the universality of its values, the strategy stressed the superiority of democracy over all other ideologies and cultures. For George W., pluralism was not an option; ideas were either right or wrong. Implicit in his thinking was the idea that obstacles to democracy must be removed. There was no doubt about the superiority of democracy and therefore democracy was destined to prevail. This view was a reflection of George W.'s evangelicalism and essentially suggested a faith-based diplomacy—a diplomacy predicated on faith in democracy, in the superiority of American values, and in the destiny of those ideas. Ultimately, the strategy included a willingness to sacrifice international stability in certain regions of the world, particularly the Middle East, in order to spread and establish democracy. Regime change, therefore, was an integral part of the Bush Doctrine.

Second, the strategy emphasized American dominance and hegemony in the world, reflecting the belief that international stability required a dominant power maintaining peace and order. According to hegemonic stability theory, the academic view of this approach, "a single Great Power is necessary to create and sustain order and openness in the international" system. In addition, "as the power of [the hegemon] declines, so also does the openness and stability of the . . . system."[121] Robert Gilpin adds, the hegemon "resolves the question of which state will govern the system, as well as what ideas and values will predominate, thereby determining the ethos of succeeding ages."[122] The Bush Doctrine incorporated these ideas into its strategy. According to George W., it was imperative that the United States dominate the world and exercise leadership in order to establish international order and promulgate the values that would sustain that order. The *National Security Strategy*, illustrating this belief, argues, "This is . . . a time of opportunity for America. We will work to translate this moment of influence into decades of peace, prosperity, and liberty. The U.S. national security strategy will be based on a distinctly American internationalism."[123]

Third, the Bush Doctrine emphasized a unilateral approach to American foreign policy. Even before September 11th and the publication of the *National Security Strategy*, George W. displayed a willingness to pursue a unilateral, go-it-alone strategy to achieve and secure American interests in spite of world public opinion. He walked away from the Kyoto Treaty on global warming, the International Criminal Court, and the protocol implementing the ban on biological weapons; in each case, he fought the tide of world opinion. Thus, the *National Security Strategy* represented the culmination and written articulation of his strong penchant for unilateralism. However, unilateralism would officially be backed by force to eradicate emerging threats to American interests. According to the *National Security Strategy*, "the United States . . . will not hesitate to act alone, if necessary, to exercise our right of self-defense."[124] George W. added, "At this moment in history, if there is a problem, [the United States] is expected to deal with it."[125]

Finally, and perhaps most controversial, the Bush Doctrine was predicated on acting preventively to deal with threats before they emerged. The *National Security Strategy* states that the United States will act "preemptively against such terrorists, to prevent them from doing harm against our people and our country."[126] The administration confused the ideas of preemption and prevention; preemption calls for a first strike when an attack is imminent, while prevention calls for a first strike before the threat emerges. According to Daniel Smith, the

"Bush Doctrine" justifying the use of military power, sets U.S. international relations on a foundation of permanent war. . . . Properly understood, the "right" of sovereign states to launch a preemptive strike when all other measures . . . have failed is a form of deterrence to war. . . . The "Bush Doctrine" upends the UN's recognition (Article 51) of "the inherent right of individual or collective self-defence if an armed attack occurs" into a presumptive right of preventive, offensive unilateral military action against any country thought to be attempting to acquire a warfighting capability [to] which Washington objects. . . . The Doctrine assumes that any nation not aligned with the U.S. that is developing or acquiring technology useful for [weapons of mass destruction] intends to attack the U.S. directly or give the weapons to "terrorist" groups to use.[127]

Essentially, administration officials were arguing that deterrence would not work against terrorists and their sponsors. Therefore, the United States had to be prepared to wage a preventive war and act before threats emerged.

With this strategy in place, the focus turned to building support for an attack on Iraq. To make that case, administration officials stressed that they already had the necessary authorization for force in past UN Security Council resolutions and congressional actions dealing with Iraq. On the domestic front, Cheney took the lead. The administration wanted to gain domestic support quickly, especially since a congressional election was nearing. With world opinion mounting up against the administration, domestic support was critical to its case. The president demanded quick action from the Congress, forcing every member to take a stand before the November election. After considerable debate, Congress passed a joint resolution supporting the enforcement of numerous UN Security Council resolutions pertaining to Iraq. It read:

> The President is authorized to use the Armed Forces of the United States as he determines to be necessary and appropriate in order to—(1) defend the national security of the United States against the continuing threat posed by Iraq; and
>
>     (2) enforce all relevant United Nations Security Council resolutions regarding Iraq.[128]

The resolution was opposed by 133 members of the House of Representatives, including 6 Republicans, and 23 members of the Senate, mostly Democrats. However, the resolution's wording essentially gave George W. a "blank check" on Iraq. With this in hand, he turned his attention to garnering world support.

This task proved far more difficult. The fact that Republicans controlled the Congress made the administration's job easier, but now they would have to face world leaders and press their case. George W. decided to pursue a new UN Security Council resolution, hoping this would solidify support. However, this proved extremely difficult, since opposition to a new resolution existed at the United Nations and within the administration itself. Cheney, in particular, was opposed to going to the United Nations, fearing that it would prevent the United States from acting. In September, he argued that "going to the U.N. would invite a never-ending process of debate, compromise, and delay. Words not action. . . . The U.N. had to be challenged . . . it's going to confront this problem or it's going to condemn itself to irrelevance."[129] Powell disagreed, arguing that it was absolutely necessary to gain UN authorization and assistance.

George W. did not fully agree with Cheney or Powell. One thing was clear: he wanted an outcome favorable for American foreign policy, and that meant that he would accept nothing less than the removal of Saddam Hussein from power. Ultimately, he was committed to regime change, and while he was prepared to accept coalition forces and world support to achieve this, he was equally ready to "go it alone." From his perspective, the UN would either "come along for the ride" or stand by as the parade marched on. There would be no compromise, no persuasion, and no backing down. The UN would accept his arguments, or accept the fact that the United States was acting without it. In his September speech at the UN General Assembly, George W. all but said this. As he told members of Congress, "I haven't given up on the U.N., but . . . it can be a diplomatic mud pit."[130]

Powell got his chance with the United Nations, but not without considerable debate. Cheney and Rumsfeld succumbed, but stressed that any resolution must contain stringent requirements for Iraq; ultimately, they argued, these requirements should trigger an automatic authorization of the use of force if Saddam Hussein failed to meet the conditions of the resolution. Powell disagreed, arguing that this was too harsh a line and would ensure that diplomacy would fail. The Security Council would not accept a resolution that was too stringent; essentially, Powell suggested, Cheney and Rumsfeld were setting him up for failure. Instead, he insisted on a softer tone, aimed at creating a resolution that would require Iraqi violations to be revisited by the UN Security Council for further consideration. According to Johanna McGeary, Powell wanted to take advantage of the "opportunities victory in the cold war offered . . . not by using our strength and position of power to get back behind our walls but by being engaged in the world."[131] And, as Richard Holbrooke explained, "These [weren't] just personal disagreements bred out of ambition and strong personality. These [were] deep, philosophical differences between two very different views of America in the world."[132] In the end, George W. sided with Cheney and Rumsfeld.

Although Powell's view resonated more closely with the views of world leaders, a new UN resolution on Iraq faced considerable debate. France, Russia, and China all expressed doubts about military action against Iraq; all three occupied permanent seats on the Security Council, had close commercial ties with Iraq, and had publicly expressed opposition to American actions to remove Saddam Hussein. As a result, Powell needed to construct a resolution that was ambiguous enough to satisfy all of the parties and prevent a permanent member from vetoing, while also satisfying the administration's concerns. The negotiations proved difficult, since the French insisted that any Iraqi breach of earlier UN resolutions should force a new Security Council meeting to determine action. This was unacceptable to George W.; he argued that the United Nations had to be forced into action with the threat of American use of unilateral force. Ongoing debate only served to reinforce his view of the irrelevance of the United Nations, making it more difficult for Powell to build international support. However, after considerable negotiation, UN Resolution 1441 emerged and was passed.[133]

Resolution 1441 was ambiguous enough to serve the administration's interests, but it also meant that the interests of the other members of the Security Council could be met, leaving open the possibility for disagreement later on. The resolution specifically found Iraq in "material breach of its obligations under relevant resolutions" and offered Iraq a "final opportunity to comply with its disarmament obligations."[134] This was satisfactory to most of the parties, but George W. remained frustrated. This resolution could be satisfied with partial disarmament, and he was convinced that partial disarmament would continue to mean that Iraq was a threat; Iraq must be totally disarmed. Typical of his worldview, George

W. sought no middle ground but remained inflexible; Iraq would be disarmed or it would face military action. George W. seized upon the last
statement in the resolution to support his case: "The Council . . . repeatedly warned Iraq that it will face serious consequences as a result of its
continued violations of its obligations."[135] The phrase *serious consequences*
convinced George W. that he had international support for military action against Iraq. Others, however, viewed things differently.

In particular, the French viewed any progress toward disarmament
as satisfying the intent of the resolution. Iraq would not be in material
breach so long as it was working toward its obligations.[136] Therefore, although Powell achieved a victory by producing a UN resolution on Iraq,
it was a hollow one. George W. was preparing to launch an attack on Iraq
as soon as Iraq breached any of its obligations, while the French were willing to grant Iraq more leeway, and more time, to disarm as long as there
were no major breaches of UN resolutions. Despite attempts by Powell to
produce broad international support, the Security Council resolution offered only veiled support. In fact, it may have made matters worse; George
W. and other administration officials were now arguing that the United
States had United Nations support for military actions. This provided the
administration with the legitimacy it had previously lacked.

In accordance with the UN resolutions, the United Nations and the
International Atomic Energy Agency (IAEA) resumed inspections on
November 27. This did not satisfy many in the administration, including Cheney, Rumsfeld, and Wolfowitz. They argued that Hans Blix, the
head of the Monitoring, Verification, and Inspection Commission, was
weak and could easily be manipulated by Saddam Hussein.[137] Cheney
continued to argue that the inspections were useless and the UN's actions a fruitless enterprise. In September, he told Tim Russert, "I'm a real
skeptic about inspections . . . if they're going to work . . . it's essential that
the inspectee . . . cooperate. And, of course, Saddam Hussein's never done
that." He went even further, criticizing the UN itself, arguing, "the United
Nations has a special problem because [it has] repeatedly . . . passed resolutions . . . sent in [inspectors] and insisted that [Saddam Hussein] must
comply. . . . And he has consistently refused . . . and there have been absolutely no consequences."[138]

It was becoming increasingly clear that Cheney was expressing not only his view but also George W.'s. In an interview with Bob Woodward, George W. explained that he was dissatisfied with the process: "I was very concerned . . . that we'd get wrapped up in [this] process and Saddam Hussein would grow stronger. I was concerned people would focus on not Saddam, not the danger that he posed, not his deception, but . . . the process and thereby Saddam would be able to . . . skate through once again . . . he would escape the trap again. And would be even stronger."[139] The door had essentially closed on a diplomatic solution. George W. was frustrated with the process and anxious to proceed. Powell would get only one more chance to convince the world that military force against Iraq was the proper course of action. George W. had already decided that it was. Richard Haass, director of policy planning in the Department of State from 2001 to 2003, explains that in July 2002 Condoleezza Rice cut him off when he was questioning the decision to attack Iraq, stating, "You can save your breath, Richard. The president has already made up his mind on Iraq."[140]

On December 7, when Iraq released its twelve-thousand-page declaration on its WMD activities, claiming that it had no banned weapons, George W. had had enough. This was precisely what those opposed to the continuing UN process had feared; on the surface, Saddam Hussein appeared to be cooperating, but George W. refused to accept the declaration and continued to push for action and clear consequences, arguing that Iraq had failed to fully comply with its obligations. Accordingly, the administration issued its own report, arguing that "Iraq's declaration is . . . inaccurate and incomplete." The report cited Iraqi noncompliance and inaccuracies, including Iraq's failure to account for 2,160 kilograms of growth media, enough to produce 26,000 liters of anthrax, 1,200 liters of botulinum toxin, and 2,200 liters of aflatoxin. In addition, the report cited that Iraq had completed 13 missile tests exceeding its 150-kilometer limit and made "efforts to procure uranium from abroad." The report also cited numerous concerns that remained unaddressed in the Iraqi declaration, including information on Iraq's mobile biological weapons program. The report concluded, "Iraq's behavior contrasts sharply with successful disarmament stories. Instead of a high-level commitment to disarm, Iraq's concealment efforts are led by Saddam's son. . . . Instead of national initiatives to disarm, Iraq's [Special Security Organization] and National

Monitoring Directorate are national programs involving thousands of people to target inspectors and thwart their duties. Instead of cooperation and transparency, Iraq has chosen concealment and deceit."[141] Essentially, George W. had made his decision long before, but now the administration was preparing for war, ensuring that two hundred thousand troops would be stationed in the Persian Gulf by early March 2003.

On January 27, 2003, the UN weapons inspectors issued their report. While critical, it was not damning; however, the administration quickly moved to use the report to confirm its beliefs and push for military action. In his testimony, Blix stated, "Iraq appears not to have come to a genuine acceptance . . . of the disarmament that was demanded of it."[142] On the following day, George W. delivered his State of the Union address, stating that he would not let Saddam Hussein elude the international community again. Citing aspects of intelligence reports and Blix's remarks, George W. argued,

> The dictator of Iraq is not disarming. To the contrary; he is deceiving. . . . Saddam Hussein has gone to elaborate lengths . . . to build and keep weapons of mass destruction. . . . The only possible . . . use he could have for [WMD] is to dominate, intimidate, or attack. . . . The day he and his regime are removed from power will be the day of [Iraqi] liberation. . . . America will not accept a serious and mounting threat to our country. . . . The United States will ask the U.N. Security Council to convene . . . to consider . . . Iraq's ongoing defiance. . . . We will consult. But let there be no misunderstanding: If Saddam Hussein does not fully disarm . . . we will lead a coalition to disarm him.[143]

His message was unequivocal. The UN process had failed. The United States was ready to use its military force against Iraq, with or without the rest of the world. George W. would lead a "coalition of the willing" to remove Saddam Hussein as a threat, whether or not the United Nations wanted him to do so. Even Powell was now prepared to proceed without the UN, albeit reluctantly. However, British prime minister Tony Blair was not; he wanted the added cover of another UN attempt before proceeding in support of George W.

On February 5, at George W.'s request, Powell went before the Security Council to press the American case one last time. Relying on human intelligence and with CIA director George Tenet sitting directly behind him, Powell asserted, "This council placed the burden on Iraq to comply and disarm. . . . What you will see is an accumulation of facts and disturbing patterns of behavior." Powell then proceeded to play tapes of alleged Iraqi "cover-ups," argued that Iraq used its twelve thousand–page declaration to "overwhelm" the international community with "useless information," and showed satellite images of alleged banned materials, weapons facilities, and mobile production laboratories. The presentation, lasting seventy-six minutes, characterized links between Iraq and Al Qaeda as "potentially more sinister. . . . Ambition and hatred are enough to bring [them] together." He concluded by offering the UN a fait accompli: "Saddam Hussein is determined to keep his weapons of mass destruction. . . . Should we take the risk that he will not someday use these weapons . . . ? The United States will not and cannot run that risk to the American people."[144]

While Powell's presentation was powerful and convincing, it would not be enough to convince the doubters. Blix contradicted numerous points in Powell's presentation. In addition, massive peace demonstrations emerged in more than six hundred cities throughout the world. Most damning, however, was that the French, Russians, and Chinese remained unconvinced. French foreign minister Dominique de Villepin argued for more inspections, stating, "No one . . . can claim the path of war . . . would lead to a safer, more just, more stable world. . . . So let us give the United Nations inspectors the time they need for their mission to succeed." Rejecting military action, Chinese foreign minister Tang Jiaxuan added, "It is the universal hope of the international community to see a political resolution of this issue within the U.N. framework." Finally, Russian foreign minister Igor Ivanov put the final nail in the coffin, arguing, "The inspectors must continue their inspections . . . this is a position shared by the overwhelming majority of states in the world."[145]

The administration's position was in serious trouble. Adding insult to injury, the administration's allies—the United Kingdom, Australia, and Spain—were facing serious domestic opposition to military action. George W., who had been "determined to invade Iraq without the second resolution,"[146] put the brakes on, arguing that a second resolution might shore up support for his key allies. Powell agreed, arguing that the administration did not have enough evidence to justify unilateral action,[147] while Cheney and Rumsfeld characteristically opposed pursuing more UN diplomacy. With the support and assistance of Spain and the United Kingdom, the United States drafted a new UN resolution calling for military action under Chapter VII of the United Nations Charter.[148] The draft continued to be met with significant opposition from the members of the Security Council. It was quickly becoming apparent that if put to a vote, the resolution would fail. George W. refused to take that risk, demanding that an ultimatum be delivered to Iraq. As negotiations wore on, George W. became increasingly agitated with the process, finally stating, "We're through."[149] He would proceed with a "coalition of the willing."

## CONCLUSION

The cautious and risk-averse approach of George H. W.'s enlightened realism contrasted sharply with the risk-acceptant approach of George W.'s cowboy liberalism. More specifically, one sees the pragmatic and flexible style of George H. W. against the ideological certitude of George W. Significantly, their variant realist perspectives are illustrated in their decisions to go to war with Iraq. George H. W. feared squandering American power and acted only after the crisis had emerged; and even then, he moved prudently in addressing the crisis. On the other hand, George W. "hit the ground running," with a plan in mind; from the beginning of his administration, he intended to use American power to foster and advance American interests and ideals. These policies reflected the characteristics of defensive and offensive realism, respectively, highlighting their differences.

In addition, George H. W.'s reliance on coalition diplomacy, international institutions, and multilateralism contrasts with George W.'s unilateralism and belief in democracy as a means to secure American interests around the world. Perhaps it is in their decisions to engage in war with Iraq that we see more clearly than anywhere else the contrasts in worldview and style between these two men. The decision to go to war highlighted this contrast; the decisions made during the wars continued to demonstrate it.

## 4

# War and Its Aftermath

Deciding to go to war is only the beginning of the decision-making process. Once the war has begun, decisions are constantly made to determine the war's course and the war's end. Presidents must remain engaged, assessing and reassessing their decisions and being prepared to change course. Wars create uncertainty and there are no guarantees; policies and visions that lead a country into war might, at the very least, need alterations. Throughout this period, George H. W. remained flexible and continued to reassess the war, but George W. continued to engage in the rhetoric of absolutes and demonstrated a reluctance to change course.

### INVASION

*1991: Operation Desert Storm*

After George H. W. received congressional support for action on January 12, 1991, the wheels were set in motion for war with Iraq. Despite preparations for war, however, the White House made a surprise announcement that Secretary Baker would be prepared to make one last effort to meet with Iraqi foreign minister Tariq Aziz in order to avoid the use of force. Within the administration, disagreement ensued over whether this would give Saddam Hussein a way to end the dispute without fully complying with the UN resolutions. Further, it might appear that the administration was reluctant to go to war, giving Saddam Hussein the advantage.

George H. W. was characteristically cautious, pursuing all diplomatic gambits before proceeding with war. In his view, he had the authority he needed to go to war, but he wanted to pursue war only as a last resort. In the end, George H. W. had made the right decision, since the Iraqi regime refused to budge. He was now able to claim that he had exhausted all diplomatic channels.

On January 15, 1991, George H. W. signed National Security Directive 54, which provided a formal set of war aims for action against Iraq. Titled "Responding to Iraqi Aggression in the Gulf," NSD-54 stated,

> This authorization is for the following purposes:
>   a. to effect the immediate, complete, and unconditional withdrawal of all Iraqi forces from Kuwait;
>   b. to restore Kuwait's legitimate government;
>   c. to protect the lives of American citizens abroad; and
>   d. to promote the security and the stability of the Persian Gulf.

What was most striking about the directive were the military aims it expressed; these went beyond liberating Kuwait and defending Saudi Arabia to include "[precluding] Iraqi . . . missiles . . . [destroying] Iraq's chemical, biological, and nuclear capabilities . . . [and eliminating] the Republican Guards as an effective fighting force."[1] Also significant was the administration's desire to keep both Israel and Jordan on the sidelines, out of the fight. Most important, the directive noted that the United States would not support efforts to alter the territorial integrity of Iraq nor would it support a replacement of Iraq's regime unless the Iraqis used WMD or carried out terrorist acts. With the war aims established, the administration pressed forward.

On January 16, Operation Desert Storm began. George H. W. began his day by consulting with and informing allies of his decision. At 7:00 p.m. Eastern Standard Time, the air war began. In his address to the nation announcing military action against Iraq, George H. W. emphasized the importance of defending international order and preventing aggression. He stressed that the world could wait no longer, citing Iraqi atrocities that had occurred during the buildup to war, and he noted the numerous attempts made by American and UN diplomats to prevent the use of force. And then he laid out a vision for the post–cold war era:

> This is an historic moment. We have in this past year made great progress in ending the long era of conflict and cold war. We have

before us the opportunity to forge for ourselves and for future generations a new world order—a world where the rule of law, not the law of the jungle, governs the conduct of nations. When we are successful, and we will be, we have a real chance at this new world order, an order in which a credible United Nations can use its peacekeeping role to fulfill the promise and vision of the U.N.'s founders.[2]

As Gary Hess has argued, unlike many of his predecessors, "Bush took the country to war without the encumbrances that had undermined their leadership. He had the advantages of unambiguous congressional authority . . . international support . . . an American military that was prepared to wage the kind of war that was at hand, and an enemy that was inferior militarily and isolated internationally."[3] George H. W.'s advantages, however, did not guarantee success. His biggest challenge was maintaining international support and keeping the UN coalition together until the objectives had been achieved. Almost immediately, this proved difficult.

Throughout the buildup to the conflict, Saddam Hussein had threatened retaliation against Israel for any allied action. As promised, on January 18, Iraq began launching Scud missile attacks on Israel. The missiles were far from accurate but caused considerable property damage and some casualties. Iraq hoped that the missile attacks would alter the character of the war, changing it from a war against Iraq for its invasion of Kuwait into a chapter in the wider Arab-Israeli conflict. If this happened, Hussein believed that Arab states would quickly drop out of the coalition against him and turn their attentions to Israel, thus causing the international coalition and Arab support for the United States to flounder. Israel's natural reaction was to retaliate, and Prime Minister Yitzhak Shamir was under considerable domestic pressure to launch an attack on Iraq. This caused great concern within the administration, which feared that Hussein's strategy would succeed and the international coalition would suffer if Israel retaliated. In a letter to Deputy Secretary of State Lawrence Eagleburger, Scowcroft explained the concerns, urging Eagleburger to reiterate them to Israel: "An Israeli retaliation . . . would threaten to break the coalition while so much remains to be done against Iraq—would yield Saddam Hussein a terrific return." Scowcroft also feared that an Israeli response would broaden the war and potentially lead to an early cease-fire.[4] George H. W. expressed his worry to Secretary of Defense Cheney: "We have worked so hard to get active participation of all coalition members. . . . I would hate to see that jeopardized." George H. W. then turned his attention to Shamir, urging him not to retaliate.[5] The president continued to pressure Israel, using tougher language to convince Shamir of the seriousness of the American position: "Absent the assumption of restraint, [the United States] would not be prepared to go ahead with other forms of enhanced cooperation and support discussed between our governments."[6] Ultimately, George H. W.'s pressure and insistent diplomacy paid off. Israel did not retaliate.

The unity of the international coalition was also threatened by Soviet efforts to curb the use of force. The administration was concerned that any efforts to end the conflict too soon would leave Iraq strong, ready to pounce again once the international coalition was dismantled. At the same time, Soviet initiatives had to be handled delicately, since the United States wanted to maintain positive American-Soviet relations. George H. W. made the assumption that Gorbachev was vital to achieving American interests; as a result, as Gorbachev faced increased internal challenges, the United States did not want to do anything that might facilitate the end of his leadership. However, Gorbachev's tepid support for American policy and pressure on the United States to pursue diplomacy proved problematic.

As the Gulf War began, Gorbachev was facing a crisis in the Baltics, where Lithuanian protestors clashed with Soviet troops. He was receiving pressure from the military and other conservatives to tighten control within the Soviet Union and reassert Soviet foreign policy, particularly in the Middle East. George H. W. was in a precarious position. Trying to restrain Gorbachev in Lithuania could lead to an open rift within the international coalition and strengthen Saddam Hussein's hand. Likewise, it could weaken Gorbachev domestically, strengthening his opponents. Thus, George H. W. chose to accommodate Gorbachev rather than risk the overall policy.

Soon after the bombing campaign against Iraq began, Gorbachev asked the United States to pause the attack to allow him to make an attempt at diplomatic reconciliation with Saddam Hussein. George H. W.

quietly rejected Gorbachev's suggestion, but he was blindsided by his own secretary of state when Baker agreed to make a joint statement with Soviet foreign minister Alexander Bessmertnykh offering a cease-fire in return for the Iraqi withdrawal from Kuwait. In addition, the statement linked the action to a settlement of Arab-Israeli issues; this had the possibility of making Saddam Hussein a hero in the Arab world, since he could argue that the invasion was justified as a means to force a resolution to the Arab-Israeli conflict. George H. W. was furious.[7] The statement fell short of Iraq's unconditional withdrawal from Kuwait and threatened to undermine the UN coalition; the White House issued a statement clarifying the Baker-Bessmertnykh proposal, explaining that it did not change the American position.

Throughout the crisis, Saddam Hussein used the Soviet overtures in an attempt to bring the war to an early end. This might mean avoiding American demands and accepting a face-saving compromise. This was unacceptable to George H. W., but for Gorbachev it offered an opportunity to restore his credibility at home and Soviet leadership abroad. On February 9, Gorbachev announced a mediation effort; two days later, he named Yevgeny Primakov, the Soviet Foreign Ministry's Arab expert, as his personal emissary to Iraq. Primakov headed to Baghdad with a proposal for Iraq's withdrawal from Kuwait within a specified timetable; in exchange, the Soviet Union would negotiate a cease-fire.

Gorbachev's overtures worried the administration. Most significant, the Soviet deal did not force Saddam Hussein to unconditionally withdraw and accept all previous UN resolutions imposed on Iraq. The Soviet mission presented enormous problems, particularly because the administration could not simply dismiss it. To make matters worse, on February 15 Radio Baghdad announced that Iraq was ready for negotiations "based on U.N. Security Council resolution 660 of 1990 to achieve a solution to the Gulf crisis, including its withdrawal from Kuwait. The willingness on the part of the RCC [Revolutionary Command Council] should be regarded as a guarantee from Iraq and coupled with an immediate and comprehensive cessation of all land, air and sea military operations."[8] However, Hussein included conditions to the Iraqi withdrawal.

George H. W. responded with calls for Saddam Hussein's overthrow, denouncing the Iraqi announcement as a "cruel ploy" and asking the

"Iraqi military and Iraqi people to take matters into their own hands and force Saddam Hussein the dictator to step aside."[9] Furthermore, in private conversations, George H. W. stressed that there had been a seven-week pause of "goodwill," leaving sufficient time for diplomacy.[10] The administration was hoping that the harsh rhetoric sent a clear message to Saddam Hussein and the world community; most significant, the United States hoped to mute further attempts by the Soviet Union to seek a negotiated solution allowing Iraq to conditionally withdraw from Kuwait.

Ultimately, Soviet efforts to pursue diplomacy were not hindered. After Tariq Aziz's February 18 trip to the Soviet Union, Gorbachev proposed a "four-point peace plan" calling for Iraq's withdrawal from Kuwait with a cease-fire taking effect the day before the withdrawal was to begin and coalition forces agreeing not to attack the retreating Iraqi forces. In addition, the proposal opposed all sanctions against Iraq and linked the "Palestinian question" to the conflict.[11] This contradicted George H. W.'s position that Iraqi forces must withdraw from Kuwait unconditionally. Gorbachev's proposal did not require Iraqi compliance with UN Security Council resolutions and included a "face-saving" opportunity for Saddam Hussein in Middle East peace. In addition, the administration remained concerned that Saddam Hussein's forces would be left intact and could be used to cause future conflict in the region. The future of the new world order could not be secured without the military defeat of Iraqi forces and punishment for Iraqi aggression.[12]

George H. W. was impatient to launch a ground war to evict Iraq from Kuwait, but he was willing to wait until the military confirmed that it was ready to proceed. His impatience was partially the result of Gorbachev's continued attempts to pursue diplomacy. On February 21, Tariq Aziz left Moscow with an Iraqi commitment to a full and unconditional withdrawal, according to UN Security Council Resolution 660; however, this would be followed by a cease-fire, the lifting of all sanctions against Iraq, and the nullification of all previous UN Security Council resolutions dealing with the conflict. The White House expressed concerns when Saddam Hussein issued a defiant speech in Baghdad; this convinced George H. W. that Iraq would continue its aggression against Kuwait. The Iraqi leader had played into George H. W.'s hands, strengthening his position regarding a ground war within the international coalition and at home.

However, Gorbachev's initiatives were capturing public support at home and throughout Europe. The window was closing fast and George H. W. feared that Iraq might snatch victory from the jaws of a certain defeat. Thus, the administration determined that the time had come to issue Saddam Hussein a final ultimatum. Despite Gorbachev's initiatives causing tensions within the coalition, Iraqi actions, including the continued attacks on civilians and Kuwaiti oil installations, helped to settle matters. On February 22, George H. W. issued an ultimatum denouncing Saddam Hussein's "scorched-earth policy." The ultimatum included the specific steps that the Iraqi regime had to take to avoid a ground war with the coalition. "Most important," George H. W. stated, "the coalition will give Saddam Hussein until noon Saturday to do what he must do: begin his immediate and unconditional withdrawal from Kuwait. We must hear publicly and authoritatively his acceptance of these terms."[13]

The ground war was about to begin, but not without serious reluctance from the Soviets, who pleaded with the administration not to proceed. The Soviets wanted to give more time for diplomacy to work and insisted that casualties in any conflict would be quite high. However, the Soviets were alone. George H. W. and Baker had worked hard to maintain the coalition's support and were moving forward with the support of the British, French, Japanese, Turkish, and numerous Arab leaders. Ten hours after the noon deadline had passed, George H. W. announced that he had "directed General Norman Schwarzkopf, in conjunction with coalition forces, to use all forces available including ground forces to eject the Iraqi army from Kuwait." George H. W. added that the decision had been made "only after extensive consultations within our coalition partnership."[14]

George H. W.'s announcement drew concern since the Pentagon had mistakenly estimated that the Iraqis had over five hundred thousand troops in Kuwait. Under these circumstances, the coalition forces could expect heavy casualties. Anxieties quickly dissipated, however, as the ground operation proved successful. While American, Saudi, British, Egyptian, and Syrian forces broke through Iraqi defenses, coalition warships in the Persian Gulf bombarded Iraqi coastal defenses in Kuwait. Surprisingly, Saddam Hussein had placed his least experienced forces in Kuwait, leaving his elite, experienced Republican Guards in reserve for a future conflict.

As the coalition forces advanced, Saddam Hussein's goal became the survival of his regime. Using the Republican Guard as a shield, the Iraqi troops began their retreat.

Although Saddam Hussein claimed that this demonstrated compliance with the UN resolutions, George H. W. angrily denounced him, arguing that Iraq "is not withdrawing. [Saddam Hussein's] defeated forces are retreating. He is trying to claim victory in the midst of a rout, and he is not voluntarily giving up Kuwait. He is trying to save the remnants of power and control in the Middle East by every means possible." George H. W. went further, arguing that Saddam Hussein was not complying with UN resolutions and thus the coalition would continue the war.[15]

While some members of Iraq's army surrendered to coalition forces, the vast majority fled toward Baghdad, under Saddam Hussein's order. The retreat quickly turned into a rout, with thousands of troops clogging the Basra Road out of Kuwait City; the Iraqi troops became an easy target for U.S. aircraft, making the road a "highway of death." On February 26–27, the coalition forces faced the Republican Guard in a massive tank battle and achieved a decisive victory, forcing a full-scale retreat. By February 27, the coalition's forces had decisively defeated the Iraqi forces and Saddam Hussein conceded defeat but remained in power. Over a decade later, George W. was engaging in war in Iraq again.

### 2003: Operation Iraqi Freedom

After making his case for war, on March 14, George W. called Prince Bandar of Saudi Arabia and explained that he was prepared to issue Saddam Hussein a final ultimatum. The Saudis expressed concern, fearing that the administration would cave to international pressure. Convincing Bandar that he was prepared to use force, George W. told him, "I am going . . . just trust me."[16] Two days later, he met with British prime minister Tony Blair and Spanish prime minister José Maria Alfredo Aznar and secured agreement to pull the plug on negotiations. On March 17, the administration asked UNMOVIC, the United Nations Monitoring, Verification, and Inspection Commission, which was mandated to gauge Iraqi compliance with UN WMD inspections, to remove its inspectors; the United States was moving forward with war. During a prime-time address that evening, George W. issued Saddam Hussein an ultimatum: he and his sons were given forty-eight hours to leave the country. The president explained, "Intelligence . . . leaves no doubt that the Iraqi regime continues to possess and conceal some of the most lethal weapons ever devised. . . . We are acting now because the risks of inaction would be far greater. In one year, or five years, the power of Iraq to inflict harm on all free nations would be multiplied many times over. With these capabilities, Saddam Hussein could choose the moment of deadly conflict when they are strongest. We choose to meet the threat now, where it arises, before it can appear suddenly in our skies and cities."[17] On the morning of March 19, George W. directed American forces to begin Operation Iraqi Freedom. The war commenced the next morning.

The invasion included 120,000 combat forces from the United States, 45,000 British troops, 2,000 Australians, and 200 Polish commandos. In addition, Kurdish groups in northern Iraq would participate, and an additional 128,000 American military personnel would be involved in intelligence, logistic, naval, and air operations. George W.'s "coalition of the willing" included forty-nine countries, with many of these governments indicating that they were influenced by Powell's February presentation at the United Nations. In reality, most countries were serving their own interests in supporting the action. Japan, for example, was concerned about its energy supply and believed that assisting the United States might help protect it. Furthermore, Japan wanted to assist with Iraqi postwar reconstruction aid to solidify its interests in oil.[18] Unlike in the first Gulf War, many other countries in the coalition offered mostly rhetorical support and contributed little to the ground combat or the financing of the operation. Also, many coalition members faced domestic public opposition. The governments in Spain and Italy, for example, lost elections due in part to their decisions to support the United States, and, in turn, both countries withdrew their forces from Iraq.

Unlike the 1991 Gulf War, in which the ground invasion was preceded by weeks of air strikes, Operation Iraqi Freedom began with simultaneous air and ground assaults. The primary approach was to identify Iraqi military equipment and personnel, destroy the targets from the air, and overwhelm the remaining forces with ground troops. The administration believed that this would diminish the morale of the Iraqi troops; once Iraq's top leaders were killed or captured, the remaining forces would surrender. Known as the "Shock and Awe" strategy, it was designed to "shock" the Iraqis into giving up control of their territory.[19] From the beginning, regime change was the goal. Richard Haass, director of policy planning at the Department of State, explains,

> Was President Bush prepared to take yes (or "uncle") for an answer? . . . It is hard to avoid the irony: Saddam resisted policy change for fear it would lead to regime change; Bush resisted accepting policy change for fear it would rule out regime change . . . most around Bush would have advised him to reject whatever Saddam offered. . . . The president opted to attack in an effort to decapitate . . . the Iraqi leadership. . . . It was not just a war of choice, but the first preventive war launched by the United States in its history. It was begun not just to disarm a regime but to oust it, in the process transforming a country and the region.[20]

The administration's plan involved ground attacks being launched from Kuwait in conjunction with British forces heading for Basra, and U.S. Army and Marine units focusing on Baghdad. In addition, hundreds of paratroopers would fight alongside opposition forces in the north. Ultimately, George W. believed that once Baghdad was captured, top Iraqi leaders were eliminated, and the city was under allied command, the Iraqi army would surrender and the Iraqi people would rally to the support of the American troops.

According to Richard Clarke, "It seemed inevitable that [the United States] would invade. Iraq was portrayed as . . . dangerous. . . . It was an idee fixe, a rigid belief, received wisdom, a decision already made and one that no fact or event could derail."[21] Now that the invasion had begun, it was clear that George W.'s beliefs were impacting the course of the war as well. His conviction that Saddam Hussein had to be removed from power was coupled with a belief in American invulnerability and effectiveness in achieving its goals. The administration failed to plan ahead and did not see alternative possibilities clearly. As Douglas Feith, former undersecretary of defense for policy, acknowledged, "Looking back on the interagency decision-making process, I am struck by its lack of clarity. On issue after issue, where there were disagreements they were not brought to the surface to be presented to the President for decision. Rather, basic disagreements were allowed to remain unresolved—as long as a degree of consensus could be produced for immediate next steps."[22] Clearly, this thinking was affecting the course of the war.

George W. and his advisors believed that the removal of Saddam Hussein would precipitate an immediate collapse of the regime and Iraqi resistance to allied forces. On March 19, the day before the invasion, an attempt was made to assassinate Saddam Hussein at a compound near Baghdad known as Dora Farms. The CIA declared that it was 99.9 percent certain that Saddam Hussein and his sons were in the compound. As a result, two F-117 stealth bombers attacked the target, while the U.S. Navy attacked with forty-five Tomahawk missiles. The mission failed since neither Saddam Hussein nor any member of his family was at the compound.[23]

Despite this failure, the drive toward Baghdad, known as Cobra II, continued. Early action supported the view that the war would be "a cakewalk."[24] The perception that the Iraqis had been badly beaten in the first Gulf War, coupled with the beliefs that Iraq was weaker in 2003 than it had been in 1990–91 and that the United States was prepared to "go the distance" in Iraq, led top policy makers, especially the president, to believe that the war would last "weeks rather than months."[25] And on *Meet the Press,* Vice President Cheney stated, "I think things have gotten so bad inside Iraq, from the standpoint of the Iraqi people . . . we will, in fact, be greeted as liberators. And the president's made it very clear that our purpose there is, if we are forced to do this, will in fact be to stand up a government that's representative of the Iraqi people, hopefully democratic due respect for human rights, and it, obviously, involves a major commitment by the United States, but we think it's a commitment worth making."[26] Following a briefing of members of the House of Representatives, Secretary of Defense Rumsfeld noted, "The people will be enormously relieved and liberated."[27] Meanwhile, American forces were decimating various Iraqi forces and had successfully destroyed hundreds of divisions of Iraqi elite units, the Republican Guards.

The plan for Baghdad had been to encircle it and destroy targets from the air before launching a ground assault on the city. However, the seemingly easy defeat of the Republican Guard units and the capture of the Baghdad International Airport led administration officials to believe that Baghdad could be captured with less fighting than anticipated. As a result, on April 5, incursions into the city began; according to American reports, about two thousand Iraqi combatants were killed, although this was disputed by Iraqi authorities, who claimed that many civilians also perished.[28] Like earlier operations, the mission was seemingly being accomplished with ease. By April 9, Baghdad was captured.

To create the appearance that the city had been liberated, a U.S. Marine colonel decided to bring down the giant Saddam statue in central Baghdad's Firdos Square. An Army Psychological Operations team quickly seized the moment to make it appear that a spontaneous Iraqi celebration had erupted. The hope was that the appearance of civilians participating in the action would place pressure on regime supporters to give up. Meanwhile, Saddam Hussein and his sons had gone into hiding and remained at large.

On the same day that the statue fell, Saddam Hussein made his last public appearance, promising a crowd of supporters that the regime would continue to resist the invasion. Then he quickly disappeared. Later, it was learned that he went to Ramadi and then the town of Hit. He and his sons were separated at this point; Qusay and Uday Hussein went to Syria, but were asked to leave and were killed by U.S. forces in July. Action throughout Iraq suggested that George W. and administration officials had been correct in their assertion that the war would be quick and American forces would be welcomed as liberators.

However, the appearance of success was giving way to the reality of problems on the ground. When Baghdad fell on April 9, many Iraqi soldiers in Kirkuk abandoned their resistance and went home; in violation of earlier understandings, Kurdish forces seized Kirkuk on April 10, causing discomfort in Turkey. Concerned about a growing problem, the Kurds were convinced to leave Kirkuk and American forces took control on April 11. Fearing that the Kurds might also attempt to seize Mosul, American forces were reinforced in the region, and on April 22, fifteen hundred American troops entered the city. General David Petraeus began negotiations with local ethnic groups and tribes in an attempt to restore order and organize a new local government.

Meanwhile, Saddam Hussein's hometown of Tikrit remained outside of American control. But after limited fighting, Tikrit was seized on April 14. Two days later, George W. announced that Iraq had been "liberated."

On May 1, 2003, in a demonstration of certainty and hubris, he flew to the U.S.S. *Abraham Lincoln,* an aircraft carrier that was returning from operations in Afghanistan and Iraq. Donning a green flight suit and landing on the carrier in a navy plane, which he briefly piloted during his flight to the carrier, George W. declared that "major combat operations in Iraq have ended" while standing in front of a large banner reading "Mission Accomplished."[29] The speech George W. made then, perhaps more than any other, was a reflection of his worldview. The view that defeating Iraq would represent an American advance in the war on terror, George W.'s certainty that American objectives and goals had been achieved, and his view of American predominance in the world were all reflected in the speech.

Despite the president's declaration that major combat operations had ended, there were signs that the war was just beginning. Many top figures in the Baathist regime were still at large, and Baghdad was clearly not under firm American control. Shortly after American forces entered the city, a wave of looting began. The looting targeted government buildings, businesses, and the national museum. Besides the desperation of the population, the fact that Saddam Hussein had released tens of thousands of prisoners in an October 2002 amnesty program contributed to the looting. The regime's law enforcement capability collapsed; this was coupled by the fact that the United States was unprepared to use its forces for the security of the general population. This proved to be a serious mistake, as hundreds of unguarded weapons arsenals were looted. A general insurrection began to develop as well. The administration was forced to move toward occupation and nation building, the very thing Governor Bush had stressed that the United States should avoid during the 2000 presidential campaign. Over a decade earlier, fearing these challenges and others, George H. W. decided to end the war before reaching Baghdad and toppling the regime.

## Ending the War

### 1991–92: Stopping Short of Baghdad

Despite routing the Iraqi forces early, George H. W. remained concerned. First, he did not want the carnage on the "highway of death" to tarnish the reputation of the United States and its coalition partners, especially among Arab populations. He was unwilling to risk the breakup of the coalition and accepted the limitations of the battlefield victory. Most important, however, he had to combine this concern with his desire not to end the war ambiguously. As George H. W. explained, "Why do I not feel elated? . . . But we need to have an end. People want that. They are going to want to know we won and the kids can come home. We do not want to screw this up with a sloppy, muddled ending."[30] In deference to his military commanders, he agreed to end the ground war after one hundred hours. While aware that he would face criticism for ending the war too early, George H. W. was determined not to exceed the UN mandate. Reflecting on the end of the war, he and Scowcroft argued, "True to the guidelines we had established, when we had achieved our strategic objectives (ejecting Iraqi forces from Kuwait and eroding Saddam's threat to the region) we stopped the fighting. . . . One more day would not have altered the strategic situation, but it would have made a substantial difference in human terms. We would have been castigated for slaughtering fleeing soldiers. . . . Trying to eliminate Saddam, extending the ground war into an occupation of Iraq, would have violated our guideline about not changing objectives in midstream . . . and would have incurred incalculable human and political costs."[31]

The victory boosted George H. W.'s popularity and his rhetoric played to these sentiments, as his approval rating reached 89 percent. George H. W. was hoping that the decisive military campaign could translate into a clear political outcome. Saddam Hussein was still in power, but intelligence estimates predicted that he would be removed from control within a year. However, Hussein's fall would not be welcomed in all quarters. Saudi Arabia and Syria, two important members of the UN coalition, feared that a coup against Hussein would bring a Shiite regime to authority in Iraq, strengthening Iran's power in the region. Meanwhile, Turkey and Iran were concerned that instability in Iraq might strengthen the Kurds in the north, and spill over into their countries. Thus, weakening Iraq was required if Saddam Hussein were to be removed from power.[32]

Punishing Iraq and reducing its military threat to the region became one of the primary goals of the postwar coalition.[33] Characteristic of George H. W.'s worldview, the United States would not do this alone. On

April 2, the UN Security Council passed Resolution 687. Unprecedented in its severity, the resolution required Iraq to accept an international commission's demarcation of its border with Kuwait and the presence of peacekeeping troops along a demilitarized zone between the two countries. Most important, Iraq was required to fully declare its involvement in the development and production of weapons of mass destruction; in practice, this meant cooperating with a UN Special Commission (UNSCOM) in the dismantling and destruction of its WMD program. Finally, nonhumanitarian sanctions remained in place, including the embargo on oil; compliance with the United Nations would determine the duration of the sanctions.[34]

By this time, however, Saddam Hussein appeared to be rebuilding his strength, and George H. W. was being criticized for his restraint. Hussein was able to preserve the elite Republican Guard units to a greater extent than was first realized. Furthermore, attempts at overthrowing Hussein from within Iraq met with failure. George H. W. had encouraged the Shiite and Kurdish rebellions that emerged after the war, but he failed to aid any revolt. In fact, when Saddam Hussein launched a counterattack against the rebellion, American troops were ordered not to assist the revolutionaries. This reflected George H. W.'s characteristic caution. He later wrote,

> I firmly believed that we should not march into Baghdad. Our stated mission, as codified in UN resolutions, was a simple one—end the aggression, knock Iraq's forces out of Kuwait, and restore Kuwait's leaders. To occupy Iraq would instantly shatter our coalition, turning the whole Arab world against us, and make a broken tyrant into a latter-day Arab hero. It would have taken us way beyond the imprimatur of international law bestowed by the resolutions of the Security Council, assigning young soldiers to a fruitless hunt for a securely entrenched dictator and condemning them to fight in what would be an unwinnable urban guerrilla war. It could only plunge that part of the world into even greater instability and destroy the credibility we were working so hard to reestablish.[35]

Baker added that the president's "absolutely correct judgment [was] enthusiastically endorsed by the military, our coalition partners, the Congress, and American public opinion."[36]

However, George H. W. was not prepared to turn his back completely on the Kurds. As pressure on the Kurds in the north mounted, he offered humanitarian aid. While he understood the symbolic importance of the relief effort, he was not willing to allow the United States to get dragged into the conflict, preferring instead to transfer the operations to the United Nations as soon as possible. In a letter to Gorbachev, George H. W. explained, "We view this initiative as temporary and solely humanitarian. We intend to transfer responsibility . . . to the UN as soon as possible. I want you to know that this effort is in no way an attempt by the U.S . . . to intervene in . . . Iraq."[37] Throughout the spring, George H. W. continued to emphasize his desire to focus on security issues, leaving the humanitarian challenges to the United Nations.[38]

George H. W. ultimately reasoned that intervention would entail too many costs and challenges. Empowering the Kurds, for example, would certainly have upset Turkey, a main coalition ally, and assisting the Shiites might have empowered Iran and risked dividing Iraq. George H. W. opted instead to stay out of Iraq, preserve the anti–Saddam Hussein coalition, promote Arab-Israeli peace, and contain Iraq through multilateral—specifically UN—diplomacy. Thus, George H. W.'s strategy relied on the "proven" lesson that containment works.

To that end, the administration's strategy aimed to continually pressure Saddam Hussein, hoping that it might convince others within Iraq that it was too costly to maintain his leadership. The idea was that the focus on Saddam Hussein would encourage cooperation among the various parties, prevent an outbreak of civil war, and lead to a united rebellion against the regime. The administration wanted to "[look] for ways to turn the screw further" without opening the door to chaos.[39] Therefore, George H. W. turned to UN actions, specifically the focus on WMD, to contain and pressure the Iraqi regime.

Beginning in April, the administration pushed for a series of Security Council resolutions aimed at containing Iraqi military capabilities. Resolution 687 declared effective a formal cease-fire and established the UN Special Commission on Weapons, which aimed to eliminate Iraq's nonconventional weapons programs. In addition, the resolution's fourth perambulatory clause required the "need to be assured of Iraq's peaceful intentions." It became known as the "Saddam Hussein clause" because

it linked the continuation of sanctions on Iraq to the survival of Saddam Hussein's regime.[40] Resolution 687 was followed by Resolution 688,
which protected the civilian populations and was used to establish no-fly
zones in the north and south of Iraq in order to protect the Kurdish and
Shia populations. While the resolution did not specifically establish these
"zones," the United States and United Kingdom used its condemnation
of the "repression of the Iraqi civilian population" as the basis for their
actions.[41]

Soon, however, the administration realized that Iraq was failing to
comply with postwar UN resolutions, and it developed a strategy to deal
with noncompliance.[42] George H. W. was concerned about maintaining
Iraqi compliance without excessive use of force; the fear was that any use
of force would be criticized, weakening the coalition and making future
support for sanctions on the regime increasingly more difficult. While
exercising caution, George H. W. wanted to ensure that Iraq could not
threaten the region or broader American interests.[43] As a result, he settled
on "carefully-targeted air strikes" against Iraq. This offered a limited approach that would not extend American objectives. As George H. W. explained to President Mitterrand of France during private conversations,
"I believe that this is a reasonable and relatively restrained approach and
that this would meet with international understanding and support . . .
it's wholly consistent, both legally and politically, with existing Security
Council resolutions."[44]

By August 1992, George H. W. had settled on the establishment of in-
definite no-fly zones and contacted numerous coalition partners to forge
a consensus. In an official cable, the administration noted, "We believe
there is a solid consensus on the need to respond to Saddam's continuing
defiance of the UN . . . the time has come for the coalition to take responsibility for monitoring Iraqi compliance. . . . We therefore propose the establishment of a no-fly zone."[45] George H. W. relied on cold war lessons in
the postwar debate. Not only was containment a vital strategy but "peace
through strength" could work in bringing about change.

By September 1992, George H. W. was convinced that the no-fly
zones were effective means of containment and that extending them
would provide greater security in the region.[46] George H. W. was establishing a policy of containment and deterrence to prevent Iraqi aggres-

sion in the region. However, in November, George H. W. would lose his bid for reelection. Thus, future presidents would be the guardians of that policy. While President Bill Clinton continued George H. W.'s policy of containment and deterrence, George W. did not.

### Beyond 2003: The Occupation of Iraq

Instead, George W. was moving to occupy Iraq, but events on the ground were impeding American policy. William Polk has suggested that the looting and chaos following the American invasion of Iraq in 2003 appeared "almost deliberate." American troops failed to stop the looting, and calls for scrapping the State Department's relatively comprehensive approach for postwar Iraq were heard within the administration; in its place, a tougher approach, intended to more radically transform Iraqi society, was initiated.[47] A number of motives may have been behind this strategy. First, the more desperate the Iraqi people were, the more willing they might be to accept American occupation and an American transformation of their society. Second, a failure of the initial policies in the region—policies promoted by the State Department and Secretary of State Powell—would allow the Defense Department to take the lead, meaning that Vice President Cheney and Secretary of Defense Rumsfeld would have greater influence over the process.

George W. selected retired army general Jay Garner to take the lead in Iraq, appointing him the director of the Office of Reconstruction and Humanitarian Assistance for Iraq (ORHA). Garner arrived in Iraq on April 21 with an advisory committee that included Ahmed Chalabi. Chalabi, a secular Iraqi Shia in exile, had supported the invasion of Iraq. Most notably, Chalabi appeared to share George W.'s views on Iraq. Chalabi came from a prominent banking family in Iraq that had lost much of its wealth after the 1958 revolution against the monarchy. In 1992, he was charged with defrauding Jordan's Petra Bank, found guilty in absentia, and sentenced to twenty-two years of hard labor.

Chalabi received help from the CIA to establish bases for his Iraqi National Congress (INC) army in Iraqi Kurdistan. But why did the administration proceed with Chalabi when there were alternatives? Most obvious, and perhaps most significant, was Chalabi's preference and support for an American invasion; in other words, he supported George W.'s already-established views on Iraq. Second, Vice President Cheney and Pentagon officials pressed for an Iraqi government led by Chalabi, an example of George W.'s reliance on his advisors. The Defense Intelligence Agency had been paying Chalabi's organization $350,000 a month to provide intelligence information. Chalabi ultimately became the source of numerous discredited intelligence information related to Iraqi weapons of mass destruction.[48] In contrast to the Pentagon's support of Chalabi, the State Department viewed him as an opportunist. Third, and perhaps most important to George W., Chalabi rhetorically supported building a secular democracy with close ties to Israel. Thus, George W. saw in Chalabi a partner for solidifying a more stable security environment for America's closest ally in the Middle East. Finally, Chalabi predicted that INC victories over Iraq's forces in the north would provoke large-scale anti–Saddam Hussein uprisings and Iraqi military defections, leading to the collapse of the regime.

However, American support for Chalabi backfired, leading to concerns about a neocolonial American puppet regime in Iraq, thus contributing to further anti-occupation insurgency. Furthermore, Chalabi campaigned for radical de-Baathification—removing Baathists from all positions of authority within the new government, including the education system.[49] This contrasted sharply with Garner's approach. Garner wanted to maintain much of Iraq's armed forces, including the Baathists, and use them for reconstruction and the maintenance of order. In addition, Garner opposed Chalabi's desire to delay elections; he wanted to move quickly to form a new Iraqi government, transferring power to the new regime.

More significant than opposition from Chalabi, Garner faced opposition from the administration itself. George W. agreed with Chalabi, wanting to rid the Iraqi regime of all the elements associated with Saddam Hussein. Thus, George W. appointed L. Paul Bremer, a retired State Department official, to serve as presidential envoy to Iraq to control the American occupation as chief of the Coalition Provisional Authority (CPA). This was designed to undercut Garner and Garner resigned, refusing to work under Bremer. Bremer had served on the post-9/11 Homeland Security Advisory Board and, more significant, had directed the conservative Heritage Foundation study, "Defending the Homeland," which focused on the war on terrorism. Bremer's appointment aimed to reinforce the connection between the invasion of Iraq and the war on terror, supporting George W.'s view.

Bremer, under directions from the White House, launched an extensive de-Baathification program, disbanded the Iraqi armed forces, and postponed the implementation of a new Iraqi government.[50] This coincided with George W.'s goals of restoring order and putting a stop to the widespread looting. On May 16, he issued CPA Order Number 1, the de-Baathification directive. The order permanently banned former Baath Party members from holding public office.[51] Drafted in the Pentagon by Douglas Feith,[52] the order reflected George W.'s view of the transformation of Iraq and the Middle East; all remnants of Saddam Hussein and his power structure had to be removed from the society and the regime had to be remade in an "American" image. According to Thomas Ricks, the CPA staffers were concerned when they received Bremer's order, believing that the government would lose its most qualified personnel at a time when the country needed these people most. Bremer hoped that the CPA could make distinctions between ideological Baathists and those who simply joined the party in order to get a job.[53]

Implementation of the order was given to the newly created Iraq Governing Council (IGC), made up of twenty-five members from the various factions within Iraq; at thirteen members, the Shia Arabs were given the largest representation. The large Shia faction within the IGC allowed Chalabi to disproportionately influence de-Baathification and CPA policies. According to Bremer, the party was one of the main vehicles of oppression and removing it, therefore, became key to establishing a democratic political system.[54] Next, the United States aimed to eliminate major Iraqi institutions.

On May 23, Bremer issued CPA Order Number 2, the "Dissolution of Iraqi Entities." Again, this reflected George W.'s desire to eliminate all elements of Saddam Hussein's regime. Order Number 2 eliminated the almost 390,000-person Iraqi military; the Ministry of Interior, which included the police and internal security forces, totaling almost 300,000 people; and the 50,000-member presidential security force.[55] This may have been the most damaging action taken, since the Iraqi Army provided a strong unifying institution in society. Its dissolution created numerous unemployed and agitated individuals who contributed to the growth of the anti-occupation insurgency. CPA Order Numbers 1 and 2 together essentially created nearly 500,000 unemployed Iraqis, antagonizing them and the families dependent on their incomes. Even more damaging, despite the fact that Sunni Arabs had dominated the regime's leadership, Sunni and Shia Arabs worked together in the armed forces; therefore, the administration's policies were helping to destroy any remaining aspects of Iraqi unity. The existence of these Iraqi institutions had limited sectarian violence.

After Order Number 2, many Iraqis felt betrayed since they had been convinced to stop fighting in the belief that they would be protected after the war. In addition, many Iraqis saw this as an extreme, intentionally humiliating act on the part of the Americans. In protest, Iraqi veterans threatened suicide attacks and military insurgency. To make matters worse, the various sectarian groups were made up of multiple, divisive factions. The Shia were divided both religiously and politically, with some adopting the Iranian Shia concept of clerical domination of the government and wanting to see closer ties to Iran. The two major rivals in the Kurdish population, the Kurdish Democratic Party and the Patriotic Union of Kurdistan, had engaged in a civil war between 1994 and 1996, and unity among the Kurds was questionable. Among the Sunni Arabs, divisions were less evident; however, the occupation of Iraq traumatized many of them since they had played a disproportionately important role in the life of the nation. Balancing these divisions and challenges was a difficult task that the administration had not prepared to confront.

After the removal of the Baath regime and the unsuccessful search for WMD, the United States failed to leave, leading many Iraqis to believe that the Americans were not there for liberation but control of their resources, especially oil. CPA actions contributed to this impression. In June 2003, the CPA halted all movement toward local elections and self-rule in the provinces in favor of appointing administrators and mayors, along with the IGC. The IGC then designated April 9, the day that Baghdad was captured, as Iraqi Freedom Day and focused on developing a temporary constitution, the Transitional Administrative Law (TAL). By the time Bremer left Iraq, one year later, an "interim" government was in place. It was a

U.S.-run operation with an "Iraqi face," consisting of 140,000 American troops and $15 billion in reconstruction funds controlled by the United States. While the interim government represented a step toward Iraqi self-rule, the American government issued over a hundred "edicts" covering everything from Iraq's legal code to elections. Significant among them was an electoral commission empowered to eliminate political parties or candidates deemed to be "unfit" to participate in the Iraqi government.

All of this reflected George W.'s views on the Middle East. From the beginning, he wanted to transform the Middle East in "an American image." Essentially, he, and others in the administration, believed that an American model of democracy in the Middle East would stabilize the region, strengthen the security of Israel, and lead to other "democratic transformations." However, Iraq's political transition was marked by confusion, delays, and flip-flopping, giving the impression that the administration lacked a clear plan of action. Ironically, this was a criticism that Governor Bush had levied against the Clinton administration's handling of various foreign policy challenges during the 2000 presidential debates.

Lacking a credible process to restore Iraqi self-rule, Iraqis turned on the CPA and American leadership. While the Pentagon could take credit for a swift and decisive military campaign to remove Saddam Hussein from power, the implementation of the occupation was flying without instruments. Chalabi blamed the State Department, arguing that Iraq's problems could have been avoided if his loyalists had been allowed to establish a government in exile; this led to the further isolation of Powell within the administration. Ironically, the State Department had argued vehemently in favor of talking to Iraqis, establishing a legitimate and broadly representative transitional structure, and involving the Iraqis from the beginning. However, George W., Cheney, and the Defense Department opposed this, and Powell was increasingly marginalized.[56]

Powell's marginalization extended to the State Department as a whole. Even when it became apparent that the Defense Department lacked the necessary language and area expertise to deal with the challenges it was now facing in Iraq, Rumsfeld refused to cooperate with the State Department and the State Department failed to appear in the CPA organizational chart.[57] Moreover, George W. did not intervene to change the situation. This proved significant. Whereas Powell and the State Department recognized the need for UN support and expertise after the war, Rumsfeld and the Pentagon did not; this, too, coincided with George W.'s doubts about the United Nations. However, at the very least, a greater presence for the United Nations could have lent legitimacy to American policies.

Throughout the summer of 2003, things went from bad to worse in Iraq, as it became increasingly clear that the administration lacked a cohesive plan for proceeding. Since the administration was unable to establish security on the ground, plans for democratization and reconstruction stalled and the lack of progress worsened the morale of Iraqis. This, in turn, fueled the insurgency and contributed to heightened violence and disorder. On August 7, a car bomb exploded at the Jordanian embassy. The UN Headquarters was attacked on August 19, and ten days later an explosion in Najaf killed many. In the fall, violence continued to spread throughout the country and George W. was under fire at home.

For the first time since September 11, 2001, George W.'s popularity fell below 50 percent.[58] Many expressed concern that American foreign policy in Iraq was without direction and that the president was no longer in control of his advisors, especially Cheney and Rumsfeld. As a result, George W. established the Iraq Stabilization Group under Condoleezza Rice's direction; the group aimed to do what Rice, the national security advisor, should have been doing all along—improving interagency coordination and cooperation, and restoring civilian control over postwar reconstruction efforts. Most concerning to many was the perceived absence of an exit strategy. George W. responded to these criticisms, arguing, "We've had a strategy from the beginning. . . . The definition of when we get out is 'when there is a free and peaceful Iraq based upon a constitution and elections,' and obviously we'd like that to happen as quickly as possible."[59] Thus, despite obstacles, George W. remained focused on transforming the Middle East through democracy.

Typical of his personality, George W. stayed on course despite criticism. His determination and his belief that ultimately his policy was the right course of action meant that criticism could be ignored. Furthermore, it meant that expertise was less important than ideology. As a result, the administration lacked a credible process to restore self-rule, and George W. appeared oblivious to the problems and challenges within Iraq. In addition, the coordination between the Departments of State and

Defense did not improve. While the Pentagon was earning high marks for its military campaign, the State Department was being blamed for American reconstruction efforts, despite having little to no role in them.

Meanwhile, self-rule was making little progress. Despite praise from the international community, the IGC was given only limited powers and the Iraqis viewed it as an extension of American policy. Therefore, it lacked legitimacy with the Iraqi people. Concerns were heightened by the insufficient representation of Sunni Arabs on the IGC, the exclusion of former Baath Party members, and the limited representation by tribal leaders. Prominent Shia clerics also rejected the IGC, arguing that elections would provide the proper representation. Ultimately, many Shia believed that the administration was stalling in order to prevent them from taking control.[60] Ironically, the administration's promise of democracy was presenting the biggest obstacle to the legitimacy of the IGC. Adding to the problems was the inability of the United States to meet basic security needs.

George W. was caught between the desire for an orderly transition—one that the United States could control—and his own rhetoric on democracy. For George W., democratizing the Arab world did not mean giving the Iraqi people control over the development of their new political structures. After all, democratic elections might produce a result that was contrary to his vision—a result that might include Sharia law as the basis of a new constitution. This, of course, became a serious problem when the administration engaged in the Israeli-Palestinian peace process (see chapter 5).

As things increasingly spun out of control in Iraq, George W. turned to the very institution he had scorned earlier, the United Nations. In part, this also reflected his worldview; the United States was not in the "business" of nation building and did not want to dirty its hands in the process. This put the UN secretary-general, Kofi Annan, in a rather uncomfortable position. He was determined not to send UN personnel into "harm's way" and had openly criticized the administration's war as "illegal."[61] At the same time, however, he understood that UN involvement could produce positive results, particularly in regards to elections, and prevent Iraq's demise.[62] Furthermore, Annan did not want the United States to fail, since a weakened America would weaken the United Nations. Perhaps most important, however, Annan had to ensure that the United Nations did not merely rubber-stamp the administration's policies.

With UN involvement, movement toward elections in Iraq proceeded. However, anti-American rage increased among the Iraqi population throughout 2004. On March 31, for example, American contractors were ambushed and killed in Fallujah, while an angry mob shouted, "Death to America! Death to occupation! Yes to Islam!"[63] The attack signaled that the United States was facing a serious challenge from insurgent forces. George W. responded by authorizing Operation Desert Scorpion, a multifaceted plan aimed at attacking insurgents and extremists, strengthening ties with local sheikhs, and expanding local police forces.

Meanwhile, George W. appeared to ignore the bad news and continued to express little doubt that the American strategy would work. While acknowledging "serious violence," George W. continued to rely on rhetoric that cast the conflict in terms of good and evil, and suggested the inevitability of American success:

> The defeat of violence and terror in Iraq is vital to the defeat of violence and terror elsewhere and vital, therefore, to the safety of the American people. Now is the time, and Iraq is the place, in which the enemies of the civilized world are testing the will of the civilized world. We must not waver. . . . We will succeed in Iraq. We're carrying out a decision that has already been made and will not change. Iraq will be a free, independent country, and America and the Middle East will be safer because of it. Our coalition has the means and the will to prevail. We serve the cause of liberty, and that is always and everywhere a cause worth serving.[64]

This was typical of George W. The world was a world of good vs. evil, and it was the destiny of the United States—and the destiny of George W. Bush—to defeat evil in the world. Furthermore, it was inevitable that the "benevolent" power would win because good always triumphs over evil.

Ultimately, the overthrow of Saddam Hussein had created a power vacuum that was more complex than the calculation of good vs. evil. The administration did as much to encourage this power vacuum as it had done to dissuade it. De-Baathification had essentially created a new class of insurgents; in addition, the administration's inability to provide basic services to the Iraqi people contributed to a renewed insurgency. Muqtada al-Sadr was more than happy to fill the void, using his network of foundations to provide food and other essential services to Iraqis. The new insurgency required a new approach, but one that would not deviate from the administration's focus on a military solution to the challenges.

By 2007, George W. settled on a surge of American troops to provide greater security to Baghdad and Al Anbar Province, where the bulk of American military and civilian personnel were stationed. Initially, George W. was resistant to the surge, supporting his military advisors who wanted to remove American forces from Iraq as quickly as possible. George W.'s tendency to defer to commanders in the field and his military advisors delayed a change in policy.[65] Developed as "The New Way Forward," George W. announced the surge in January 2007. Three months earlier, in November 2006, an election had brought Democratic majorities to both houses of Congress. A substantial majority of Americans and the news media viewed the election as a referendum on Iraq, suggesting that a policy change was necessary.[66] Facing a Democratic Congress that wanted to bring the war to an end,[67] George W. uncharacteristically changed course. After the U.S. midterm congressional election, on December 6, 2006, the Iraq Study Group issued its report, calling for a change in policy, including a significant increase in the number of U.S. military personnel imbedded in and supporting Iraqi Army units.[68] Throughout December, George W. met with State Department officials, experts on Iraq, and the Joint Chiefs of Staff in hopes of devising a new strategy.

On January 10, 2007, he announced, "America will change our strategy to help the Iraqis carry out their campaign to put down sectarian violence and bring security to the people of Baghdad. This will require increasing American force levels."[69] On the same day, the administration distributed a fact sheet that outlined the objectives of the policy, including protection of the Iraqi population, isolation of extremists, and letting the Iraqis take the lead.[70] Initially, the policy proved ineffective. Despite a massive security crackdown, the monthly death toll rose in March.[71] Three months after the surge began, American troops controlled less than one-third of the capital and violence continued in western Baghdad, where there were mixed Sunni-Shiite neighborhoods. Moreover, improvements were not widespread across Baghdad or throughout Iraq more generally.[72]

By the beginning of 2008, however, the tide had turned. George W. naturally attributed this success to his change in policy. American policy, according to George W., had prevailed. However, the claims of success were fragile. As Bob Woodward pointed out, at least three other factors impacted success in Iraq. First, in 2007 the U.S. military launched a series of covert operations designed to eliminate key leaders in the insurgency. According to reports, these operations significantly reduced the violence in Iraq. Second, the Anbar Awakening, in which tens of thousands of Iraqis worked with the United States against the insurgents, served to lessen the violence; Al Qaeda in Iraq had essentially made a strategic error when it began terrorizing the local population, leading to a backlash against it. Finally, Muqtada al-Sadr's order to suspend operations, an act of charity, according to General Petraeus, furthered the reduction of insurgent attacks. Despite this, the administration continued to demonstrate its rigid thinking, with Stephen Hadley, the president's national security advisor, arguing that the surge was the most important factor in any change in Iraq.[73] True to form, George W. was unwilling to see things differently.

Over the course of the next year, George W. would continue to defend his policy in Iraq, maintaining his steadfast resolution. According to Bob Woodward, "His strategy was to make repeated declarations of optimism and avoid adding to any doubts."[74] During his farewell speech to the nation, George W. focused on consistent themes: "Good and evil are present in this world, and between the two there can be no compromise."[75] And in a November 2010 interview with Matt Lauer, he held to his convictions, stating, "I don't believe [Operation Iraqi Freedom] was the wrong decision. . . . I will say definitely the world is better off without Saddam Hussein in power, as are 25 million people who now have a chance to live in freedom."[76] George W. was comfortable with his decision, convinced that he had done the right thing. There was no wavering—there was no second-guessing.

## CONCLUSION

Like their decisions to go to war with Iraq, the decisions made during war reflected the worldviews of George H. W. and George W. Most notable is the fact that George H. W. decided to end the war without marching to Baghdad and removing Saddam Hussein from power. Alternatively, George W. made it his primary aim to change the regime in Baghdad and oust Saddam Hussein. This reflected the differences in their views on the use and aims of American power. George H. W.'s defensive realist view of the world lent itself to a more cautious and reactionary approach; for example, he was unwilling to advance beyond the UN mandates, fearing that it would cause a breakup of the war coalition. More significant, George H. W. wanted to secure political capital and use it to advance the Middle East peace process. George W.'s offensive realist view of the world, on the other hand, aimed to expand American power and interests. George W. wanted to rebuild Iraq in an American image, reflecting his beliefs in the sanctity of democracy. In doing so, he squandered American credibility; this impacted the Middle East peace process, as his focus on the war on terror and his staunch belief in democracy prevented progress on the issue.

# 5

# Searching for Peace

The manner in which George H. W. Bush and George W. Bush approached the Middle East peace process also reflected their worldviews. George H. W., although characteristically cautious, maintained flexibility in his policy, using the breakup of the Soviet Union and the subsequent Gulf War to attempt to reshape the political atmosphere in the region. George W., on the other hand, saw no need to engage directly in the Middle East peace process. In fact, he viewed the invasion of Iraq as the key to Middle East peace, arguing that a transformation of Iraq would create a more peaceful security environment for Israel and resolve many of the issues and challenges in the region.

## OPENING GAMBITS

### 1989–90: The Road to Madrid

When George H. W. arrived in the Oval Office, his characteristic caution and pragmatism was evident in his approach to Middle East peace. Early on, his policy reflected traditional American interests. George H. W. initially encouraged the Israelis to set the agenda, fearing that American pressure might derail any Israeli support for the peace process. In April 1989, Israeli prime minister Yitzhak Shamir offered a four-point proposal as the basis for continued peace talks. The plan called for a recommitment to the Camp David Accords, called upon Arab states to negotiate with Israel with an aim toward normalized relations, offered to ensure a "satisfactory solution" to the humanitarian challenges in the region, and called for free Palestinian elections to select a non–Palestine Liberation Organization (PLO) government. However, the Shamir proposal was also

Israel and the occupied Palestinian territories

adamant that an international peace conference would not take place.[1] While the administration continued American support of Israel, it began to show signs of its willingness to pressure Israel toward a greater peace. George H. W.'s preference for multilateral solutions to international challenges and his pragmatic approach to foreign policy suggested that he would support a negotiated solution to the Israeli-Palestinian conflict that relied on an international peace conference.

Throughout 1989, George H. W. expressed his willingness to move forward. In letters to various constituents writing to the White House, opposition to current Israeli practices was stressed. For example, in a letter to Mr. Ramsey Hakim in July, the administration stated, "We oppose the use of excessive force. . . . Our opposition to this is well-known to Israel."[2] This was not an isolated incident, and other letters reiterate this point.[3] Further, George H. W. and his advisors understood the importance of seizing the opportunity to move the peace process forward in the Middle East. As early as March 1989, Scowcroft emphasized the importance of using the changing global political climate, particularly the easing of tensions with the Soviet Union, as a means to resolve the Israeli-Palestinian conflict through peace and negotiation. Scowcroft suggested that pressure by both the United States and the Soviet Union could advance the peace process significantly.[4]

However, the policy also reflected the characteristic caution and pragmatism of George H. W., which permeated the administration as the president set the tone for his advisors. In a February 1989 interview in *Time,* Secretary of State Baker illustrated this caution: "The U.S. is and can be the most influential player [in the Middle East peace process]. But it is important that we not permit the perception to develop that we can deliver peace, that we can deliver Israeli concessions. If there is going to be a lasting peace, it will be the result of direct negotiations between the parties, not something mandated or delivered by anyone from the outside. . . . It is not the role of the U.S. to pressure Israel. At the same time, it is in Israel's interest to resolve the issue. Both sides have got to find a way to give something."[5] This pragmatism was also reflected in the administration's deputies at the State Department and on the National Security Council. Most significant among those deputies were Dennis Ross, the head of Baker's policy planning staff, and Richard Haass, senior director for Near East and South Asian affairs on the staff of the National Security Council. Ross and Haass had contributed to the 1988 Washington Institute for Near East Policy's *Building for Peace: An American Strategy for the Middle East*. Like Baker, they urged caution and patience: "The next president will need to proceed with caution, acting to reshape the political environment . . . stabilize the Middle East military balance and help construct a postwar framework of stability in the Gulf. . . . The immediate task of the next president should be to help create the conditions for an eventual negotiation rather than attempting to bring that negotiation about in short order. . . . The next president will need to demonstrate his commitment to peacemaking while clearly indicating that the U.S. is looking to the parties themselves to recondition the political environment."[6] As a result, qualities that proved effective in the Gulf War did not initially prove effective in the peace process, and those looking for George H. W. to jump-start the peace process would have to wait until 1990. Thus, the same strengths that led to success with Iraq would often cause frustration in the peace process.

Over the summer and throughout the fall of 1989, signs that the administration was preparing to move forward slowly emerged but remained mainly rhetorical. However, Baker delivered a speech to the American Israel Public Affairs Committee (AIPAC) that jolted Israel and its supporters and demonstrated the administration's willingness to seek new solutions to the age-old problem. Baker's speech, backed by George H. W., made it clear that the administration would seek a balanced approach to the issue. Most significant, Baker called on Israel to "lay aside, once and for all, the unrealistic vision of greater Israel," including the West Bank and the Gaza Strip. He continued, arguing, "Forswear annexation; stop settlement activity; allow schools to reopen; reach out to the Palestinians as neighbors who deserve political rights." To conclude, Baker called upon Palestinians to "reach out to Israelis and convince them of your peaceful intentions."[7] The speech laid out Baker's five-point plan, which the administration intended to be a fair perspective on problems in the Middle East. However, attempts to offer a balanced approach to the conflict fell on deaf ears.

As 1990 unfolded, George H. W. decided to exert more pressure on Israel to stop unilateral actions, particularly settlement activity in the region, while continuing to pressure the Palestinians on terrorism.[8] This marked an important shift, as George H. W. was now pushing forward with the peace process, hoping to get both sides to the table for negotiations. In addition, it meant that George H. W. was willing to use his credibility and leadership to exert pressure on Israel. George H. W.'s personal diplomacy played an important role throughout the process, as it had during the Persian Gulf War, but it was particularly evident in his relations with Israeli prime minister Shamir.

In the Gulf War, personal relations had proved to have a positive impact. However, personal diplomacy can also backfire. In this case, George H. W.'s personal dislike of Shamir made negotiations and diplomacy more difficult. On the other hand, it made George H. W. more willing to exert pressure on Shamir and less concerned about cultivating a close personal relationship with him. In early 1990, Shamir expressed his desire to continue building Israeli settlements in the occupied territories. Baker met with Shamir to urge him to declare his willingness to meet with Palestinians without new Palestinian elections, withdraw from southern Lebanon, end settlement activity in the occupied territories, and consider negotiations on the Golan Heights. In order to demonstrate the administration's seriousness on these issues, Baker also met with a Palestinian delegation during his trip. Ultimately, this presented serious challenges to Shamir's unity government. Faced with pressure from the Right to continue current Israeli policies and pressure from the Left to reverse many of those policies, Shamir refused to commit to American suggestions. Ultimately, Shamir's government increased the settlement activity in the occupied territories, angering many in the administration, particularly George H. W. Most important, it led George H. W. to see Shamir as an obstructionist in the process.

In addition to the problems with the Shamir government, Benjamin Begin, the son of former Israeli prime minister Menachem Begin, publicly blasted Baker and the American administration, further souring relations between the United States and Israel. On March 3, 1990, George H. W. entered the fray, criticizing Israeli settlement activity in the West Bank and East Jerusalem.[9] While this had consistently been American policy, George H. W. was the first president to single out East Jerusalem settlement activity publicly. Shamir responded with a decidedly strong denunciation of George H. W.'s condemnation. As a result, the peace process was put on hold and, by May, Shamir's government moved further to the right, making peace even more difficult.

In addition to the challenges from Israel, Arab support for the peace process was weak. Anti-American sentiment throughout the Arab world was high, reflected in the growing appeal of Islamic radicalism and its anti-Western, anti-Israel rhetoric. Adding to the challenges, the Israelis thwarted two Palestinian commando units attempting to land on a beach outside Tel Aviv, in what was clearly an attempted act of terrorism.[10] At the same time, Palestinian leader Yasir Arafat was seeking American support for a UN resolution calling on the secretary-general to take action to prevent further violence against Palestinians in the occupied territories. Prior to the attempted assault on Tel Aviv, George H. W. was leaning toward supporting the resolution, but after the event, he was compelled to veto it, creating resentment in U.S.-Palestinian relations.

Despite the veto, however, George H. W. exerted additional pressure on Israel. In an oral message delivered to Prime Minister Shamir in July, George H. W. pushed the Israeli government to act in a positive way for peace. In particular, he prodded Shamir to accept an American suggestion of negotiating with a joint Jordanian-Palestinian delegation; Shamir, however, refused direct negotiations of any kind with the Palestinians. George H. W. responded, "In all candor, Mr. Prime Minister, the US cannot and will not be engaged in a process that simply creates the illusion of . . . progress. . . . We believe the best way to advance the prospects for peace is by your agreeing to the formulation . . . we have suggested."[11] At the same time, George H. W. was exerting pressure on the Palestinians to take steps to stop acts of terrorism. According to George H. W., "The PLO [had] not provided a credible accounting . . . or undertaken [appropriate] actions." Most notably, he was concerned that the PLO had not disassociated itself from the Palestine Liberation Front.[12] Thus, the summer had produced few results and Secretary Baker expressed the administration's frustration with great candor: "I have to tell you," he wrote, "that everybody over there should know that the telephone number is 1-202-456-1414. When you're serious about peace, call us."[13] Events in the region would soon prod the administration forward. Likewise, events in the region would affect George W.'s approach to the peace process, but in a vastly different way.

*2001–5: "All Those Old Issues"*

On December 5, 2008, George W. addressed the Brookings Institution's Saban Forum in Washington, DC. His address focused on the Middle East and the accomplishments of his administration in the region. He argued that the "primary threat" had become "violent religious extremism," and the "old approach of promoting stability [was] unsuited to this new danger."[14] Further, he claimed to have forged a successful American foreign policy in the region, stressing the effectiveness of the war on terror and the decision to invade Iraq, rapprochement with Libya, and the Annapolis peace process. However, his claims of success are questionable. By the end of his administration, the Middle East peace process in particular was arguably in a worse position than it had been when his administration began. Much of this was the result of the president's worldview and its impact on the administration's foreign policy.

Early in his administration, George W. was unwilling to engage in the Middle East peace process; in fact, he never demonstrated any serious interest in bringing peace to the region until late in his administration, when he saw the peace process as a political instrument to achieve his larger goals in the region. He was often dismissive of the issues and challenges surrounding the peace process, describing them as "all those old issues,"[15] and saw the process as marginal to the larger issue of "reforming" the Middle East by introducing democracy to the region. As a reflection of his position on the issue, the term *peace process* was banned from use during his tenure. Further, George W. associated any discussion of Middle East peace with the Clinton administration, and adopted the ABC—Anything but Clinton—policy on the Middle East. Adding to George W.'s unwillingness to seriously engage in the process was his diplomatic bias toward Israel; this was not unusual for an American administration, but George W. took his bias to a new level by labeling the Palestinian leadership terrorists and refusing to deal directly with them. From the Oval Office, George W. saw a Middle East hardened by conflict and driven by anger. During his tenure, however, the administration would not merely disengage from the process; it would redefine American perceptions about and policy in the region.

There is some irony in George W.'s disengagement from the Middle

East. Unlike his predecessors, he declared his support for a two-state solution. Ultimately, however, the issue became peripheral to his larger vision for transforming the Middle East. As a result, the flexibility required
in peace negotiations was sacrificed to ideological rigidity, and George W.
left his successor with an even worse hand than he had been dealt.

For George W., the Israeli-Palestinian conflict and the larger issues
associated with the conflict were marginal to other, more significant issues. Also, the peace process was a "losing issue," as the Clinton administration's policies had demonstrated. Martin Indyk, a National Security
Council staffer in the Clinton administration, explains, "Clinton's handoff
to . . . Bush . . . left a lot to be desired. Negotiations had broken down,
and the Palestinian territories were in flames. For good measure, Clinton
warned his successor against dealing with Arafat."[16] Clinton's difficulty in
achieving a successful outcome, coupled with his warnings about Arafat, contributed to George W.'s already existing bias against the Clinton
administration's policies and resulted in the establishment of the ABC
policy. To be fair, a quick assessment of Clinton's record would have given
any new administration pause, and George W. gave no clear indication
that he would be investing political capital with very little chance of a
return on the investment.

Contributing to his unwillingness to advance the Middle East peace
process was his diplomatic tilt toward Israel. As governor of Texas, George
W. had traveled to Israel in 1998 and was "blown away by how small and
vulnerable Israel was."[17] In addition, his election to the presidency cor-
responded with the election of Ariel Sharon as prime minister of Israel.
From the outset, George W. stood steadfastly by Sharon and his policies.
This was evident even before September 11, 2001, but became increasingly more evident afterward. This reflected George W.'s determinism
and ideological rigidity, demonstrated the downside of personal politics,
and illustrated his predisposition upon entering office. George W.'s close
relationship with Sharon often blinded him to alternatives in the region.
In May 2001, for example, the Mitchell Plan emerged out of an international commission appointed by President Clinton and headed by former
senator George Mitchell. The plan called for "an unconditional cessation
of violence" and suggested numerous confidence-building measures to
foster peace and stability in the region. Most controversial, however, it

called upon Israel to "freeze all settlement activity, including the 'natural growth' of existing settlements."[18] This was in direct opposition to Sharon's policy. In his inauguration, Sharon argued, "I would be remiss if I failed to mention the generations of our parents and grandparents, whose Zionist vision brought them to the homeland. Here they walked and, with their ten fingers, established a mighty settlement enterprise. I was born and raised in one of these settlements . . . and I am an inseparable part of it. It is important to the State of Israel and personally dear to me. I will make every effort to preserve and strengthen it." He went on to argue that his position on settlements and a settlement freeze was clear and "well known," particularly with regard to "the Golan Heights, the Jordan Valley and other security zones."[19] Sharon suggested that any negotiation on substantive issues must be preceded by an end to Palestinian violence. George W. and his advisors supported Sharon's position without question. Secretary of Defense Rumsfeld began discussing the "so-called occupied territory" when referring to the issue, for example.[20] This directly contrasted with the policy of George H. W. In fact, when George W. entered office, the Arab world was optimistic, hoping that he would follow in his father's footsteps, clashing openly with the Israeli leadership. However, optimism soon dissipated as a "special assistant" for the Middle East, William Burns, was not appointed until May.

The Palestinians hopes were dashed further when in March the United States vetoed a UN Security Council resolution calling for an observer force to protect Palestinian civilians in Gaza and the West Bank because Israel opposed the force. The United States argued that the resolution was "unbalanced, unworkable and unwise."[21] Also, when Sharon visited Washington, George W. assured him that the United States would not force the peace process forward. In May, the administration publicly acknowledged that George W. did not want to get directly involved in the region's problems, and officials stated that they were unwilling to ask Sharon to freeze Israeli settlements. Essentially, George W. was giving Israel a free hand to operate. The United States had set the tone on Israeli-Palestinian negotiations by supporting Sharon's position that Palestinian violence had to end before Israel would discuss substantive issues.[22]

In fact, American support for Sharon's policies set the tone for all future dealings on Middle East peace. George W. entered the peace process with blinders on and he lacked the flexibility to change. The president's personal relationship with Sharon, and their shared view on issues like terrorism, added to that inflexibility. In addition, George W's belief in democracy as transformative led him to support the primary "democracy," no matter how nominal, in the region. In June 2001, CIA director George Tenet proposed a plan that fostered a cease-fire and mutual security. The Tenet plan called upon Israel and the Palestinian Authority to "resume security cooperation," "take immediate measures to enforce . . . adherence to the declared cease-fire," and act aggressively against violent acts.[23] George W's support for Sharon's position that Palestinian violence would have to stop before negotiations could proceed meant that the Tenet plan was dead from the beginning. Likewise, Assistant Secretary of State William Burns and former Marine general Anthony Zinni's mission to meet with Israeli and Palestinian leaders to reach a cease-fire as the basis for future peace negotiations was unsuccessful.

George W's priorities had changed after September 11, and any progress on the Israeli-Palestinian issue would be tied to progress in the war on terror. The events of 9/11 reinforced George W's inflexibility and his predisposed views of the Middle East. Therefore, the Zinni mission ended almost as soon as it started. To make matters worse, upon his arrival, Palestinian violence erupted. On November 27, two Palestinians killed three Israelis and wounded thirty others in Afula. Further, while Zinni was meeting with Arafat, Palestinian gunmen fired on an Israeli neighborhood in Jerusalem.[24] On November 29, three more Israelis were killed as a suicide bomber attacked a bus near Hadera.[25] Zinni responded by pressuring Arafat, arguing that "those responsible for planning and carrying out these attacks must be found and brought to justice. This is an urgent task and there can be no delay or excuses for not acting decisively."[26] On December 2, fifteen Israelis were killed in another suicide attack on a bus. In response, Israel attacked Palestinian Authority headquarters in the West Bank and Gaza. Ari Fleischer, George W's press spokesman, responded in a manner that became characteristic of the administration and reflected the president's views: "Israel had the right to defend herself. And the President understands that."[27] Further, over a week earlier, Fleischer had explained that the "President thinks it is very important that Palestinian jails not only have bars on the front, but no longer have revolving doors at the back."[28] Despite American warnings, the suicide attacks did not stop. By mid-December, the Israeli government had cut all contacts with Arafat.[29] The peace negotiations were effectively at a dead end. On December 15, Secretary Powell ended the mission, returning Zinni and Burns to the United States. Powell, without backing from George W., did not want to put his own personal capital on the line.

To complicate matters further, on January 2, 2002, the Israelis captured the *Karine-A,* a ship carrying fifty tons of weapons, alleging it was for the Palestinian Authority. Arafat denied the allegations, but this denial undermined his credibility with the United States. Cheney and Rumsfeld, in particular, pressed for Arafat's isolation.[30] This distanced the United States from the Palestinian Authority and increased America's support for Israel. Meanwhile, Hamas attacked an Israeli outpost in Gaza, killing four Israeli soldiers.[31] Israel responded with air strikes, an action that drew criticism. The United States rushed to defend the Israelis, calling their actions defensive in nature, and warned Arafat that a "heavy burden rests on [him] to deal with these charges" and end the violence against Israel.[32]

In March 2002, the Saudis proposed a peace initiative that was unanimously accepted at an Arab summit meeting. Again, U.S. policy undermined the initiative. After a trip to the region, Cheney concluded that Arafat could not be a force for peace and that dealing with him was inconsistent with the war on terror.[33] And George W. argued, "I'm not going to spend my political capital on losers, only winners. I'm still in a war mode, and the war is terrorism. If people don't fight terrorism, I am not going to deal with them."[34]

However, reflecting his concern with politics and in an effort to appease the region and his domestic critics, George W. sent Zinni to make another attempt at achieving a cease-fire. To facilitate the visit, George W. convinced Sharon to lift his demand for a weeklong cessation of violence before talks could resume. Further, on March 12, the administration introduced a new UN Security Council resolution calling for a two-state solution.[35] However, all of this ultimately failed to move the process forward. Once again, the war on terror intervened and George W.'s focus on that issue prevented any progress.

On March 27, the first night of Passover, a Palestinian suicide bomber killed 30 and wounded 140 in Netanya. Suicide bombings also occurred in Jerusalem, Tel Aviv, and Haifa over the next couple of days, killing close to 20 and wounding an additional 80 people. Israel responded with attacks on Arafat's compound, aptly dubbed "Operation Defensive Shield." As had been the pattern, the United States backed the Israeli actions. Powell argued, "Sharon made concessions, while Arafat backed terrorism."[36] And Bush denounced Arafat, adding, "The chairman of the Palestinian Authority has not consistently opposed or confronted terrorists nor has he renounced terror as he agreed to do at Oslo."[37]

Several days later, however, George W. demanded an Israeli withdrawal, only to face severe criticism at home. Neoconservatives in the public, particularly the evangelical Christians who had been prominent George W. supporters, attacked his position and urged greater support for Israel.[38] Prominent members of the administration also expressed strong support for Israel. Almost a year later, for example, Attorney General John Ashcroft made his support for Israel very clear: "When we experienced the horror of September 11th . . . Israel was among those countries capable of understanding our national pain and our national thirst for justice."[39] In addition, George W. faced congressional criticism for his apparent reversal of policy.[40] George W. quickly backtracked and once again supported Israeli policy, accusing Arafat of sponsoring terrorism. On May 26, George W. stated, Arafat "doesn't deliver. He had a chance to secure the peace as a result of the hard work of President Clinton and he didn't. He had a chance to fight terrorism and he hasn't."[41] Essentially, George W. gave Israel a free hand; he proved that his rhetorical criticism of Israeli policy would only go so far. And much of the criticism was politics—George W.'s desire to maintain and increase support for American foreign policy initiatives in the region, particularly as they related to Iraq.

Almost one month later, George W. called on the Palestinian Authority to replace its leadership:

> For the sake of all humanity, things must change in the Middle East. It is untenable for an Israeli citizen to live in terror. It is untenable for Palestinians to live in squalor and occupation. And the current situation offers no prospect that life will improve. Israeli citizens will continue to be victimized by terrorists, and so Israel will continue to defend herself. . . . Peace requires a new and

different Palestinian leadership, so that a Palestinian state can be born. I call on the Palestinian people to elect new leaders, leaders not compromised by terror. . . . And when the Palestinian people have new leaders . . . the United States of America will support the creation of a Palestinian state. . . . Today, Palestinian authorities are encouraging, not opposing terrorism. This is unacceptable. And the United States will not support the establishment of a Palestinian state until its leaders [are] engaged in a sustained fight against the terrorists and dismantle their infrastructure.[42]

George W. placed the burden of peace on the Palestinians, requiring nothing of Israel, reversing his earlier pressure—albeit tepid pressure—on the Israeli government. In addition, he made a clear link between Middle East peace and the war on terror. Further, he offered a transformative vision of the Middle East, stressing the power of democracy to redefine the region. Finally, he formally eliminated Arafat as an effective partner in the peace process, ordering all U.S. diplomats to cease dealing with Arafat altogether.

As the summer wound down, the administration began working with the European Union, Russia, and the United Nations as part of a "Quartet" to develop a peace process. This reflected George W.'s desire to gain support for his Iraq policy throughout the summer and fall of 2002 and into early 2003. In particular, George W. understood that support for Middle East peace was important to Prime Minister Tony Blair; Blair needed the peace initiative to convince his Labour Party to support the invasion of Iraq. However, American unwillingness to deal with Arafat continued to delay any progress, and the administration never intended to actually engage in the Israeli-Palestinian issue. What finally emerged on April 30, 2003, became known as the "Road Map." The "Road Map" called for three phases and a variety of benchmarks in the movement toward a Palestinian state. Once again, however, the war on terrorism dominated the peace process; in addition, the war on Iraq was now central to George W.'s transformative vision of the Middle East. The Road Map required Palestinians to "declare an unequivocal end to violence and terrorism and undertake visible efforts on the ground to arrest, disrupt, and restrain individuals and groups conducting and planning violent attacks on Israelis anywhere." In addition, it asked the Palestinian Authority to establish an "empowered" prime minister and a strong parliamentary democracy. For its part, Israel was required to cease deportations and attacks on civilians.[43] Arafat acceded to the demand to establish a prime minister, Abu Mazen, but the prime minister was not sufficiently empowered to combat terrorism. In essence, Arafat retained control. In order to build support for the Road Map, George W. went to the Middle East in June 2003. However, at the end of June terrorist attacks once again thwarted any progress. Since the Palestinian Authority failed to adequately crack down on terrorism, George W. increasingly viewed Mazen as a puppet of Arafat. Further, Arafat himself was dubbed a terrorist by American leaders. The Road Map was essentially dead.

As a result, George W. moved even closer to Sharon. This move brought criticism from mainstream Republican policy makers. Scowcroft, George H. W.'s national security advisor, argued that George W. had become "mesmerized" by Sharon. "Sharon just has [Bush] wrapped around his little finger. . . . When there is a suicide attack . . . Sharon calls the president and says, 'I'm on the front line of terrorism,' and the president says, 'Yes you are.'"[44] By 2004, George W. supported the Israeli settlement policy and the policy refusing the Palestinians a right to return to Israel.[45] Ultimately, the tilt toward Israel, coupled with the war in Iraq, which began in March 2003, damaged American credibility in the region, making it more difficult to pursue progress in the peace process.

In December 2004, Arafat died and Mahmoud Abbas replaced him as Palestinian president. Also, after George W.'s election to a second term, Rice replaced Powell as secretary of state in January 2005. There was a sense of new hope and opportunities on the horizon. Despite this, there was little progress on Middle East peace. After Abbas's election, George W. once again stressed the importance of ending terrorism and reforming the Palestinian Authority as the basis for peace in the region. "The new Palestinian president," he argued, "face[s] critical tasks ahead, including fighting terrorism, combating corruption, building reformed and democratic institutions, and reviving the Palestinian economy."[46] To this end, in his February State of the Union address, George W. requested $350 million to "support Palestinian political, economic, and security reforms." Reform was just one half of the equation, however, as George W. also stressed fighting the "common threat of terror" in the region.[47] Over a decade earlier, George H. W. was preparing for war with an eye toward peace.

## Progress and Regress

### 1990–91: The Madrid Peace Process

By August 1990, events in the region had overtaken any administration attempts at peace. The Iraqi invasion of Kuwait led to an international coalition that evicted Iraq from Kuwait and aimed to restrict Saddam Hussein's power in the region (see chapters 3 and 4). The invasion, and the subsequent war to reverse it, gave a needed jump-start to the peace process. In October, the administration was trying to build and maintain a coalition that included Arab states against Iraq. To that end, they supported a UN Security Council Resolution, 672, condemning Israeli acts of violence in the occupied territories and calling upon Israel to abide by its legal obligations.[48]

In addition, it quickly became apparent that Syrian cooperation was pivotal not just to sustain a coalition to evict Iraq from Kuwait but also to move the peace process forward. Meeting with President Hafez al-Assad of Syria in November, George H. W. stressed the importance of a peace conference following Iraq's withdrawal, or eviction, from Kuwait. The meeting proved crucial since Assad committed to a peace conference as long as Israeli occupation was on the table for negotiation.[49]

As the war in Iraq developed, the peace process took shape as well. At the conclusion of the Persian Gulf War, George H. W. decided that the time was ripe to force the issue and move the peace process forward. As Baker explains, the moment offered "an unprecedented window of opportunity" created by the congruence of a number of factors that emerged as a result of the war.[50] First, pursuing the Gulf War through the United Nations process proved effective and enhanced America's reputation. In addition, Arab radicalism, particularly the radicalism of Saddam Hussein, was discredited to some extent, allowing the strengthening of the more moderate Arab voices and letting more moderate Arab countries take the lead. Most significant, Arafat's power was severely weakened, since he had supported Saddam Hussein during the crisis. This would allow Arab states to exert considerable pressure on him during the peace process. These factors were coupled with the end of the cold war and the transformation of Eastern Europe and the Soviet Union, which strengthened American credibility and leadership in the world.

In February 1991, George H. W. showed that he was prepared to exert significant pressure on Israel to foster peace in the region by opposing Israeli loan guarantees as long as Israel continued to build settlements in the occupied territories, including East Jerusalem. According to internal administration documents, it was the "President's judgment that a pause in considering absorption assistance was in the best interest of the historic opportunity for peace that lies before us."[51]

In late February, the administration laid out its strategy. According to the administration's thinking, there was a great opportunity for resolving or at least reducing the Israeli-Palestinian conflict. The United States supported a two-track approach to the peace process, emphasizing both state-to-state relations and negotiations over the challenges faced by Palestinians. In particular, George H. W. wanted to avoid an American-dominated process; this, he feared, would lead to a rejection of the peace process as being biased toward Israel. As a result, he proposed an international conference, jointly hosted by the United States and the Soviet Union.[52] As in war, George H. W.'s preference for multilateral processes would prevail in peace.

Addressing a joint session of Congress on March 6, 1991, George H. W. outlined his goals for the peace process: "On the night I announced Operation Desert Storm, I expressed my hope that out of the horrors of war might come new momentum for peace. . . . By now, it should be plain to all parties that peacemaking . . . requires compromise. . . . We must do all that we can to close the gap between Israel and the Arab States— and between Israel and Palestinians." Stressing the two-track approach, he continued, noting that American policy would require grounding a comprehensive peace in the parameters of UN Security Council Resolutions 242 and 338, and the principle of territory for peace. He concluded his remarks with a guarantee that his administration would work hard toward a "stable peace in the region."[53]

One week later, Baker was "on the road" negotiating with the various parties involved in the peace process. His first meetings were in Riyadh, Saudi Arabia, with members of the Gulf Cooperation Council. Baker noted an "improved Arab attitude" toward the peace process and negotiated Arab support for the two-track approach to peace.[54] It was quickly becoming clear that the greater challenge would be getting Israel to the negotiation table. Baker met with Israeli foreign minister David Levy and Prime Minister Shamir. In meetings with Levy, Baker expressed concern about increased Israeli settlement activities and reports that Israel was planning on greatly expanding these activities. It concerned Baker that Levy claimed to know nothing of these reports. The meetings led Baker to note that the United States would "have to keep up the heat on Shamir," who was "more interested in talking about what the Arabs should do." Most significant about his meetings was that Baker met separately with a Palestinian delegation—minus leaders of the PLO—from the West Bank and Gaza, signaling the administration's willingness to engage Palestinians in the process.[55]

In meetings with Syria, Baker was faced with another challenge. President Assad expressed concern about Arab reconciliation with Israel and did not want to pursue peace prematurely. However, Assad was very open to an international conference hosted by the United States and the Soviet Union.[56] By April, the administration's strategy was in place. The administration would propose an international conference offering a "menu" approach to negotiations, rather than a specific set of steps each of the parties had to take. The menu approach included various confidence-building measures and would give the parties greater ownership and control over the process. The administration made clear that it did not want to force the parties into specific choices.[57]

In April, George H. W. personally got involved, sending letters to President Assad of Syria, King Fahd of Saudi Arabia, King Hussein of Jordan, President Mubarak of Egypt, and Prime Minister Shamir of Israel. All of the letters urged the leaders to engage in the peace process and work toward an international conference.[58] By the end of April, everyone had accepted the two-track approach and the need for a conference. The next step involved getting the Soviets on board as the cohosts of the conference.[59] While the Soviets were willing to host a conference with the United States, many obstacles to the peace process remained.

Most significant, Israeli settlements continued to present a challenge to peace.

In May, George H. W. pressured Prime Minister Shamir directly. In a letter, he noted concern for Israel's "momentous strategic task," but argued that "a climate of peace would do much to facilitate this task." He went on to emphasize that peace making "entail[ed] risks"; however, those risks were shared by other parties as well. Most notably, George H. W. ended the letter with a clear message: "King Hussein . . . is being asked to take on the PLO, the fundamentalists, and maybe the Syrians, and he needs some symbols to point to. Frankly, he would not need these symbols . . . if he could say there would be a freeze on settlement activity once negotiations begin."[60] Throughout the summer, the administration would continue to stress its opposition to Israeli settlement activity, increasing the pressure on Israel.[61] By the fall, George H. W. was personally pressuring members of Congress to delay loan guarantees to Israel as a way to convince the Israelis to halt settlements.[62] In addition, George H. W. offered the Israeli government a "letter of assurances" prior to any negotiations; the assurances were meant to protect the vital interests of Israel in the region.

Meanwhile, George H. W. focused on garnering Arab support for a peace conference despite Israeli intransigence. In his response to a letter from Syrian President Assad, George H. W. pushed for Syrian participation, noting that the United States would not "change its fundamental policy position . . . nor [its] non-recognition of Israel's purported 'annexation' of the Golan Heights." George H. W. continued by offering an American "security guarantee of the border that Israel and Syria mutually agree upon."[63] Further, in letters to King Fahd of Saudi Arabia, King Hussein of Jordan, and President Mubarak of Egypt, George H. W. demonstrated his willingness to use American credibility to build a comprehensive peace. In each letter, he stressed the need of the parties to offer symbolic gestures to move the process forward.[64] George H. W.'s inclination to pursue personal diplomacy became increasingly significant throughout the process.

By September, George H. W. was becoming increasingly concerned that he would fail to get a peace conference. Israeli intransigence continued and the Palestinians were unresponsive to calls for peace. Secretary Baker was instructed to make another trip to the region in an effort to jump-start the peace process. In meetings with Jordan's King Hussein,

Baker was instructed to express George H. W.'s determination to "get to conference and negotiations." He was to remind the Arab leaders that George H. W. drew "the line on loan guarantees." Further, Baker told the Jordanians, "We simply can't afford to let Israel and its lobbyists and supporters in Congress force that issue now."[65]

George H. W.'s determination, coupled with intense personal diplomacy, finally produced results. On October 30, 1991, Israel, Syria, Lebanon, Jordan, and a Palestinian delegation met at a conference in Madrid, Spain, jointly sponsored by the United States and the Soviet Union. At the opening of the conference, George H. W. set forth a set of principles to help move the process forward:

1. The negotiations were directed toward peace agreements; diplomatic, cultural, and economic ties; and investment in development and tourism.
2. A comprehensive peace could only be achieved through direct negotiation and territorial compromises.
3. Any peace would have to come from negotiation and would not be imposed from the outside.
4. Peace must be based on fairness toward both the Israelis and the Palestinians, allowing the Palestinian people to control their lives and destiny, while ensuring Israeli security and recognition.[66]

Despite getting the parties to the peace table, the conference did not achieve a significant substantive agreement. However, it did bring together Israeli and Palestinian negotiators for the first time; this opened the door for future peace negotiations. George H. W.'s personal involvement and diligence proved significant throughout the process, and helped jump-start the process. Almost a decade later, George W., faced with a serious breakdown in the peace process, would choose a different path.

### 2005–9: The Peace Slips Away

George W.'s second term initially saw little change in his policy toward the Palestinians and Israelis. In April 2005, Mohammad Dahlan, a Palestinian minister, visited Washington, DC, in preparation for Mahmoud

Abbas's May meetings with George W. Martin Indyk, a former Clinton advisor and two-time ambassador to Israel, advised Dahlan to emphasize the administration's "democracy and governance agenda," noting that "the President sincerely believes that genuine reform by Palestinians is a prerequisite for moving towards negotiations for a Palestinian state." Furthermore, Indyk explained that in George W.'s view, Israeli occupation was the result of "Palestinian deficiencies—bad leadership, an unwillingness to end terrorism and violence, and dysfunctional institutions."[67]

The following month Mahmoud Abbas visited Washington. George W. praised his "rejection of terrorism," announcing that "the United States [would] provide to the Palestinian Authority $50 million to be used for new housing and infrastructure projects in Gaza. These funds will be used to improve the quality of life of the Palestinians living in Gaza, where poverty and unemployment are very high."[68] Abbas, however, did not want words and money. He wanted the ability to fight back against Israeli attacks. George W. was unsympathetic to his requests. Abbas, like Arafat before him, was proving to be a disappointment, as terror attacks failed to wane and Hamas still remained strong. Taking Indyk's advice, Abbas exploited George W.'s zeal for democracy. He proposed a plan to deal with Hamas by bringing elections to the Palestinians.

While George W. was supportive of the plan, it had one major flaw. It assumed that Abbas and his supporters would win the January 2006 elections. But the Israeli unilateral withdrawal from Gaza allowed Hamas to grow and flourish, since Gaza was its main stronghold. Furthermore, Hamas took credit for the Israeli withdrawal, arguing that their tactics had produced results. By November 2005, relations between Israelis and Palestinians had failed to improve. Sharon cut contacts with Abbas, arguing that the Palestinian Authority had not cracked down on militants. At this point, it was Rice who decided to intervene in an attempt to reverse the backslide in the peace process. She made the decision on her own, with hardly any involvement from George W. himself; this was an illustration of the fact that George W.'s foreign policy inexperience often left him at the mercy of his advisors. Since he and Rice had a much better relationship than he and Powell had, George W. was more willing to let Rice engage in the Israeli-Palestinian issue. However, it did not mean that he would seriously engage the issue.

In fact, the surprising results of the January 2006 Palestinian legislative elections encouraged George W.'s further disengagement from the process. Prior to the election, most assumed that Hamas would win a considerable number of seats but remain in the minority. The administration even funded a $2 million program of civic activities in the West Bank, including street cleaning, food distribution, and a national youth soccer tournament, through the Agency for International Development in an effort to improve Fatah's image and enhance the credibility of other "secular" Palestinian candidates.[69] Despite these efforts, Hamas candidates won 74 of the 132 seats available; the victory caught the United States and many other countries off guard and created a dilemma, since George W. argued that one of his primary foreign policy objectives was the promotion of democracy through fair elections in the Middle East. This victory was preceded by victories won by Shiite Islamists with ties to Iran in Iraq and gains by the Muslim Brotherhood in Egypt. George W. was compelled to support the outcomes of these elections as a result of his overall policy; ultimately, his support for democracy backfired, raising the specter that democracy might encourage rather than discourage radical Islamist governments to emerge in the region.

However, George W. decided not to push for a negation of the elections and expressed hope that Hamas could become a responsible government authority, recognizing Israel, renouncing violence, and honoring previous agreements made by Israel and Palestinian delegates. Thus, George W. continued to argue that democracy could transform the Middle East; in this case, democracy would transform Hamas itself in its attitude and its objectives. However, George W. made clear that Hamas could not be a legitimate partner in the peace process without achieving this transformation. During a news conference on the day after the elections, he stated,

So the Palestinians had an election yesterday, and the results of which remind me about the power of democracy. You see, when you give people the vote, you give people a chance to express themselves at the polls. And if they're unhappy with the status quo, they'll let you know. That's the great thing about democracy; it provides a look into society. And yesterday the turnout was significant, as I understand it. And there was a peaceful process as people went to the polls, and that's positive. But what was also positive is, is that it's a wake-up call to the leadership. Obviously, people were not happy with the status quo. The people are demanding honest government. . . . And so the elections should open the eyes of the old guard there in the Palestinian territories. I like the competition of ideas. . . . On the other hand, I don't see how you can be a partner in peace if you advocate the destruction of a country as part of your platform. And I know you can't be a partner in peace if you have a—if your party has got an armed wing. And so the elections just took place. We will watch very carefully about the formation of the government. But I will continue to remind people about what I just said, that if your platform is the destruction of Israel, it means you're not a partner in peace. And we're interested in peace.[70]

As a result, George W. pressured Hamas to transform by instructing Israel to withhold Israeli tax payments of $55 million per month to the beleaguered Palestinian Authority. This clearly had some impact, as Hamas engaged in an internal debate about its direction.

Meanwhile, in Israel, Kadima won the most seats in the March 28 Knesset election. Kadima, a new political party led by Sharon, was able to beat the two traditional parties, Likud and Labor. In the weeks leading up to the election, Kadima exploited Ariel Sharon's promise that he would make the Palestinian problem disappear. Ehud Olmert, Kadima's leader (Sharon had taken ill and was in a coma), boldly determined that Kadima would unilaterally decide Israel's international borders. According to Neve Gordon, "Kadima had a straightforward message and the Israeli public bought it. The thrust of its claim is that there is a contradiction between Israel's geographic and demographic aspirations: as the settlement project deepened its hold on the Occupied Territories, the very idea of Israel as a Jewish state, where Jews are the majority, has been undermined. In other words, the fact that the majority of people living between the Jordan Valley and the Mediterranean Sea are not Jewish underscores the impossibility of achieving the vision of a greater Israel while maintaining a Jewish state."[71] Kadima suggested it would remake the geographic and demographic reality in Israel, redrawing the boundaries. George W. viewed this as a positive step in the peace process; however, he ignored the realities of such a plan. This plan would have restricted Palestinian rights further, eliminating them from the decision-making process altogether.

Despite this, the administration supported the plan. Secretary of State Rice went to the region in hopes of restarting the stalled peace process. However, Rice found that the Palestinians were unwilling to talk to or trust the United States; in addition, the Israeli position had only hardened further. After her trip to the region, Rice was able to get the two sides to agree to talks, but little else. The talks were viewed as confidence-building measures, with the hope that they would lead to more substantive negotiations.

Kadima's election also brought renewed troubles with Lebanon, further reversing the peace process. Initially, Lebanon was a success story for George W. It had become a symbol of democracy in the Middle East, reflecting George W.'s belief in democracy's "transformative" power. In mid-2004, French president Jacques Chirac told the visiting American president, "You're always talking about democracy in the Middle East. . . . There's one true democracy in the Middle East that's occupied by foreign forces. We ought to be doing something about that."[72] After discussions, George W. agreed, seeing an opportunity to promote democracy in the region. In September 2004, the United States and France sponsored Security Council Resolution 1559, demanding the withdrawal of all foreign forces from Lebanon and the "disarmament" of all armed groups, including Hezbollah.[73] On February 14, 2005, Lebanese prime minister Rafic Hariri was assassinated. The assassination offered an opportunity for the United States to promote Lebanese independence from Syria, since the Syrian government was allegedly involved in the assassination.

On April 27, Syria ended its twenty-nine-year military presence, withdrawing its forces from Lebanon. For George W., it was a clear victory and reinforced his vision of transformation in the Middle East. He declared, "Any who doubt the appeal of freedom in the Middle East can look to Lebanon."[74] In July, as a show of support for the new government, Secretary of State Rice visited Beirut. Despite Resolution 1559's demand that Hezbollah disarm, Rice did not press the government on this issue. Hezbollah was actually gaining strength, but the administration was preoccupied with events in Iraq and Lebanon's problems had not risen to crisis proportions—yet. The victory would be short-lived.

One year later, in July 2006, Hezbollah commandos in Lebanon attacked across the Israeli border, abducting two Israeli soldiers and killing four others. The Israelis reacted strongly, wanting to send a message to all of Lebanon in hopes that the Lebanese people would no longer support Hezbollah. This put George W. in a difficult position. The president believed that Israel had a right to defend itself against terrorists but was concerned about the fragility of democracy in Lebanon.[75] George W. began working the phones, telling leaders in the region that he would try to calm the situation and prevent Israel from toppling the Lebanese government, but he reminded leaders that "the real culprit . . . is the militant wing of Hamas and Hezbollah."[76] Again, the war on terror, and George W.'s worldview, took precedence in the crisis. Initially, George W.'s diplomacy was working, with world leaders blaming Hezbollah for the crisis and tacitly supporting Israel's response. However, the crisis spun out of control.

George W. watched and waited, understanding that he might eventually have to intervene in the crisis but wanting to ensure that the Israelis were given enough time to wage a successful campaign against Hezbollah; the issue was now linked to the larger policy of the war on terror. According to Glenn Kessler, "Bush . . . was convinced that the Israeli effort would be seen as successful because Hezbollah would no longer be able to control southern Lebanon."[77] This meant that he was slow to respond to calls for American intervention to end the crisis. With some reluctance, Rice would go to the Middle East. However, George W. was not looking to restore the pre–July 2006 status quo in the region; instead, he hoped that Rice's visit could provide a more permanent solution to the challenge of Hezbollah.

During her visit, Rice explained that the administration would not accept an immediate cease-fire; instead, she insisted on the disarmament of Hezbollah as the first step to a comprehensive solution to the crisis.[78] This angered many throughout the region, especially in Lebanon, and led to angry demonstrations against American support for Israel and its war.[79] The administration's policy was unraveling. On the one hand, George W. supported democracy; on the other hand, he refused to let Hezbollah participate in that democracy. To the Lebanese the American president was signaling his support for the Israelis. Rice gave the Lebanese further reason to be suspicious of American diplomacy when she suggested that the Lebanese election was peculiar since Hezbollah had gained seats.[80]

From Beirut, Rice headed to Israel, where she met with Prime Minister Olmert. Little came of the meeting. Notably, Rice did not go to Damascus. Clearly, Syria still played a hidden role as a key source of the problem, yet George W. was unwilling to engage with its government, suggesting that Syria was behind the Hezbollah attack.[81] Ultimately, the United States was playing a delicate balancing act, trying to give Lebanon control over its territory and remove the threat to Israel along its northern border.

On July 29, Rice returned to Israel for discussions with Olmert. George W. was still hoping to find a diplomatic solution that did not require any immediate action by the Israelis, but placed the onus of response on Hezbollah and the Syrians. Meanwhile, the French were working on a United Nations resolution calling for an immediate cease-fire; this diverted significantly from George W.'s desire to create a political settlement isolating Hezbollah as a part of any cease-fire. The administration now had a mess on its hands, as Israel was increasing its attacks, resulting in civilian deaths, and the French were demanding a cease-fire. Now the United States was being criticized for delaying a cease-fire. As a result, George W. pressured Israel to cease its air strikes for forty-eight hours and provide a twenty-four-hour period of safe passage for refugees. However, Hezbollah continued to launch rockets into Israel, and the Israelis continued to strike at targets in Lebanon.

The French proposal meant that the United States would need two UN resolutions—one calling for a cease-fire and one providing an international force in the region. Over dinner, Rice and George W. discussed the situation. On August 6, the administration debated whether to pressure Israel to halt its offensive. In the end, George W. chose to give Israel the ability to harm Hezbollah further and continue the war; the war on terror took precedence over events on the ground.[82] Ultimately, George W.'s policy of refusing to negotiate with countries or groups linked to terrorists constrained his maneuverability. Earlier in the year, in the 2006 *National Security Strategy* report, the administration argued, "In the world today, the fundamental character of regimes matters as much as the distribution of power among them. The goal of our statecraft is to help create a world of democratic, well-governed states that can meet the needs of their citizens and conduct themselves responsibly in the international system. This is the best way to provide enduring security for the American people."[83] Thus, countries like Syria and Iran—backers of Hezbollah—that could apply pressure on Hezbollah to halt its attacks on Israel could not be approached, making a solution to the conflict even more difficult.

Now the French and Americans were floating different ideas and resolutions, complicating the problem further. Meanwhile, on the ground, the Israelis continued their assault on Lebanon. Amid a flurry of negotiations, Security Council Resolution 1701 emerged, calling on Israel to withdraw its forces from Lebanon "in parallel" with the deployment of United Nations peacekeepers. The international force had a mandate to use firepower but no explicit role in disarming Hezbollah. According to the resolution, the UN force could take "all necessary action" to ensure that there were no "hostile activities of any kind." The resolution also authorized the troops to protect civilians and ensure the flow of humanitarian assistance.[84]

However, American credibility suffered throughout the region as a result of its handling of the crisis. George W.'s unwillingness to pressure Israel to end the conflict earlier made it appear as if Israel was acting as an American proxy against Hezbollah. To make matters worse, the war resulted in the deaths of 1,100 Lebanese compared to 160 Israelis, and forced many in southern Lebanon to flee their homes. Moderate Arab states felt betrayed by the American policy and Hezbollah reinforced this view by decorating the mountains of rubble across south Beirut with giant banners declaring, MADE IN USA, THE NEW MIDDLE EAST, and SMART BOMBS FOR DUMB MINDS.[85]

Thus, the United States came out of the conflict in a significantly weaker position in the region. First, Hezbollah had not been eliminated; in fact, it appeared stronger. Second, Iran was emboldened to resist the international effort to restrain its nuclear program, turning down the American offer to join European-led talks in exchange for suspending nuclear enrichment. Finally, and perhaps most significant, American credibility was damaged, making attempts at Middle East peace increasingly more difficult. Ultimately, the war forced Israel to abandon its plan to withdraw from large sections of the West Bank, since it had not achieved a decisive outcome against Hezbollah and its allies. To make matters worse, like Hamas in the Palestinian Authority earlier, Hezbollah was elected into the Lebanese government.

By 2007, it appeared that George W. was far from achieving success in the Middle East peace process. The Hamas victory, coupled with the Israel-Lebanon war, brought the road map to a halt. George W. almost completely disengaged. Despite pleas from Abbas and his supporters for leeway in dealing with Hamas, George W. refused any dealings, arguing that Hamas remained a terrorist group. George W. was determined to halt all but humanitarian aid to the Palestinians until Hamas accepted Israel's existence, ended violence, and acknowledged previous agreements. This made it harder for the United States to convince Arab governments to pressure the Palestinians to move forward with peace negotiations. The leverage that the United States had had after 9/11 was almost nonexistent now.

Despite this, George W. encouraged Secretary Rice to take the lead in negotiating a meeting between the various parties. First, however, the administration had to contend with the "Hamas problem." Throughout the spring and summer, George W. continued to pressure the Palestinians on the inclusion of Hamas in its unity government by authorizing a political and economic boycott of the Palestinian Authority. On June 14, Palestinian president Mahmoud Abbas dissolved the Fatah-Hamas unity government and removed Hamas leader Ismail Haniyeh from his position as prime minister. On June 17, Hamas took control of the Gaza Strip and Fatah retained control of the West Bank. On June 18, George W. authorized lifting the political and economic boycott of the Palestinian Authority, signaling a willingness to conduct negotiations with Abbas and Fatah.

In addition, George W. announced his desire to hold a conference in the fall to conduct negotiations between the Israelis and Palestinians. He invited regional neighbors to attend but stressed the importance of Israelis and Palestinians taking the lead throughout the process. However, George W. continued to insist that Hamas not be involved. Hamas, in turn, called upon Arab countries to boycott the conference.

In November 2007, Israelis and Palestinians, along with other invitees, met for a one-day conference at Annapolis, Maryland. George W. came to the table with very low credibility and expectations. Yet his aims were ambitious. George W. had decided to push the Israelis and Palestinians toward an agreement, at least in principle, on a final peace treaty. The peace conference's aims were out of reach, however, since issues such as security, the Palestinian refugees' right of return, the fate of Jerusalem, and Hamas's control of the Gaza Strip remained impediments. It appeared that George W. wanted to solidify his legacy in the Middle East with nothing short of a revolutionary agreement that would have reversed almost sixty years of history.

To make matters worse, George W.'s approval rating was 30 percent going into the conference, and Arabs were distrustful of his actions. The Iraq war and George W.'s seemingly uncompromising support for Israel made trust difficult. Furthermore, George W.'s sporadic involvement in the peace process gave the appearance that the United States was convening the conference only for political expediency and historical legacy. In addition, the administration undermined its own policy with internal divisions. While Rice believed that a long-term solution to the region's problems began with the resolution of the Israeli-Palestinian conflict, Cheney and Elliot Abrams, the National Security Council's Middle East policy advisor, did not. Both considered the Annapolis Conference unrealistic and cautioned against it; furthermore, both favored the hard-line Israeli policy.[86] In his opening address to the conference, George W. made clear that Israel must do its part, but emphasized the need for Palestinian reforms and renunciation of extremism.

> The time is right because a battle is underway for the future of the Middle East—and we must not cede victory to the extremists. With their violent actions and contempt for human life, the extremists are seeking to impose a dark vision on the Palestinian people—a vision that feeds on hopelessness and despair to sow chaos in the Holy Land. If this vision prevails, the future of the region will be endless terror, endless war, and endless suffering. . . . Standing against this dark vision are President Abbas and his government. They are offering the Palestinian people an alterna-

tive vision for the future—a vision of peace, a homeland of their own, and a better life. . . . If Palestinian reformers cannot deliver on this hopeful vision, then the forces of extremism and terror will be strengthened, a generation of Palestinians could be lost to the extremists, and the Middle East will grow in despair. We cannot allow this to happen. Now is the time to show Palestinians that their dream of a free and independent state can be achieved at the table of peace—and that the terror and violence preached by Palestinian extremists is the greatest obstacle to a Palestinian state.[87]

In the end, however, George W. deferred to Israeli policies, meaning that little could be accomplished at Annapolis.

As George W.'s final year came into focus, little progress on Middle East peace was made. His focus on the war on terror and the establishment of democracy in Iraq as the key to ending the region's problems left little room for anything else. Furthermore, by 2006, the idea of democracy in the Middle East was rapidly losing credibility as the elections of Hamas and Hezbollah undermined George W.'s position. Ultimately, the war on terror became the driving force of George W.'s Middle East policy and it sealed the fate of any chances at peace in the region.

## CONCLUSION

As they were in war, the worldviews of George H. W. and George W. were reflected throughout the peace process. While the pragmatism of George H. W. vs. the ideological definitiveness of George W. impacted the outcomes, differences in personal diplomacy also affected their policies significantly. In the case of George H. W., his intense dislike of Shamir made it easier for him to pursue a policy that pressured Israel into the peace process. Likewise, George W.'s personal friendship with Sharon, and later Olmert, led to a policy that supported Israel, often without question, and stalled the peace process. Perhaps more than any other case, the Israeli-Palestinian issue demonstrates the importance of personal diplomacy to presidential politics and policy. The personal politics of foreign policy—the relationships that presidents have with world leaders—can alter the course of a president's policy, both negatively and positively. One might suppose that a close personal relationship would facilitate positive results, but ironically, in the case of the Israeli-Palestinian peace process, the opposite was true. Close friendship stalled the peace process, while tension moved it forward; George W.'s close personal relationship with Sharon negatively impacted the process, while George H. W.'s tense one with Shamir had the opposite effect.

# 6

# Comparing the Bush
# Presidencies

In 1830, John Quincy Adams wrote about the collision course between the West and the Islamic world. He argued that Islamic civilization would not accept the West's notions of liberty and equality, and the West had a right to defend its values and interests against Islam. According to Adams, "Between [Christianity and Islam], thus contrasted in their characters, a war of twelve hundred years has already raged. That war is yet flagrant; nor can it cease but by the extinction of that imposture, which has been permitted by Providence to prolong the degeneracy of man. While the merciless and dissolute dogmas of the false prophet shall furnish motives to human action, there can never be peace upon earth, and good will towards men. . . . The precept of the Koran is, perpetual war against all who deny, that Mahomet is the prophet of God."[1] Although I disagree with Adams's premise, his words are particularly prescient when one considers the foreign policies of the George H. W. Bush and George W. Bush presidencies. Both presidents left a legacy of war and peace in the Middle East. In 1988, one would have been hard-pressed to believe that George H. W. Bush and George W. Bush would both be president and even more hard-pressed to predict that American foreign policy after the cold war would be defined, to a large measure, by interactions with a major state in the Middle East, Iraq. Moreover, that the two conflicts in Iraq would be undertaken by presidents related as father and son would have been unimaginable. Despite this unique situation, the conflicts in Iraq were commenced in very different ways with very different results. Likewise, the two Bush administrations' approaches to the Middle East peace process were also very different.

## On War

Richard Haass, a participant in both Bush administrations, has astutely labeled the two wars in Iraq as respectively a war of necessity and a war of choice.[2] George H. W. was confronted with an unavoidable crisis when Iraq invaded Kuwait, and the president pursued a measured response. George W., on the other hand, sought a crisis with Iraq. Saddam Hussein had no association with the devastating attacks of 9/11, yet George W. chose to invade Iraq under false pretenses of an Iraqi association with Al Qaeda and the belief that Iraq posed a potential future threat, perhaps using weapons of mass destruction.

A number of points can be drawn from the analysis of the decisions to engage in these two wars. First, the person in the Office of the Presidency matters; the character and worldview of the president sets the tone and determines the direction of the administration. It is not enough for a president to surround himself with "strong" advisors; strong advisors can mislead the president or "feed" the president's personal beliefs in order to maintain their positions within the administration. In the case of the first Gulf War, George H. W. had the experience necessary to navigate the murky waters of war. His experience was tempered by advisors who worked well together and confidently expressed beliefs, even those in opposition to the president's. George H. W.'s experience gave him the confidence to listen to opposing views and the knowledge to assess the facts before him.

By contrast, George W.'s lack of experience often left him at the mercy of his advisors and, more significant, trapped within his own inflexibility and certainty of thinking. When confronted with an opposing view, he often battened the hatches, refusing to budge. His "my way or the highway" approach prevented an adequate evaluation of the problem at hand and an exploration of alternatives for dealing with the problem. His father may have been mocked for "prudence" and his lack of the "vision thing," but the reality is that his measured approach allowed a diplomatic process to unfold. Only when the diplomatic process had reached its conclusion did the elder Bush pursue the use of force. George W. had decided to pursue the use of force before most, if any, alternative options were evaluated. We may want confidence in our presidents; in fact, we may want clear direction and vision. However, this can also mean the loss of measured analysis and, in the case of George W., it meant just that.

Second, the approach to the two wars demonstrates the contrast between enlightened realism and the cowboy liberal. The enlightened realist, George H. W., emphasized external relations between states. The domestic politics of a state does not matter in foreign policy calculations. In fact, George H. W. did not believe that he could modify the nature of another state; this was far too ambitious for American foreign policy. On the other hand, George W. pursued a foreign policy aimed at altering the nature of Iraq—making it into a democracy modeled on American democracy. His view was highly moralistic and aimed to expand freedom and democracy throughout the Middle East. This approach was significantly more ambitious than George H. W.'s. That ambition came with much higher costs, including the squandering of American reputation and credibility throughout the world. George H. W.'s willingness to pursue diplomacy through the United Nations left the United States in a more credible position. While George H. W. may be criticized for lacking a forward-thinking policy, his approach gained power and prestige for the United States. George W.'s policy was certainly ambitious and forward thinking, but it was also costly to American power. After 9/11, the United States had an opportunity to shape and lead the world, but by pursuing a unilateral policy, the United States, in many ways, mirrored the actions of the rogues it was trying to deter.

I believe that the Persian Gulf War was largely successful. Strategically, the United States responded to Iraqi aggression and prevented Iraqi dominance of the Middle East. Inaction could have set a dangerous precedent. Diplomatically, the United States responded without damaging American reputation and credibility. In fact, George H. W. went to extraordinary measures to build a coalition to evict Iraq from Kuwait; in doing so, he cultivated trust, increased American power, and created an atmosphere supporting continued American leadership in a post–cold war world. In addition, George H. W. accomplished his war aims: the eviction of Iraq from Kuwait and the restoration of the Kuwaiti government.

This does not eliminate potential criticisms of the policy. Most certainly, one could suggest that George H. W. was too cautious in his approach to Iraqi aggression. Also, American intelligence vastly underestimated Iraq's intentions and motivations leading up to the invasion of Kuwait. Furthermore, one could argue that it was a mistake to end the war prior to disarming or destroying most of the Iraqi army. Finally, signals to the Shia in the south and the Kurds in the north could certainly have been clearer, and potentially could have lessened the humanitarian catastrophe at the war's end.

However, George H. W.'s possible mistakes do not undermine the fact that his policy produced far better results than that of George W.'s. Not only was the second Iraq war ill advised, but no alternatives were considered and George W. went into the war without assessing its probable outcomes. If the administration had simply examined the likelihood of success, it would have realized the enormous consequences associated with its choice. George W. inherited the presidency with a budgetary surplus, a growing economy, and a world relatively at peace; in addition, the United States had a strong reputation and could exercise its persuasive influence in the world. After eight years in office, he left the White House with a massive deficit and debt (brought on mainly by the pursuit of two wars), an economic recession, a military stretched to the limits, and a world in which American credibility was declining and anti-Americanism was on the rise. The 2003 war in Iraq contributed to the emergence of a world in which American power is diminished.

George W.'s leadership during the war must also face serious scrutiny. He had entered the presidency with serious misgivings about nation building but set precisely that course with regard to Iraq. The administration's beliefs that the war in Iraq would be simple and quick were dashed, yet there were no contingency plans in the event of the policy's failure. It was only after considerable prodding that the administration considered the surge in forces to deal with the challenges on the ground.

Much of the difference between the policy and the conduct of the two wars can be attributed to the worldviews of George H. W. Bush and George W. Bush; the outcomes in each war were more than a matter of process. It is vital that a policy maker understand the assumptions that go into a chosen policy. In the cases of George H. W and George W., these assumptions were radically different and, in the end, they had a significant impact on the policy outcomes. Most notably, the issue of America's role in the world highlights the profound differences between George H. W.

and George W. George H. W.'s enlightened realism focused on the actions of states beyond their borders. Accordingly, the state's regime type is of only secondary importance; attempting to modify the internal nature of a state and its society is too ambitious and difficult a task and should be undertaken only in circumstances where there is no choice. Consequently, George H. W. did not attempt to use direct means to topple the Iraqi government; while he would have supported the removal of Saddam Hussein, his instincts cautioned against it.

George W.'s cowboy liberal worldview, on the other hand, emphasized the domestic structure of the state. The nature of the state and society matters because there are "moral" and "immoral" governments and societies. George W. accepted the view that democracies are not only moral but also more peaceful, thus resulting in a better world. However, George W. overlooked the simple fact that American democracy is neither universal nor inevitable. In Iraq, democracy still remains tenuous and reflects the sectarian challenges inherent in Iraqi society. This was also true for the Middle East as a whole; democracy in the Palestinian Authority or Lebanon did not produce what the administration had hoped for. In fact, democracy might bring adversaries to power, as it did with Hamas and Hezbollah.

## On Peace

George H. W. Bush and George W. Bush's approaches to peace were also reflective of their thinking. First, in their approaches to ending the Iraq wars, George H. W. and George W. took different paths. George H. W. had clearly established goals and parameters for ending the Persian Gulf War; completing the UN mandates meant that George H. W. had achieved success. George W. also had goals, but it was unclear what constituted success and the achievement of those goals. Early on, he suggested that the mission was "accomplished," yet the conflict was far from over. Moreover, the measure of success shifted once the Iraqi insurgency emerged. While a democratic Iraq appeared to be the goal of American policy, what constituted democracy was never clearly explained to the American people or the world. In addition, the administration sent mixed messages about democracy through its policies. Once the insurgency emerged, it was clear that the administration was more interested in securing American interests than in promoting Iraqi democracy. George W. was very concerned about the democracy that was emerging in Iraq and sought to limit the damages.

Likewise, regarding the Israeli-Palestinian peace process, George H. W. was less concerned than George W. about the internal structure of either Israel or Palestine and more concerned with the actions that each took toward the other. George W.'s beliefs prevented any real progress toward peace. First, and perhaps most important, in contrast to George H. W., pragmatism and flexibility were sacrificed to ideology. The emphasis on the war on terror clouded George W.'s vision. Once the war in Iraq began, George W.'s views became increasingly inflexible. Further, he identified Palestinian leaders as terrorists, making it nearly impossible to pursue peace.

Second, in this instance, personal diplomacy harmed the peace process. George W.'s relationship with Sharon proved fatal to progress. Personal diplomacy isolated Arafat and Abbas, leading the administration to support the Israeli position without question. On the other hand, George H. W.'s personal diplomacy ironically served to facilitate the peace process; his opposition to Israeli settlement activity, which was integral to convincing the Palestinians that he was serious about the peace process, was enhanced by his dislike of Shamir.

In addition, George W.'s emphasis on unilateralism lent itself to a "my way or the highway" approach to Middle East peace. Either the Palestinians accepted and complied with George W.'s positions on peace, or progress would not occur. George H. W., ironically, exhibited a similar tendency with his approach to Israel throughout the peace process. However, he was more willing to exhibit cooperation and to pursue various angles for negotiation.

## FINAL ANALYSIS

One might argue that a study of the two Bush presidencies is exceptional and offers little in the way of generalizations and lessons. However, we must remember that these two presidents had many of the same advisors, but very different outcomes. Thus, examining George H. W. Bush and George W. Bush offers both specific and general conclusions; one should not overlook the value of the study simply because it focuses on an unusual relationship in presidential history. Moreover, understanding presidential worldviews offers insights into future presidential candidates and presidents. To more fully understand the two Bush presidencies, I have suggested an approach that examines the realist and liberal elements of a president's worldview. This approach highlights the significant differences between these two presidents.

Some have suggested that September 11, 2001, changed everything for George W., for example. I disagree. Prior to 9/11, George W. had a worldview that guided his foreign policy. Rather than "changing" George W.'s worldview, 9/11 reinforced it. By taking an approach that examines the worldviews of presidents and presidential candidates, we gain a clearer understanding of the personal foreign policy goals that they see for the United States. There is no doubt that some presidents are more successful at achieving those goals than others; in the case of the Bush presidencies, one cannot deny the significance of the international context in allowing each president to proceed. The approach I have taken here is merely one look into the policies of the Bush presidencies; it does not deny other approaches or models. However, it is important to understand that many scholars underestimate the heavy weight of "personality" factors on presidential choices. The assumption often is that misguided or failed policies are the result of naïveté or contextual pressures and issues. This reflects the proclivity toward rational choice models as a way of approaching foreign policy analysis. Yet these models often leave the reader with more questions than answers. Still, the events in Iraq since 1990 cannot be attributed solely to presidential worldviews; decisions do not take place in a vacuum—situation matters.

So what do we learn from this study? What does it explain? What lessons does it yield? First, both presidents operated in an environment that increased the impact of their worldviews. In other words, without the crises of the end of the cold war and 9/11, both presidents would have had greater difficulty leaving such an indelible mark on American foreign policy. Crises allow individual policy makers to exercise greater influence over the direction of policy. It is then that the worldviews of presidents are particularly important. Since we cannot predict crises, especially crises like 9/11, it is helpful to know how a president sees the world and how he or she might respond to challenges in it. This does not, of course, guarantee the future, but it does provide some signposts to help guide our understanding of the policy options that presidents may choose.

George W.'s worldview was well developed prior to 9/11. Rather than changing his views of the world, 9/11 reinforced them and provided opportunities for his administration to implement them. Before 9/11 the administration had set a course regarding Iraq; however, it was only after 9/11 that the administration was able to implement its policy. Prior to 9/11 George W. had begun the process of transforming American foreign policy in his "image." He had pulled the United States out of the Anti-Ballistic Missile and Kyoto treaties, illustrating his desire to pursue a unilateral approach to American foreign policy, for example. In addition, his administration had already begun to pursue a policy of regime change in Iraq; 9/11, however, made "selling" that policy very easy.

Likewise, George H. W.'s characteristic pragmatism was evident before the collapse of the Soviet Union. His caution toward the changes taking place throughout Europe illustrates this well. And even with the changes taking place throughout the Soviet Union, George H. W. initially exercised caution toward Iraq. His vision of a new world order of stability and maintaining the status quo was reflected in his cautious worldview. Moreover, George H. W.'s multilateral inclinations were present early in his career, as evidenced by his experiences at the United Nations.

This leads to a second, crucial point—experience matters. This is important, since many presidential candidates run a campaign capitalizing on being an outsider, someone who does not have "Washington" experience. But "Washington" experience is not always a bad thing. George H. W. was arguably one of the most experienced presidents in history. His experience made an important impact on foreign policy. He not only understood the significance of coalitions and the use of American power on the world stage, he also was sensitive to the perspectives of other countries. This was particularly important during the Gulf crisis, when George H. W. maintained the support of Arab states. Experience also frees the individual from rigid ideological thinking. George W.'s lack of experience meant that he often relied on his instinctual ideological views and rarely reassessed policies once he had chosen his direction. His lack of experience also led him to rely on advisors more readily than George H. W. did. A lack of experience can lead a president to fall back on an "old reliable" way of thinking and might prevent the flexibility and creativity that is often required in foreign policy.

Third, it should come as no surprise that I see greater benefits in multilateralism than in unilateralism. Particularly since the end of the cold war, the United States requires an international approach that stresses leadership but not domination. Multilateralism is not only a smarter alliance strategy, it is a better strategy for dealing with the dangers inherent in today's world. Defeating terrorism, for example, requires cooperation, and a unilateral strategy only serves to alienate important actors on the world stage. Furthermore, the benefits of multilateralism are multiple. As Stewart Patrick explains, "For all its overwhelming power, the United States cannot by itself stem the proliferation of weapons of mass destruction, preserve regional stability, enforce international law and human rights standards, maintain an open and nondiscriminatory trading system, ensure the stability and liquidity of global financial markets, protect the 'global commons,' stop global warming, stem transnational trafficking in narcotics, thwart organized crime syndicates, slow global population growth, regulate immigration flows, respond to humanitarian catastrophes, stem pandemics, or promote sustainable development."[3] Relative to the scale of these problems, American power is rather limited. It is in the best interest of the United States to cooperate with the international community in order to deal with these challenges. Also, American unilateral action negatively impacts the collective efforts of the international community. American noncompliance with international actors will have a tremendous impact on the group, even if no other actors defect. The United States has both a great incentive and a great responsibility to cooperate with the other countries of the world to arrive at multilateral agreements in order to protect both our common future and American national interests.

With this in mind, we must think seriously about our presidential candidates' worldviews. For example, in 2008, we witnessed vast differences in the worldviews of Senators John McCain and Barack Obama, the Republican and Democratic presidential candidates, which would have produced drastically different foreign policies. Take their positions on Iran and its nuclear program, for example. On July 18, 2007, for example, Senator McCain argued, "And every option must remain on the table. Military action isn't our preference. It remains, as it always must, the last option. We have some way to go diplomatically before we need to contemplate other measures. But it is a simple observation of reality that there is only one thing worse than a military solution, and that, my friends, is a nuclear armed Iran. The regime must understand that it cannot win a showdown with the world."[4] And in June 2008, McCain added, "Emboldened by nuclear weapons, Iran would feel unconstrained to sponsor terrorist attacks. Its flouting of the Nuclear Nonproliferation Treaty would render that agreement obsolete and could induce others to join a nuclear arms race. There would be the possibility that Tehran might pass nuclear materials or weapons to terrorist networks. An Iranian nuclear bomb would pose an existential threat to Israel. . . . Rather than sitting down unconditionally with the Iranian President or Supreme Leader, John McCain will work to create real-world pressures to peacefully but decisively change Iran's behavior."[5] By contrast, on his campaign Web site in July 2008, Senator Obama argued, "We have not exhausted our non-military options in confronting this threat; in many ways, we have yet to try them. That's why [I] stood up to the Bush administration's warnings of war, just like [I] stood up to the war in Iraq." Furthermore, he noted that he was the "only major candidate who supports tough, direct presidential diplomacy with Iran without preconditions." This included offering "incentives like membership in the World Trade Organization, economic investments, and a move toward normal diplomatic relations." Ultimately, Senator Obama argued that diplomacy could secure a "comprehensive settlement" with Iran.[6]

While one could argue that President Obama has reversed course somewhat regarding Iran, the two candidates' statements revealed something deeper about their worldviews and told us about their potential approaches to foreign policy. Senator McCain's statement suggests a greater willingness to use force, or perhaps "saber-rattle"; McCain might have been more willing to use the American military to secure American interests abroad. On the other hand, Senator Obama suggested a more cautious approach that relied on diplomatic pressure in the form of sanctions and international institutions as a means of solving the challenges the

United States faces abroad. The gleanings we get from examining these brief statements could have told us something about each man's response to the crisis in Libya. While supporting President Obama's actions in Libya, McCain argued that the United States was not going far enough. In fact, McCain suggested using American ground troops to assist in overthrowing Libyan leader Muammar Gaddafi. This stood in contrast to President Obama's multilateral approach, allowing European countries to take the lead on a Western response to Libya.

This example serves only to highlight the significance of investigating the experiences and worldviews of presidential candidates. Too often, the American electorate gets caught up in "form" to the neglect of "substance." Presidential elections have become popularity contests and the results can be dangerous. In recent years, "popularity" polls have been conducted, asking potential voters which presidential candidate they would rather have a beer with. In 2004, 57 percent of undecided voters answered George W. Bush.[7] In January 2008, the National Beer Wholesalers Associated conducted a similar poll. Barack Obama led the poll with 13 percent, followed by Rudy Giuliani at 12 percent, and John McCain at 10 percent. Craig Purser, president of the beer wholesalers, explained, "With all the rigors of a campaign—attack ads, phone calls, direct mail—Americans know sometimes it just comes down to who you want to have a beer with. We hope this campaign reminds voters that at the end of the day, while issues are very important, so is conversation, civility and character. Having a beer with someone represents getting to know someone better, and that's what the campaign season is all about—getting to know these candidates better."[8] However, civility may not be the best judge of decision-making style and worldview. And while knowing the candidate's stances on various issues provides a guide, a more intimate portrait of the candidate's worldview can provide a clearer road map. We must take care when choosing our presidents. The danger lies in not knowing where each candidate wants to take the country. Analyzing worldviews provides an important opportunity to examine the type of decision maker a potential president might be.

After all, many others in the same position as George W. would not have made the same decisions. George H. W. and Scowcroft clearly did not, and it is unlikely that Al Gore, Bill Clinton, or Jimmy Carter would have followed George W.'s path. Strong characteristics, motivational goals, and values that formed a coherent worldview led George W. to make his decisions. George W.'s presumption that democracies were more law abiding, more predictable, and friendlier than other states had significant consequences for the Middle East. Not only did it lead the United States into a war in Iraq, but it also prevented any serious progress on Middle East peace. As long as the Palestinian Authority was unable to meet the requirements of a stable democracy, George W. could not accept its leaders as viable diplomats. He refused to deal with Arafat and Abbas because they were associated with antidemocratic values. Ironically, embracing democracy meant the reality of a Hamas electoral victory. In the end, George W.'s approach to the Middle East was blinded by his worldview, which closed off alternatives and prevented any real analysis or understanding of the region.

Thus, we can conclude that personality matters. The individual traits one possesses, the personal goals one pursues, and the value system one espouses create a framework that guides actions. In the end, this matters because presidents have the potential to impose their visions on the world. And ultimately, these visions have consequences, both good and bad, that can shape the course of history.

# Acknowledgments

Writing a book is, at times, a lonely process. It is easy to forget that the completion of a book takes more than one person and that while the actual writing can be lonely, you are never alone. I owe many debts to many people. Like many first books, this one began with my doctoral dissertation at the University of Virginia. My dissertation analyzed the decisions and worldview of the George H. W. Bush administration as the cold war came to an end. In many ways, this book is an extension of my earlier research. I owe much to the University of Virginia Department of Government and Foreign Affairs (now the Department of Politics) and my dissertation committee: Dr. Michael Joseph Smith, the director of the committee; Dr. David Newsom; Dr. James Ceasar; and Dr. Philip Zelikow. I would be remiss if I did not also mention Dr. Whittle Johnston, the first director of my dissertation committee; he died from cancer during the process, but I will never forget his guidance.

In some ways, a dissertation does not begin in graduate school, and I owe an important debt to my undergraduate institution, the State University of New York College at Geneseo. The faculty members in the Department of Political Science were always supportive and encouraged me to pursue a graduate degree. Most significant was Dr. Bob Goeckel; Bob epitomizes the ideal of the teacher-scholar and he has served as my model both in and out of the classroom. For his friendship and mentorship, I am indebted to him.

It would be thoughtless not to mention the many institutions involved in my career's trajectory. They include Virginia Commonwealth University, Southern Illinois University at Carbondale, the University of Wisconsin–Stevens Point, Georgetown College, and Transylvania University. I spent the first decade of the twenty-first century at Georgetown College. Georgetown financially supported some of my research on this project, including that at the George Bush Presidential Library at Texas

155

A&M University. I am particularly indebted to Dr. Lindsey Apple, emeritus professor of history; Michael Taylor Rains, who accompanied me to the George Bush Presidential Library and assisted in the research process; and Thomas Brawner, who read some of the manuscript and offered his ideas.

In 2010, I joined the faculty at Transylvania University in Lexington, Kentucky. I am thankful to my colleagues in the Division of Social Sciences and especially those in the Political Science Program for their support: Dr. Jeffrey Freyman and Dr. Don Dugi. I am thankful for our wonderful administrative assistant, Katie Banks, who provided assistance in the completion of this book. Dr. William Pollard, vice president and dean, has in many ways impacted my career more significantly than most. He hired me at Georgetown College in 2001 when he was Georgetown's provost and hired me again at Transylvania University in 2010. I owe him a debt of gratitude for believing in a young scholar and taking another chance on me later in my career. I also thank the Dr. Byron and Judy Young Faculty Development Program for funding the completion of this project. Lastly, I thank the students at Transylvania who challenge me every day.

My thanks also go to those associated with the George Bush Presidential Library in College Station, Texas. The Scowcroft Institute at Texas A&M University provided an O'Donnell travel grant to support my research at the library. Rebecca Sams and Thaddeus Romansky, archives technicians at the library, and Elizabeth Myers, an archivist, were extremely helpful in finding and identifying materials for research.

A debt is also owed to the staff of the University Press of Kentucky. Steve Wrinn, the director, has offered guidance and encouragement since the beginning of this process. In addition, the many other staff members at UPK have always been helpful, especially Allison Webster, David Cobb, Robin DuBlanc, Cameron Ludwick, and Mack McCormick. I am also extremely grateful for the assistance of the press's reviewers, who helped guide my revisions of the book.

Finally, I wish to thank my family. My parents encouraged and supported my desire to pursue a PhD and developed in me the sense of critical thinking necessary to be a scholar. Most important, my bride, Carey, has been my rock throughout this process. She has lovingly cajoled me toward completion of the book and "edited" multiple drafts of the manuscript. Her love and support have made me a stronger person. And lastly, I thank my children, Max and Sophia. They remind me to have fun, even when I'm working. Ultimately, my family has been patient with the angst often associated with completing a book. This book is for them.

# Notes

## Introduction

1. Stanley Renshon, *High Hopes: The Clinton Presidency and the Politics of Ambition* (New York: New York University Press, 1996), 4, 38.

2. See Richard E. Neustadt, *Presidential Power and the Modern Presidents: The Politics of Leadership from Roosevelt to Reagan* (New York: Free Press, 1990), 3–4.

3. Alexander L. George, *Bridging the Gap: Theory and Practice in Foreign Policy* (Washington, DC: United States Institute of Peace Press, 1993), xx.

4. Patrick Callahan, *Logics of American Foreign Policy: Theories of America's World Role* (New York: Pearson Longman, 2004), 4.

5. Kerry, quoted in Jack Snyder, "One World, Rival Theories," *Foreign Policy* 145 (November–December 2004): 54.

6. Michael Joseph Smith, *Realist Thought from Weber to Kissinger* (Baton Rouge: Louisiana State University Press, 1986), 165.

7. See, for example: Henry Kissinger, *Nuclear Weapons and Foreign Policy* (Garden City, NY: Doubleday, 1957); Henry Kissinger, *The Necessity for Choice: Prospects for American Foreign Policy* (New York: Harper Brothers, 1960); and Henry Kissinger, *American Foreign Policy: Three Essays* (New York: Norton, 1969).

8. George F. Kennan, *American Diplomacy, 1900–1950* (Chicago: University of Chicago Press, 1951), 95.

9. Hedley Bull, *The Anarchical Society: A Study of Order in World Politics* (New York: Columbia University Press, 1977), 106–7.

10. John Mearsheimer, *The Tragedy of Great Power Politics* (New York: Norton, 2001), 35.

11. Michael W. Doyle, "Liberalism and World Politics," *American Political Science Review* 80, no. 4 (1986): 1155–56.

12. See Michael W. Doyle, "Kant, Liberal Legacies, and Foreign Policy," *Philosophy and Public Affairs* 12, nos. 3–4 (1983): 205–35.

13. See Robert O. Keohane and Joseph S. Nye, *Power and Interdependence,* 3rd ed. (New York: Longman, 2001).

14. Ibid., 8, 22, 24.

15. Ibid., 30–32.

16. *The National Security Archive,* George Washington University, http://www.gwu.edu/~nsarchiv/index.html (accessed August 1, 2011).

## 1. Formative Experiences

1. Ann Richards, "Democratic Presidential Convention Keynote Address," *American Rhetoric,* July 19, 1988, http://www.americanrhetoric.com/speeches/annrichards1988dnc.htm (accessed October 29, 2007).

2. John Robert Greene, *The Presidency of George Bush* (Lawrence: University Press of Kansas, 2000), 12.

3. Randall Rothenberg, "In Search of George Bush," *New York Times Magazine,* March 6, 1988, 30, http://www.nytimes.com/1988/03/06/magazine/in-search-of-george-bush.html (accessed December 19, 2011).

4. Hugh Sidey, "The Presidency," *Time,* November 30, 1992, http://www.time.com/time/magazine/article/0,9171,977128,00.html (accessed April 29, 2009).

5. George Bush with Victor Gold, *Looking Forward: An Autobiography* (New York: Bantam Books, 1987), 23, 25.

6. Bush, quoted in Herbert S. Parmet, *George Bush: The Life of a Lone Star Yankee* (New York: Scribner, 1997), 42.

7. Bush, *Looking Forward,* 30.

8. Ibid., 36–37.

9. "George Bush: A Sense of Duty," Arts and Entertainment Network's *Biography* series (first broadcast November 1996).

10. Parmet, *George Bush,* 59.

11. Tony Carnes, "A Presidential Hopeful's Progress," *Christianity Today,* October 2, 2000.

12. Stephen Mansfield, *The Faith of George W. Bush* (New York: Jeremy P. Tarcher/Penguin, 2003), 29.

13. Nicholas D. Kristof, "A Philosophy with Roots in Conservative Texas Soil," *New York Times,* May 21, 2000, http://movies.nytimes.com/library/politics/camp/052100wh-gop-bush-bio.html (accessed December 19, 2011).

14. George W. Bush, *A Charge to Keep* (New York: William Morrow, 1999), 15.

15. George Lardner Jr. and Lois Romano, "Tragedy Created Bush Mother-Son Bond," *Washington Post,* July 26, 1999, http://www.washingtonpost.com/wp-srv/politics/campaigns/wh2000/stories/bush072699.htm (accessed December 19, 2011).

16. Lois Romano and George Lardner Jr., "Bush: So-So Student but a Campus Mover," *Washington Post,* July 27, 1999, http://www.washingtonpost.com/wp-srv/politics/campaigns/wh2000/stories/bush072799.htm (accessed December 19, 2011).

17. Bush, *A Charge to Keep,* 22.

18. Evans Thomas and Martha Brant, "A Son's Restless Journey," *Newsweek*, August 7, 2000, http://www.thedailybeast.com/newsweek/2000/08/06/a-son-s-restless-journey.html (accessed December 19, 2011).

19. Nicholas D. Kristof, "The 2000 Campaign: The Texas Governor—Ally of an Older Generation amid the Tumult of the 60's," *New York Times*, June 19, 2000, http://www.nytimes.com/2000/06/19/us/2000-campaign-texas-governor-ally-older-generation-amid-tumult-60-s.html (accessed December 19, 2011).

20. Elizabeth Mitchell, *W.: The Revenge of the Bush Dynasty* (New York: Hyperion, 2000), 87.

21. See Sam Howe Verhovek, "Is There Room on the Republican Ticket for Another Bush?" *New York Times*, September 13, 1998, http://www.nytimes.com/1998/09/13/magazine/is-there-room-on-a-republican-ticket-for-another-bush.html (accessed December 19, 2011).

22. Bush, *A Charge to Keep*, 50.

23. Bill Minutaglio, *First Son: George W. Bush and the Bush Family Dynasty* (New York: Times Books, 1999), 115.

24. Ibid., 116.

25. Parmet, *George Bush*, 117–21.

26. Fitzhugh Green, *George Bush: An Intimate Portrait* (New York: Hippocrene Books, 1989), 135.

27. Bush, *Looking Forward*, 119–20.

28. See Gerald R. Ford, *A Time to Heal: The Autobiography of Gerald R. Ford* (New York: Harper and Row, 1979), 142–46.

29. Bush, *Looking Forward*, 128, 134, 140.

30. Letter, Bush to Henry Kissinger, November 1975, reprinted in Greene, *Presidency of George Bush*, 21.

31. Parmet, *George Bush*, 193, 195.

32. Ibid., 194, 206.

33. Mansfield, *Faith of George W. Bush*, 41–56.

34. Ibid., 51.

35. Alexander Moens, *The Foreign Policy of George W. Bush: Values, Strategy, and Loyalty* (Burlington, VT: Ashgate, 2004), 7.

36. George Lardner Jr. and Lois Romano, "Bush Name Helps Fuel Oil Dealings," *Washington Post*, July 30, 1999, http://www.washingtonpost.com/wp-srv/politics/campaigns/wh2000/stories/bush073099.htm (accessed December 19, 2011).

37. Lois Romano and George Lardner Jr., "Young Bush, a Political Natural, Revs Up," *Washington Post*, July 29, 1999, http://www.washingtonpost.com/wp-srv/politics/campaigns/wh2000/stories/bush072999.htm (accessed December 19, 2011).

38. Eric Pooley and S. C. Gwynne, "How George Got His Groove," *Time*, June 21, 1999, http://www.cnn.com/ALLPOLITICS/time/1999/06/14/bush.groove.html (accessed December 19, 2011).

39. Mansfield, *Faith of George W. Bush*, 76–77.

40. Bush, *A Charge to Keep*, 6.

41. Pooley and Gwynne, "How George Got His Groove."

42. Jim Pinkerton, interview, PBS, "The Choice 2000," *Frontline*, October 2, 2000, http://www.pbs.org/wgbh/pages/frontline/shows/choice2000/bush/pinkerton.html (accessed November 10, 2007).

43. Tom Grieve, interview, PBS, "The Choice 2000," *Frontline*, October 2, 2000, http://www.pbs.org/wgbh/pages/frontline/shows/choice2000/bush/grieve.html (accessed November 10, 2007).

44. Nicholas D. Kristof, "The 2000 Campaign: Running Texas—A Master of Bipartisanship with No Taste for Details," *New York Times*, October 16, 2000, http://www.nytimes.com/2000/10/16/us/2000-campaign-running-texas-master-bipartisanship-with-no-taste-for-details.html (accessed December 19, 2011).

## 2. Beliefs and Style

1. Excerpt taken from *Inside the Obama White House: Brian Williams Reports*, NBC, June 2 and June 3, 2009.

2. Ivo H. Daalder and James M. Lindsay, *America Unbound: The Bush Revolution in Foreign Policy* (Washington, DC: Brookings Institution Press, 2003), 19.

3. Quoted in Gerald M. Boyd, "Pledging Tolerance, Bush Officially Joins 1988 Race," *New York Times*, October 13, 1987, http://www.nytimes.com/1987/10/13/us/pledging-tolerance-bush-officially-joins-1988-race.html (accessed December 19, 2011).

4. Bush, *Looking Forward*, xiii–xiv.

5. George Bush and Brent Scowcroft, *A World Transformed* (New York: Random House, 1998), 190–91, 186–87.

6. Philip Zelikow and Condoleezza Rice, *Germany Unified and Europe Transformed: A Study in Statecraft* (Cambridge, MA: Harvard University Press, 1995), 126.

7. Michael R. Beschloss and Strobe Talbott, *At the Highest Levels: The Inside Story of the End of the Cold War* (Boston: Little, Brown, 1993), 264.

8. Scott McClellan, *What Happened: Inside the Bush White House and Washington's Culture of Deception* (New York: Public Affairs, 2008), 127.

9. Dan P. McAdams, *George W. Bush and the Redemptive Dream: A Psychological Portrait* (New York: Oxford University Press, 2011), 127.

10. Justin A. Frank, *Bush on the Couch: Inside the Mind of the President* (New York: Harper, 2007), 13.

11. Ibid., 63, 69.

12. Zbigniew Brzezinksi, *Second Chance: Three Presidents and the Crisis of American Superpower* (New York: Basic Books, 2007), 138.

13. For this and similar examples, see Ron Suskind, "Faith, Certainty, and the Presidency of George W. Bush," *New York Times Magazine*, October 17, 2004, http://

www.nytimes.com/2004/10/17/magazine/17BUSH.html?_r=1 (accessed December 19, 2011).

14. Robert Jervis, "The Remaking of a Unipolar World," *Washington Quarterly* 29, no. 3 (2006–7): 15.

15. Natan Sharansky, *A Case for Democracy: The Power of Freedom to Overcome Tyranny and Terror* (New York: Public Affairs, 2004).

16. Bob Woodward, *Bush at War* (New York: Simon and Schuster, 2002), 257–58.

17. Ron Suskind, "Without a Doubt," *New York Times,* October 17, 2004, http://www.hereinstead.com/Suskind-WithoutaDoubt.htm (accessed December 19, 2011).

18. Charles W. Kegley Jr., "The Bush Administration and the Future of American Foreign Policy: Pragmatism or Procrastination?" *Presidential Studies Quarterly* 19, no. 4 (1989): 726.

19. See Nicholas King, *George Bush: A Biography* (New York: Dodd, Mead, 1980), 14.

20. Parmet, *George Bush,* 250.

21. Ibid., 290–92.

22. Bush and Scowcroft, *A World Transformed,* 73–74.

23. See Rebecca Leung, "Rise of the Righteous Army," *CBS News,* February 8, 2004, http://www.cbsnews.com/stories/2004/02/05/60minutes/main598218.shmtl (accessed June 11, 2009).

24. Suskind, "Faith, Certainty and the Presidency of George W. Bush."

25. Stephen J. Rubenzer and Thomas R. Faschingbauer, *Personality, Character, and Leadership in the White House: Psychologists Assess the Presidents* (Washington, DC: Brassey's, 2004).

26. David Frum, *The Right Man: The Surprise Presidency of George W. Bush* (New York: Random House, 2003), 91–92.

27. Frank, *Bush on the Couch,* 43–44, 124–25.

28. Suskind, "Faith, Certainty and the Presidency of George W. Bush."

29. Richard A. Shweder, "George W. Bush and the Missionary Position," *Daedulus* 133, no. 3 (2004): 27.

30. George W. Bush, "President Bush's Letter on the Regulation of Carbon Dioxide," *FYI: The AIP Bulletin of Science Policy News,* March 15, 2001, http://www.aip.org/fyi/2001/029.htm (accessed June 11, 2009).

31. Parmet, *George Bush,* 150.

32. Daalder and Lindsay, *America Unbound,* 46–47.

33. George W. Bush, "President Sworn-in to Second Term," January 20, 2005, http://georgewbush-whitehouse.archives.gov/news/releases/2005/01/20050120-1.html (accessed December 19, 2011).

34. Bob Woodward, *Plan of Attack* (New York: Simon and Schuster, 2004), 88–89.

35. Bush, *Looking Forward*, 201–2.

36. *The National Security Strategy of the United States*, March 1990, http://bushlibrary.tamu.edu/research/pdfs/national_security_strategy_90.pdf (accessed July 14, 2007).

37. Frank, *Bush on the Couch*, 82, 159.

38. Lloyd C. Gardner, "Truman Era Foreign Policy: Recent Historical Trends," in *The Truman Period as a Research Field: A Reappraisal, 1972*, ed. Richard S. Kirkendall (Columbia: University of Missouri Press, 1974), 69–70.

39. See, for example, Kenneth N. Waltz, *Theory of International Politics* (New York: McGraw-Hill, 1979).

40. Louis J. Halle, *The Cold War as History* (New York: Harper and Row, 1967), 75–76.

## 3. Boots on the Ground

1. "Declaration of Howard Teicher," United States District Court, Southern District of Florida, January 31, 1995, http://www.overcast.pwp.blueyonder.co.uk/print/spiderweb/teicher.htm (accessed April 29, 2008).

2. See Alan Friedman, *Spider's Web: The Secret History of How the White House Illegally Armed Iraq* (New York: Bantam Books, 1993), 27–38.

3. National Security Directive 26, October 2, 1989, http://bushlibrary.tamu.edu/research/pdfs/nsd/nsd26.pdf (accessed April 29, 2008).

4. Bush and Scowcroft, *A World Transformed*, 307.

5. "Confrontation in the Gulf: Excerpts from Iraqi Document on Meeting with U.S. Envoy," *New York Times*, September 23, 1990, http://www.nytimes.com/1990/09/23/world/confrontation-in-the-gulf-excerpts-from-iraqi-document-on-meeting-with-us-envoy.html (accessed December 19, 2011).

6. Letter, Embassy, Baghdad to Secretary of State, July 25, 1990, OA/ID#CF01937, 1998-0099-F, National Security Council: Richard N. Haass Files, Bush Presidential Records, George Bush Presidential Library, Texas A&M University, College Station.

7. Glaspie, quoted in Michael Ross, "Glaspie Says She Warned Hussein on Kuwait Issue," *Los Angeles Times*, March 21, 1991, http://articles.latimes.com/1991-03-21/news/mn-658_1_saddam-hussein (accessed December 19, 2011).

8. Glaspie, quoted in Leslie H. Gelb, "Foreign Affairs: Mr. Bush's Fateful Blunder," *New York Times*, July 17, 1991.

9. Bob Woodward, *The Commanders* (New York: Simon and Schuster, 1991), 209, 220.

10. See letter, Embassy, Baghdad to SECSTATE, July 26, 1990, OA/ID#CF01937, 1998-0099-F, National Security Council: Richard N. Haass Files; and memo, Re: Iraq-Kuwait Tensions—What's Really at Stake? July 26, 1990, OA/ID# CF01937, 1998-0099-F, National Security Council: Richard N. Haass Files.

11. Telephone call, President Bush to King Fahd, August 2, 1990, OA/ID#CF01478, 1998–0099-F, National Security Council: Richard N. Haass Files. See also notes, National Security Council Meeting, August 3, 1990, ID#CF01478, 1998-0099-F, National Security Council: Richard N. Haass Files.

12. Transcript, National Security Council Meeting, August 4, 1990, OA/ID#CF01478, 1998-0099-F, National Security Council: Richard N. Haass Files.

13. Telephone call, President Bush to King Fahd, August 4, 1990, OA/ID#CF01478, 1998-0099-F, National Security Council: Richard N. Haass Files.

14. Transcript, National Security Council Meeting, August 5, 1990, OA/ID#CF01478, 1998-0099-F, National Security Council: Richard N. Haass Files.

15. Margaret Thatcher, *Statecraft: Strategies for a Changing World* (London: HarperCollins, 2002), 29–30.

16. Margaret Thatcher, *The Downing Street Years* (New York: HarperCollins, 1993), 816–22.

17. Bush and Scowcroft, *A World Transformed,* 303–4.

18. "Remarks and a Question-and-Answer Session with Reporters in Aspen, Colorado, Following a Meeting with Prime Minister Margaret Thatcher of the United Kingdom," in *Public Papers of the Presidents of the United States: George H. W. Bush,* 1990/2 (August 2, 1990), 1087–88, http://bushlibrary.tamu.edu/research/public_papers.php?id=2124&year=1990&month=8 (accessed April 20, 2012). Also see notes, National Security Council Meeting, August 6, 1990, OA/ID#CF01478, 1998-0099-F, National Security Council: Richard N. Haass Files.

19. See letter, POTUS to Mikhail Gorbachev, October 1990, OA/ID#CF01584, 1998-0099-F, National Security Council: Richard N. Haass Files.

20. "Remarks at the Aspen Institute Symposium in Aspen, Colorado," *Public Papers of the Presidents: George H. W. Bush,* 1990/2 (August 2, 1990), 1093.

21. Bush and Scowcroft, *A World Transformed,* 303.

22. See, for example, meeting with President al-Assad of Syria, November 23, 1990, OA/ID#CF01584, 1998-0099-F, National Security Council: Richard N. Haass Files.

23. Memorandum to conversation, Secretary Baker/Foreign Minister Shevardnadze, August 9, 1990, OA/ID#CF01478, 1998-0099-F, National Security Council: Richard N. Haass Files.

24. Bush and Scowcroft, *A World Transformed,* 318.

25. James A. Baker III with Thomas DeFrank, *The Politics of Diplomacy: Revolution, War and Peace, 1989–1992* (New York: G. P. Putnam's Sons, 1995), 278–79.

26. Mikhail Gorbachev, *Memoirs* (New York: Doubleday, 1995), 450, 564.

27. Memo, country-by-country paper concerning Gulf crisis, October 30, 1990, OA/ID#CF00946–006, 1999-0578-F, National Security Council: Robert M. Gates Files, Bush Presidential Records, George Bush Presidential Library, Texas A&M University, College Station.

28. *Iraq Liberation Act of 1998*, HR 4655, 105th Cong., *Library of Congress*, http://thomas.loc.gov/cgi-bin/query/z?c105:H.R.4655.ENR (accessed June 4, 2008).

29. "The First Gore-Bush Presidential Debate," October 3, 2000, *Commission on Presidential Debates*, http://www.debates.org/pages/trans2000a.html (accessed June 6, 2008).

30. See Seymour Hersh, "The Iraq Hawks," *New Yorker*, December 24 and 31, 2000, 59.

31. See Ron Suskind, *The Price of Loyalty: George W. Bush, the White House, and the Education of Paul O'Neill* (New York: Simon and Schuster, 2004), 72–75.

32. Memorandum, U.S. Department of State, Bureau of Near Eastern Affairs, Edward S. Walker Jr. to Colin Powell, "Origins of the Iraq Regime Change Policy," January 23, 2001, http://www.gwu.edu/~nsarchive/NSAEBB/NSAEBB326/doc03.htm (accessed January 19, 2011).

33. Richard A. Clarke, *Against All Enemies: Inside America's War on Terror* (New York: Free Press, 2004), 264; Suskind, *Price of Loyalty*, 70–75.

34. McClellan, *What Happened*, 98.

35. Memorandum, U.S. Department of State, from Robert J. Einhorn and James A. Larocco to Colin Powell, "Update on Efforts to Prevent Iraqi Procurement of Aluminum Tubes," June 29, 2001, http://www.gwu.edu/~nsarchive/NSAEBB/NSAEBB326/doc04.htm (accessed January 19, 2011).

36. Memorandum, U.S. Department of State, from Van Van Diepen, James A. Larocco, and James A. Kelly to Colin Powell, "Update on Efforts to Prevent Iraqi Procurement of Aluminum Tubes," July 2, 2001, http://www.gwu.edu/~nsarchive/NSAEBB/NSAEBB326/doc05.htm (accessed January 19, 2011).

37. Memorandum, U.S. Department of Defense, Donald Rumsfeld to Condoleezza Rice, "Iraq," July 27, 2001, http://www.gwu.edu/~nsarchive/NSAEBB/NSAEBB326/doc06.htm (accessed January 19, 2011).

38. McClellan, *What Happened*, 98.

39. See John C. Henry, "America Responds: Letter Signals Broader Effort; Action Could Extend beyond Afghanistan, U.N. Told," *Houston Chronicle*, October 9, 2001.

40. U.S. Department of Defense, Office of the Under Secretary for Policy, notes from Stephen Cambone [Rumsfeld's comments], September 11, 2001, http://www.gwu.edu/~nsarchiv/NSAEBB/NSAEBB326/doc07.pdf (accessed January 19, 2011).

41. Cullen Murphy and Todd S. Purdum, "Farewell to All That: An Oral History of the Bush White House," *Vanity Fair*, February 2009, http://www.vanityfair.com/politics/features/2009/02/bush-oral-history200902 (accessed March 31, 2011).

42. Jane Mayer, "The Manipulator," *New Yorker*, June 7, 2004.

43. See, for example, Robert Kagan and William Kristol, "An Administration of One," *Weekly Standard*, December 1, 2003, 7–8; and Robert Kagan and William Kristol, "Toward a Neo-Reaganite Foreign Policy," *Foreign Affairs* 75, no. 4 (1996): 18–32.

44. "Statement of Principles," *Project for the New American Century,* June 3, 1997, http://www.newamericancentury.org/statementofprinciples.htm (accessed March 6, 2008).

45. "Letter to President Clinton on Iraq," *Project for the New American Century,* January 26, 1998, http://www.newamericancentury.org/iraqclintonletter.htm (accessed April 2, 2008).

46. Robert Draper, *Dead Certain: The Presidency of George W. Bush* (New York: Free Press, 2007), 173.

47. Bush, quoted in Clarke, *Against All Enemies,* 32.

48. Michael R. Gordon and Bernard E. Trainor, *Cobra I* (New York: Pantheon Books, 2006), 17.

49. For a further discussion of the effects of the anthrax attacks on administration policy, see McClellan, *What Happened,* 108–12.

50. Jacob Weisberg, *The Bush Tragedy* (New York: Random House, 2008), 191.

51. As quoted in Karen Hughes, *Ten Minutes from Normal* (New York: Viking, 2004), 246.

52. Woodward, *Plan of Attack,* 64–66.

53. George W. Bush, "President Delivers State of the Union Address," January 29, 2002, http://georgewbush-whitehouse.archives.gov/news/releases/2002/01/20020129-11.html (accessed December 5, 2011).

54. Daniel Eisenberg, "We're Taking Him Out," *Time,* May 5, 2002, http://www.time.com/time/world/article/0,8599,235395,00.html (accessed December 19, 2011).

55. Michael Elliott et al., "First Stop Iraq," *Time,* March 31, 2003, http://www.time.com/time/magazine/article/0,9171,1004567,00.html (accessed December 19, 2011).

56. George W. Bush, "President Bush Delivers Graduation Speech at West Point," June 1, 2002, http://georgewbush-whitehouse.archives.gov/news/releases/2002/06/20020601-3.html (accessed December 5, 2011).

57. Bush and Scowcroft, *A World Transformed,* 318.

58. See Michael R. Gordon and Bernard E. Trainor, *The General's War: The Inside Story of the Conflict in the Gulf* (Boston: Little, Brown, 1995), 31–33; and Cecil V. Crabb and Kevin V. Mulcahy, "George Bush's Management Style and Operation Desert Storm," *Presidential Studies Quarterly* 25, no. 2 (1995): 258.

59. See James Mann, *Rise of the Vulcans* (New York: Penguin, 2004), 187.

60. Gordon and Trainor, *The General's War,* 35, 126. Also see Baker and DeFrank, *The Politics of Diplomacy,* 280–81.

61. Baker and DeFrank, *The Politics of Diplomacy,* 281.

62. See memo, Brent Scowcroft to George Bush, August 1990, OA/ID#CF00946, 1999-0578-F, National Security Council: Robert M. Gates Files.

63. See, for example, memo, James Baker to George Bush, Re: Gulf Trip, No-

vember 6, 1990, OA/ID#CF00946-006, 1999-0578-F, National Security Council: Robert M. Gates Files.

64. For the administration's domestic strategy, see Communications Plan—Gulf Policy, November 28, 1990, OA/ID#06837-022, 1998-0099-F, White House Office of Media Affairs: Subject Files, Bush Presidential Records, George Bush Presidential Library, Texas A&M University, College Station.

65. United Nations Security Council Resolution 661, August 6, 1990, http://daccessdds.un.org/doc/RESOLUTION/GEN/NR0/575/10/IMG/NR057510 .pdf?OpenElement (accessed May 16, 2008).

66. George H. W. Bush, "Address to the Nation Announcing the Deployment of United States Armed Forces to Saudi Arabia," August 8, 1990, http://bushlibrary. tamu.edu/research/public_papers.php?id2147&year=1990&month=8 (accessed May 21, 2008).

67. George H. W. Bush, "Remarks and an Exchange with Reporters on the Persian Gulf Crisis," August 11, 1990, http://bushlibrary.tamu.edu/research/public_ papers.php?id2158&year=1990&month=8 (accessed May 21, 2008).

68. See Middle East—Economic Strategy, OA/ID#CF00946-002, 1999-0578-F, National Security Council: Robert M. Gates Files.

69. See diary notations for September 7 in George Bush, *All the Best, George Bush: My Life in Letters and Other Writings* (New York: Scribner, 1999), 478–79.

70. Thatcher, *Downing Street Years,* 821. Also see letter, James A. Baker III to POTUS, Re: London Meetings, November 10, 1990, OA/ID#CF01584, 1998-0099-F, National Security Council: Richard N. Haass Files.

71. United Nations Security Council Resolution 665, August 25, 1990, http://daccessdds.un.org/doc/RESOLUTION/GEN/NR0/575/15/IMG/NR057515 .pdfOpenElement (accessed May 21, 2008).

72. Bush and Scowcroft, *A World Transformed,* 382.

73. Ibid., 362–68.

74. See Jeremy M. Sharp, "Iraq: A Compilation of Legislation Enacted and Resolutions Adopted by Congress, 1990–2003," *CRS Report for Congress,* March 27, 2003, http://www.fpc.state.gov/documents/organization/19131.pdf (accessed July 4, 2009).

75. Schwarzkopf, quoted in Milan Rai, *War Plan Iraq: Ten Reasons against War on Iraq* (New York: Verso, 2002), 155.

76. See Woodward, *The Commanders,* 307–8.

77. Scowcroft is quoted in David Wood, "Bush Forges Ahead on Iraq Attack Plan," *Seattle Times,* May 4, 2002, http://community.seattletimes.nwsource.com/ archive/?date=20020504&slug=iraqcivilians04 (accessed May 22, 2008). The article offers a comparison and reflection on the Persian Gulf War during the buildup to the invasion of Iraq in 2003.

78. Bush and Scowcroft, *A World Transformed,* 381.

79. Ibid., 390, 393.

80. Ibid., 396.

81. See Neil A. Lewis, "Mideast Tensions: Sorting out Legal War concerning Real War," *New York Times,* November 15, 1990, http://www.nytimes.com/1990/11/15/world/mideast-tensions-sorting-out-legal-war-concerning-real-war.html?src=pm (accessed December 19, 2011).

82. Bush and Scowcroft, *A World Transformed,* 402.

83. Ibid., 403–4.

84. Baker and DeFrank, *The Politics of Diplomacy,* 305.

85. See letter, James A. Baker III to POTUS, Re: Cairo Meetings, November 7, 1990, OA/ID#CF01584, 1998-009-F, National Security Council: Richard N. Haass Files.

86. Gorbachev, *Memoirs,* 555–56.

87. Thatcher, *Downing Street Years,* 821.

88. Baker and DeFrank, *The Politics of Diplomacy,* 314.

89. Ibid., 326.

90. United Nations Security Council Resolution 678, November 29, 1990, http://daccessdds.un.org/doc/RESOLUTION/GEN/NR0/575/28/IMG/NR057528.pdf?OpenElement (accessed August 23, 2008).

91. Woodward, *The Commanders,* 331.

92. George H. W. Bush, "The President's News Conference," November 30, 1990, http://bushlibrary.tamu.eduresearch/public_papers.php?id=2516&year=1990&month=11 (accessed December 5, 2011).

93. Letter, POTUS to Mubarak, Fahd, Amir Jaber, Ozal, Major, Mitterrand, and Gorbachev, December 2, 1990, OA/ID#CF01584, 1998-0099-F, National Security Council: Richard N. Haass Files.

94. See Patrick E. Tyler, "Standoff in the Gulf: Iraq Says Talks with U.S. Are Postponed Indefinitely," *New York Times,* December 14, 1990.

95. Bush, *All the Best,* 497–98.

96. Ibid., 499–500.

97. See memorandum of conversation between James Baker and Tariq Aziz with other participants, January 9, 1991, OA/ID#CF00946, 1999-0578-F, National Security Council: Robert M. Gates Files.

98. Bush, *All the Best,* 501–2.

99. *Authorization for the Use of Military Force against Iraq Resolution,* S.J. Res. 2, Joint Resolution, 102nd Cong., 1st sess., January 12, 1991, *The Library of Congress,* http://thomas.loc.gov/cgi-bin/query/D?c102:1:./temp/~c10288xHeE (accessed June 4, 2008).

100. Donald H. Rumsfeld, "Prepared Testimony by the U.S. Secretary of Defense Donald H. Rumsfeld," Senate Armed Services Committee Hearings on Iraq, September 19, 2002, http://www.globalsecurity.org/military/library/congress/2002_hr/rumsfeld919.pdf (accessed June 20, 2008).

101. DOD/OUSDP memorandum, "Read Ahead for Secretary Rumsfeld RC

Meeting, Tuesday April 16, 2002: 'Necessity for Full Range of Training for Iraqi Opposition,'" April 12, 2002, http://www.waranddecision.com/doclib/20080420_ Readaheadontrainingopp.pdf (accessed April 22, 2011). Also see Department of Defense, Secretary of Defense, memorandum for Vice President, Secretary of State, and Assistant to the President for National Security Affairs, "Iraq Inspections/ UN Strategy," n.d., http://www.gwu.edu/~nsarchiv/NSAEBB/NSAEBB328/II-Doc08.pdf (accessed April 22, 2011); and Department of Defense paper, "Dealing with Iraqi WMD: The Inspection Option," n.d., http://www.gwu.edu/~nsarchiv/ NSAEBB/NSAEBB328/II-Doc09.pdf (accessed April 22, 2011).

102. Condoleezza Rice, "Rice on Iraq, War and Politics," *Online News Hour,* September 25, 2002, http://www.pbs.org/newshour/bb/international/july-dec02/rice-9–25.html (accessed June 20, 2008).

103. United Kingdom, Cabinet Office, Overseas and Defense Secretariat, "Iraq: Options Paper," March 8, 2008, http://www.gwu.edu/~nsarchiv/NSAEBB/ NSAEBB328/II-Doc01.pdf (accessed April 22, 2011). Also see United Kingdom Government, Prime Minister's Office, memorandum, David Manning—Tony Blair, March 14, 2002, http://www.gwu.edu/~nsarchiv/NSAEBB/NSAEBB328/ II-Doc05.pdf (accessed April 22, 2011); and United Kingdom, Washington Embassy, memorandum, Christopher Meyer—David Manning, "Iraq and Afghanistan, Conversation with Wolfowitz," March 18, 2002, http://www.gwu .edu/~nsarchiv/NSAEBB/NSAEBB328/II-Doc06.pdf (accessed April 22, 2011).

104. Michael Duffy and Massimo Calabresi, "Clash of the Administration Titans," *Time,* April 5, 2003, http://www.time.com/time/printout/0,8816,441132,00 .html (accessed June 20, 2008).

105. "Final Report of the National Commission on Terrorist Attacks upon the United States," in *The 9/11 Commission Report,* July 22, 2004, http://www.gwu .edu/~nsarchiv/NSAEBB/NSAEBB326/doc14.pdf (accessed January 19, 2011).

106. Fred Kaplan, "The Tragedy of Colin Powell: How the Bush Presidency Destroyed Him," *Slate,* February 19, 2004, http://www.slate.com/id/2095756 (accessed June 21, 2008).

107. Ewen MacAskill, "George Bush: 'God Told Me to End the Tyranny in Iraq,'" *Guardian,* October 6, 2005, http://www.guardian.co.uk/world/2005/ oct/07/iraq.usa (accessed August 1, 2011).

108. Colin Powell with Joseph E. Persico, *My American Journey* (New York: Random House, 1995), 491.

109. See Todd S. Purdum, "Embattled, Scrutinized, Powell Soldiers On," *New York Times,* July 25, 2002, http://www.nytimes.com/2002/07/25/world/embattled-scrutinized-powell-soldiers-on.html (accessed December 19, 2011).

110. Woodward, *Plan of Attack,* 25, 26–27, 79.

111. Richard B. Cheney, "The Vice President Appears on *Meet the Press* (NBC)," March 24, 2002, http://georgewbush-whitehouse.archives.gov/vicepresident/ news-speeches/speeches/vp20020324.html (accessed December 5, 2011).

112. Department of State, Bureau of Intelligence and Research, Intelligence Assessment, "Western Europe: Publics Support Action against Iraq," April 10, 2002, http://www.gwu.edu/~nsarchiv/NSAEBB/NSAEBB328/II-Doc12.pdf (accessed April 22, 2011).

113. Richard B. Cheney, "Vice President Speaks at the VFW 103rd National Convention," August 26, 2002, http://georgewbush-whitehouse.archives.gov/news/releases/2002/08/20020826.html (accessed December 5, 2011).

114. Donald H. Rumsfeld, "Secretary of Defense Donald H. Rumsfeld at the United States Air Force Academy Commencement Ceremony," *U.S. Department of Defense,* May 29, 2002, http://www.defenselink.mil/speeches/speech.aspx?speechid=244 (accessed June 23, 2008).

115. George W. Bush, "President's Remarks at the United Nations General Assembly," September 12, 2002, http://georgewbush-whitehouse.archives.gov/news/releases/2002/09/20020912-1.html (accessed December 5, 2011).

116. John R. Bolton, "The International Aspects of Terrorism and Weapons of Mass Destruction," November 1, 2002, http://www.nti.org/e_research/official_docs/dos/bolton_rogue.pdf (accessed June 25, 2008).

117. John R. Bolton, "The New Strategic Framework: A Response to 21st Century Threats," July 2002, http://www.nti.org/e_research/official_docs/dos/792JB.DOS.pdf (accessed June 25, 2008).

118. Condoleezza Rice, "Dr. Condoleezza Rice Discusses President's National Security Strategy," October 1, 2002, http://georgewbush-whitehouse.archives.gov/news/releases/2002/10/20021001-6.html (accessed December 5, 2011).

119. "Introductory Letter," in *The National Security Strategy of the United States of America,* September 2002, http://georgewbush-whitehouse.archives.gov/nsc/nss/2002/ (accessed December 5, 2011).

120. "Overview of America's International Strategy," in *The National Security Strategy of the United States of America,* September 2002, http://georgewbush-whitehouse.archives.gov/nsc/nss/2002/ (accessed December 5, 2011).

121. G. John Ikenberry, "Rethinking the Origins of American Hegemony," *Political Science Quarterly* 104, no. 3 (1989): 377.

122. Robert Gilpin, *War and Change in World Politics* (New York: Cambridge University Press, 1981), 203.

123. "Overview of America's International Strategy."

124. "Strengthen Alliances to Defeat Global Terrorism and Work to Prevent Attacks against Us and Our Friends," in *The National Security Strategy of the United States of America,* September 2002, http://georgewbush-whitehouse.archives.gov/nsc/nss/2002/ (accessed December 5, 2011).

125. Quoted in Woodward, *Bush at War,* 281.

126. "Strengthen Alliances to Defeat Global Terrorism and Work to Prevent Attacks against Us and Our Friends."

127. Colonel Daniel Smith, USA (Ret.), "Preemption vs. Prevention: A Short

Primer on the Bush War Doctrine," *Friends Committee on National Legislation,* April 16, 2003, http://www.fcnl.org/issues/int/sup/iraq_bush-war-doctrine.htm (accessed June 14, 2008).

128. *Authorization for the Use of Military Force against Iraq Resolution of 2002,* Public Law 107-243, October 16, 2002, 102nd Cong., 1st sess., http://c-span.org/resources/pdf/hjres114.pdf (accessed June 26, 2008).

129. Woodward, *Plan of Attack,* 161.

130. Ibid., 189.

131. Johanna McGeary, "Odd Man Out," *Time,* September 10, 2001, http://www.time.com/time/magazine/article/0,9171,1000708–3,00.html (accessed May 3, 2011).

132. Holbrooke, quoted in Todd S. Purdum, *A Time of Our Choosing: America's War in Iraq* (New York: Times Books, 2003), 34.

133. See Michael Elliott and James Carney, "First Stop, Iraq," *Time,* March 24, 2003, http://www.time.com/magazine/article/0,9171,435968–7,00.html (accessed June 27, 2008).

134. United Nations Security Council Resolution 1441, S/Res/1441, November 8, 2002, http://daccessdds.un.org/doc/UNDOC/GEN/N02/682/26/PDF/N0268226.pdf?OpenElement (accessed June 27, 2008).

135. Ibid.

136. Elliott and Carney, "First Stop, Iraq."

137. See Woodward, *Plan of Attack,* 223–27.

138. "Transcript of Interview with Vice President Cheney on *Meet the Press,*" September 8, 2002, http://www.mtholyoke.edu/acad/intrel/bush/meet.htm (accessed June 29, 2008).

139. Woodward, *Plan of Attack,* 251.

140. Richard N. Haass, *War of Necessity, War of Choice: A Memoir of Two Iraq Wars* (New York: Simon and Schuster, 2009), 5.

141. "What Does Disarmament Look Like?" January 2003, http://georgewbush-whitehouse.archives.gov/infocus/iraq/disarmament/printer.html (accessed December 5, 2011).

142. "War in Iraq: Transcript of Blix's Remarks," *CNN.com/US,* January 27, 2003, http://www.cnn.com/2002/US/01/27/sprj.irq.transcript.blix/index.html (accessed July 1, 2008).

143. George W. Bush, "President Delivers 'State of the Union,'" January 28, 2003, http://georgewbush-whitehouse.archives.gov/news/releases/2003/01/20030128–19.html (accessed December 5, 2011).

144. Colin Powell, "U.S. Secretary of State Colin Powell Addresses the U.N. Security Council," February 5, 2003, http://georgewbush-whitehouse.archives.gov/news/releases/2003/02/20030205–1.html (December 5, 2011).

145. "Reactions to Interim Iraq Weapons Report," *CNN.com/US,* February 14, 2003, http://www.cnn.com/2003/US/02/14/sprj/irq/un.quotes/ (accessed July 4, 2008).

146. Don Van Natta Jr., "Bush Was Set on Path to War, British Memo Says," *New York Times*, March 27, 2006, http://www.nytimes.com/2006/03/27/world/europe/27iht-wev.0327memo.html (accessed December 19, 2011).

147. "Another Iraq Memo Revealed: Colin Powell Opposed War without Second U.N. Resolution," *Think Progress*, March 28, 2006, http://thinkprogress .org/2006/03/28/new-iraq-memo/ (accessed July 6, 2008).

148. "Iraq: U.S./U.K./Spain Draft Resolution," *U.S. Department of State*, February 24, 2003, http://www.state.gov/p/io/rls/othr/17937.htm (accessed July 8, 2008).

149. Woodward, *Plan of Attack*, 343.

## 4. War and Its Aftermath

1. National Security Directive 54, January 15, 1991, http://bushlibrary.tamu .edu/research/pdfs/nsd/nsd54.pdf (accessed November 13, 2009).

2. George H. W. Bush, "Address to the Nation Announcing Allied Military Action in the Persian Gulf," January 16, 1991, http://bushlibrary.tamu.edu/research/ public_papers.php?id=2625&year=1991&month=01 (accessed November 13, 2009).

3. Gary R. Hess, *Presidential Decisions for War: Korea, Vietnam, and the Persian Gulf* (Baltimore: Johns Hopkins University Press, 2001), 199–201.

4. Cable, White House to COS/Jerusalem, Re: Cable to Deputy Secretary Eagleburger from General Scowcroft, January 23, 1991, OA/ID#CF00946, 1999-0578-F, National Security Council: Robert M. Gates Files.

5. Bush and Scowcroft, *A World Transformed*, 454, 455. Also see letter, White House to COS/Jerusalem, Re: Letter from George Bush to Prime Minister Shamir, January 23, 1991, OA/ID#CF00946, 1999-0578-F, National Security Council: Robert M. Gates Files.

6. Message from White House to COS/Jerusalem, Re: Message for Eagleburger, January 24, 1991, OA/ID#CF00946, 1999-0578-F, National Security Council: Robert M. Gates Files.

7. Bush and Scowcroft, *A World Transformed*, 460–61.

8. Statement quoted from "War Chronology: February 1991," *U.S. Navy in Desert Shield/Desert Storm*, http://www.history.navy.mil/wars/dstorm/dsfeb.htm (accessed November 14, 2009).

9. George H. W. Bush, "Exchange with Reporters in Andover, Massachusetts, on the Iraqi Offer to Withdraw from Kuwait," February 15, 1991, http://bushlibrary .tamu.edu/research/public_papers.php?id=2710&year=1991&month=2 (accessed January 12, 2010); "The Presidents: George H. W. Bush," *American Experience*, http://www.pbs.org/wgbh/amex/presidents/video/ghw_bush_19. html#v271 (accessed January 12, 2010).

10. Memo, list concerning contacting other countries, January 1991, OA/ ID#CF00946, 1999-0578-F, National Security Council: Robert M. Gates Files.

11. "U.S. Studies Soviet Peace Bid: Plan Demands Iraq Withdrawal from Kuwait," *Milwaukee Sentinel,* February 19, 1991, http://news.google.com/newspapers?nid=1368&dat=19910219&id=yd4VAAAAIBAJ&sjid=uBIEAAAAIBAJ&pg=6037,4743239 (accessed January 13, 2010).

12. On U.S.-Soviet disagreements, see memorandum of telephone conversation between Secretary Baker and Soviet Foreign Minister Bessmertnykh, February 23, 1991, OA/ID#CF00946, 1999-0578-F, National Security Council: Robert M. Gates Files; telcon between George Bush/James Baker and Mikhail Gorbachev, February 23, 1991, OA/ID#CF00946, 1999-0578-F, National Security Council: Robert M. Gates Files; and telcon with President Mikhail Gorbachev of the USSR on February 23, 1991, 11:15–11:43 a.m., OA/ID#CF01584, 1998-0099-F, National Security Council: Richard N. Haass Files.

13. George H. W. Bush, "Remarks on the Persian Gulf Conflict," February 22, 1991, http://bushlibrary.tamu.edu/research/public_papers.php?id=2729&year=1991&month=2 (accessed January 15, 2010).

14. George H. W. Bush, "Address to the Nation Announcing Allied Military Ground Action in the Persian Gulf," February 23, 1991, http://bushlibrary.tamu.edu/research/public_papers.php?id=2734&year=1991&month=2 (accessed January 18, 2010).

15. George H. W. Bush, "Address to the Nation on the Iraqi Statement on Withdrawal from Kuwait," February 26, 1991, http://bushlibrary.tamu.edu/research/public_papers.php?id=2739&year=1991&month=2 (accessed January 18, 2010).

16. Woodward, *Plan of Attack,* 348.

17. George W. Bush, "President Says Saddam Hussein Must Leave Iraq within 48 Hours," March 17, 2003, http://georgewbush-whitehouse.archives.gov/news/releases/2003/03/20030317-7.html (accessed December 19, 2011).

18. Yukiko Miyagi, "Japan: A Bandwagoning 'Lopsided Power,'" in *The Iraq War: Causes and Consequences,* ed. Rick Fawn and Raymond Hinnebusch (Boulder, CO: Lynne Rienner, 2006), 105–7.

19. See Anthony H. Cordesman, *The Iraq War: Strategy, Tactics, and Military Lessons* (Washington, DC: Center for Strategic and International Studies, 2003), 253–349.

20. Haass, *War of Necessity, War of Choice,* 246.

21. Clarke, *Against All Enemies,* 265.

22. Douglas J. Feith, *War and Decision: Inside the Pentagon at the Dawn of the War on Terrorism* (New York: Harper, 2008), 245.

23. Michael R. Gordon and Bernard E. Trainor, *Cobra II: The Inside Story of the Invasion and Occupation of Iraq* (New York: Pantheon Books, 2006), 164–81.

24. Ken Adelman, "Cakewalk in Iraq," *Washington Post,* February 13, 2002. Adelman was an assistant to Donald Rumsfeld.

25. Vice President Dick Cheney, interview with Bob Schieffer, *Face the Nation,*

March 16, 2003, http://www.cbsnews.com/stories/2003/03/17/ftn/main544228.shtml (accessed June 10, 2010).

26. Vice President Dick Cheney, interview, NBC, *Meet the Press*, March 16, 2003, http://www.mtholyoke.edu/acad/intrel/bush/cheneymeetthepress.htm (accessed June 10, 2010).

27. *Weapons of Mass Destruction (WMD)*, GlobalSecurity.org, March 20, 2003, http://www.globalsecurity.org/wmd/library/news/iraq/2003/iraq-030320-3618cdd3.htm (accessed June 10, 2010).

28. See Thomas E. Ricks, *Fiasco: The American Military Adventure in Iraq* (New York: Penguin, 2006), 126.

29. George W. Bush, "President Bush Announces Major Combat Operations in Iraq Have Ended," May 1, 2003, http://georgewbush-whitehouse.archives.gov/news/releases/2003/05/20030501-15.html (accessed December 19, 2011).

30. Michael R. Gordon and Bernard E. Trainor, "How Iraq Escaped to Threaten Kuwait Again," *New York Times*, October 23, 1994, http://www.nytimes.com/1994/10/23/international/middleeast/23ITEX.html?pagewanted=1 (accessed February 1, 2010).

31. Bush and Scowcroft, *A World Transformed*, 488–89.

32. The Bush administration had acknowledged this early in the crisis. See letter, US Mission USUN New York to Secretary of State, Re: US Objectives: Iraq-Kuwait Settlement, August 30, 1990, OA/ID#CF01478, 1998-0099-F, National Security Council: Richard N. Haass Files.

33. See Arms Control After the War, February 8, 1991, OA/ID#CF01584, 1998-0099-F, National Security Council: Richard N. Haass Files.

34. United Nations Security Council Resolution 687, April 3, 1991, http://daccess-dds-ny.un.org/doc/RESOLUTION/GEN/NR0/596/23/IMG/NR059623.pdf?OpenElement (accessed February 1, 2010).

35. Bush and Scowcroft, *A World Transformed*, 464.

36. Baker and DeFrank, *The Politics of Diplomacy*, 435–38.

37. Letter, SECSTATE to AmEmbassy Moscow, Re: Letter from POTUS to President Gorbachev, April 17, 1991, OA/ID#CF01584, 1998-0099-F, National Security Council: Richard N. Haass Files.

38. See memo, Nancy Bearg Dyke to Brent Scowcroft, Re: Telephone call to UN Secretary-General Pérez de Cuéllar, April 24, 1991, OA/ID#CF01584, 1998-0099-F, National Security Council: Richard N. Haass Files; telcon with Javier Pérez de Cuéllar, UN Secretary-General, April 25, 1991, 3:35–3:45 p.m., OA/ID#CF01584, 1998-0099-F, National Security Council: Richard N. Haass Files; meeting with Secretary-General Javier Pérez de Cuéllar of the UN, May 9, 1991, 11:35 a.m.–12 noon, OA/ID#CF01585, 1998-0099-F, National Security Council: Richard N. Haass Files; and memcon, Script of Conversation between POTUS and Secretary-General Javier Pérez de Cuéllar at the White House, May 9, 1991, OA/ID#CF01077-019, 1998-0099-F, National Security Council: Nancy Bearg

Dyke Files, Bush Presidential Records, George Bush Presidential Library, Texas A&M University, College Station.

39. Keeping Pressure on Saddam Hussein's Regime: Strategy and Actions, May 24, 1991, OA/ID#CF01585, 1998-0099-F, National Security Council: Richard N. Haass Files.

40. United Nations Security Council Resolution 687, April 3, 1991, http://daccess-dds-ny.un.org/doc/RESOLUTION/GEN/NR0/596/23/IMG/NR059623.pdf?OpenElement (accessed February 1, 2010).

41. United Nations Security Council Resolution 688, April 5, 1991, http://daccess-dds-ny.un.org/doc/RESOLUTION/GEN/NR0/596/24/IMG/NR059624.pdf?OpenElement (accessed August 18, 2010).

42. See UN Iraq resolutions monitoring report, July 26, 1991, OA/ID#CF00946, 1999-0578-F, National Security Council: Robert M. Gates Files.

43. See Responding to Iraqi non-Compliance with UNSCR 687, July 1991, OA/ID#CF01585, 1998-0099-F, National Security Council: Richard N. Haass Files.

44. Telephone conversation with President Mitterrand of France, September 25, 1991, 2:55–3:50 p.m., OA/ID#CF01585, 1998-0099-F, National Security Council: Richard N. Haass Files. See also telephone conversation with PM Major of Great Britain, September 25, 1991, 4:45–5:00 p.m., OA/ID#CF01585, 1998-0099-F, National Security Council: Richard N. Haass Files.

45. Cable to London and Paris Embassies, Secretary of Defense, Joint Chiefs, Riyadh, Kuwait, Manama, and Doha Embassies, August 13, 1992, OA/ID#CF01585, 1998-0099-F, National Security Council: Richard N. Haass Files.

46. Memo, Re: Expansion of Security Zone, September 28, 1992, OA/ID#CF01585, 1998-0099-F, National Security Council: Richard N. Haass Files.

47. William R. Polk, *Understanding Iraq* (New York: Harper Perennial, 2005), 178.

48. See George Tenet, *At the Center of the Storm: My Years at the CIA* (New York: HarperCollins, 2007); and "The Times and Iraq," *New York Times,* May 26, 2004, http://nytimes.com/2004/05/26/international/middleeast/26FTE_NOTE.html (accessed December 19, 2011).

49. See Ricks, *Fiasco,* 154.

50. Ibid., 158–66.

51. *Coalition Provisional Authority Order Number 1: De-Ba'athification of Iraqi Society,* May 16, 2003, http://www.iraqcoalition.org/regulations/20030516_CPAORD_1_De-Ba_athification_of_Iraqi_Society_.pdf (accessed June 16, 2010).

52. See Michael Isikoff and David Corn, *Hubris: The Inside Story of Spin, Scandal, and the Selling of the Iraq War* (New York: Crown, 2006), 224.

53. Ricks, *Fiasco,* 159–61.

54. "The Invasion of Iraq: Operation Iraqi Freedom," *Frontline,* February 26, 2004, http://www.pbs.org/wgbh/pages/frontline/shows/invasion/cron (accessed June 16, 2010).

55. *Coalition Provisional Authority Order Number 2: Dissolution of Entities,* May 23, 2003, http://www.iraqcoalition.org/regulations/20030823_CPAORD_2_Dissolution_of_Entities_with_Annex_A.pdf (accessed June 16, 2010).

56. See David L. Phillips, *Losing Iraq: Inside the Postwar Reconstruction Fiasco* (New York: Basic Books, 2005), 169–70.

57. See L. Elaine Halchin, "The Coalition Provisional Authority (CPA): Origin, Characteristics, and Institutional Authorities," *CRS Report for Congress,* April 29, 2004, http://fpc.state.gov/documents/organization/32338.pdf (accessed August 20, 2010).

58. See "Historical Bush Approval Ratings," June 20, 2008, http://www.hist.umn.edu/~ruggles/Approval.htm (accessed August 20, 2010).

59. Bush, quoted in Scott Wilson, "Bremer Adopts Firmer Tone," *Washington Post,* May 26, 2003, A13.

60. See Jonathan S. Landay, "The Administration Split over How to Restore Iraqi Self-Rule," *Knight Ridder/Tribune News Service,* January 27, 2004.

61. "Iraq War Illegal, Says Annan," *BBC News,* September 16, 2004, http://news.bbc.co.uk/2/hi/middle_east/3661134.stm (accessed October 6, 2010).

62. "Elections in Iraq on Track, Annan says," *UN News Centre,* October 19, 2004, http://www.un.org/apps/news/story.asp?NewsID=12272&Cr=iraq&Cr1= (accessed October 6, 2010).

63. John F. Burns, "The Long Shadow of a Mob," *New York Times,* April 4, 2004, http://www.nytimes.com/2004/04/04/weekinreview/04burn.html?pagewanted=all (accessed October 7, 2010).

64. George W. Bush, "President Addresses the Nation in Prime-time Press Conference," April 13, 2004, http://georgewbush-whitehouse.archives.gov/news/releases/2004/04/20040413-20.html (accessed December 19, 2011).

65. See "Iraq 'Surge' Followed Sharp Internal Debate: Report," *Reuters,* August 31, 2008, http://www.reuters.com/article/2008/08/31/us-iraq-bush-report-idUSB8275620080831 (accessed August 1, 2011).

66. See, for example, Adam Nagourney and Megan Thee, "With Election Driven by Iraq, Voters Want New Approach," *New York Times,* November 2, 2006, http://www.nytimes.com/2006/11/02/us/politics/02poll.html?ex=1320123600&en=307df668f49e0b07&ei=5088&partner=rssnyt&emc=rss (accessed October 15, 2010); "U.S. Elections: Democrats in Control," *Worldpress.org,* November 9, 2006, http://www.worldpress.org/Americas/2557.cfm (accessed October 15, 2010).

67. Nancy Pelosi, "Bringing the War to an End Is My Highest Priority as Speaker," *Huffington Post,* November 17, 2006, http://www.huffingtonpost.com/rep-nancy-pelosi/bringing-the-war-to-an-en_b_34393.html (accessed October 15, 2010).

68. James A. Baker III, Lee H. Hamilton, Lawrence S. Eagleburger, Vernon E. Jordan Jr., Edwin Meese III, Sandra Day O'Connor, Leon E. Panetta, William J.

Perry, Charles S. Robb, and Alan K. Simpson, *The Iraq Study Group Report: The Way Forward—A New Approach* (New York: Vintage Books, 2006), 70–74.

69. George W. Bush, "President's Address to the Nation," January 10, 2007, http://georgewbush-whitehouse.archives.gov/news/releases/2007/01/20070110-7.html (accessed October 15, 2010).

70. "Fact Sheet: The New Way Forward in Iraq," January 10, 2007, http://georgewbush-whitehouse.archives.gov/news/releases/2007/01/20070110-3.html (accessed October 15, 2010).

71. Salam Faraj, "Iraq Toll Up 15% Despite Crackdown," *Relief Web*, April 1, 2007, http://www.reliefweb.int/rw/RWB.NSF/db900SID/KHII-6ZV4DW (accessed October 15, 2010).

72. See David S. Cloud and Damien Cave, "Commanders Say Push in Baghdad Is Short of Goal," *New York Times*, June 4, 2007, http://www.nytimes.com/2007/06/04/world/middleeast/04surge.html?_r=1 (accessed October 15, 2010).

73. Bob Woodward, "Why Did Violence Plummet? It Wasn't Just the Surge," *Washington Post*, September 8, 2008, http://www.washingtonpost.com/wp-dyn/content/article/2008/09/07/AR2008090701847.html (accessed October 20, 2010).

74. Bob Woodward, *State of Denial: Bush at War, Part III* (New York: Simon and Schuster, 2006), 480.

75. George W. Bush, "President Bush Delivers Farewell Address to the Nation," January 15, 2009, http://georgewbush-whitehouse.archives.gov/news/releases/2009/01/20090115-17.html (accessed December 19, 2011).

76. "'Decision Points': Former President George W. Bush Reflects on the Most Important Decisions of His Presidential and Personal Life," *MSNBC*, November 8, 2010, http://www.msnbc.msn.com/id/40076644/ns/politics-decision_points/ (accessed May 24, 2011).

## 5. Searching for Peace

1. "Special Document—The Shamir Four-Point Plan," *Journal of Palestine Studies* 20, no. 4 (1991): 149–50.

2. Letter, John L. Hirsch to Mr. Ramsey Hakim, July 6, 1989, ID#046493, 2003-0261-F, White House Office of Records Management: Alphabetical File, Bush Presidential Records, George Bush Presidential Library, Texas A&M University, College Station.

3. See, for example, draft letter, Nancy Bearg Dyke to Rev. C. Charles Vache, ID#CF01473-001, 2003-0261-F, National Security Council: Subject Files, Bush Presidential Records, George Bush Presidential Library, Texas A&M University, College Station; and letter, Robert Gates to Larry Monk, August 1, 1989, ID#8905869, 2003-0621-F, National Security Council: Subject Files.

4. Letter, Brent Scowcroft to Joe Hale, March 1, 1989, ID#028445, 2003-0261-F, White House Office of Records Management Category: Palestine, Islamic Republic of, Bush Presidential Records, George Bush Presidential Library, Texas A&M University, College Station.

5. Michael Kramer, John Stacks, Christopher Ogden, and James Baker, "I Want to Be the President's Man," *Time*, February 13, 1989, http://www.time.com/time/magazine/article/0,9171,956930,00.html (accessed July 15, 2008).

6. Washington Institute for Near East Policy, "Executive Summary," in *Building for Peace: An American Strategy for the Middle East*, 1988, http://www.washingtoninstitute.org/templateC04.php?CID=9 (accessed July 15, 2008).

7. See "Excerpts from Baker's Mideast Talk," *New York Times*, May 23, 1989, http://query.nytimes.com/gst/fullpage.html?res=950DE5D6123AF930A15756C0A96F948260 (accessed July 21, 2008); and "A Mideast Speech to Remember," *New York Times*, May 24, 1989, http://query.nytimes.com/gst/fullpage.html?res=950DE6DD103EF937A15756C0A96F948260 (accessed July 21, 2008).

8. See memo, Brent Scowcroft to Fred McClure, June 18, 1990, ID#9004892, 2003-0261-F, National Security Council: PRS Files, Bush Presidential Records, George Bush Presidential Library, Texas A&M University, College Station. Also see Letter, Robert Gates to Seymour Reich, ID#9001798, 2003–0261-F, National Security Council: PRS Files.

9. See "The President's News Conference Following Discussions with Prime Minister Toshiki Kaifu of Japan in Palm Springs, California," March 3, 1990, http://bushlibrary.tamu.edu/research/public_papers.php?id=1612&year=&month= (accessed July 29, 2008).

10. See Daniel Williams, "Israelis Thwart Beach Assault Near Tel Aviv," *Los Angeles Times*, May 31, 1990, http://articles.latimes.com/1990–05–31/news/mn-911_1_tel-aviv (accessed June 24, 2010).

11. Oral message from Secretary of State to American Embassy, Tel Aviv, Re: Oral message from the President to PM Shamir, July 1990, OA/ID# CF01394-001, 1998-0497-F, National Security Council: Edmund J. Hull Files, Bush Presidential Records, George Bush Presidential Library, Texas A&M University, College Station.

12. Letters, Bush to Max M. Fisher, George Klein, Richard Fox, Abraham H. Foxman, and Mayer Mitchell, July 11 and 12, 1990, ID#160106, 2003-0261-F, White House Office of Records Management, Bush Presidential Records, George Bush Presidential Library.

13. See Baker and DeFrank, *The Politics of Diplomacy*, 131.

14. George W. Bush, "George W. Bush: 'America Reshaped Our Approach to the Middle East,'" *Middle East Quarterly*, Spring 2009, http://www.meforum.org/2137/george-w-bush-america-reshaped-approach-middle-east (accessed August 25, 2009).

15. See Glenn Kessler, *The Confidante: Condoleezza Rice and the Creation of the Bush Legacy* (New York: St. Martin's, 2007), 123.

16. Martin Indyk, *Innocent Abroad: An Intimate Account of American Peace Diplomacy in the Middle East* (New York: Simon and Schuster, 2009).

17. Aaron David Miller, *The Much Too Promised Land: America's Elusive Search for Arab-Israeli Peace* (New York: Bantam Books, 2008), 323–24.

18. "Sharm el-Sheikh Fact-Finding Committee: The Mitchell Plan, April 30, 2001," http://www.yale.edu/lawweb/avalon/mideast/mitchell_plan.htm (accessed August 3, 2008).

19. "Inauguration Speech of Israeli Prime Minister Ariel Sharon," March 7, 2001, http://www.docstoc.com/docs/35791124/Inauguration-Speech-of-Prime-Minister-Ariel-Sharon-in-the-Knesset (accessed December 23, 2011).

20. Miller, *The Much Too Promised Land,* 330.

21. Colum Lynch, "U.S. Vetoes U.N. Observer Force to Protect Palestinians," *Washington Post,* March 28, 2001, A19.

22. Jane Perlez, "Mitchell Report on Mideast Violence May Thaw the Ice; U.S. Gingerly Discusses Taking More Active Role," *New York Times,* May 17, 2001, http://www.nytimes.com/2001/05/17/world/mitchell-report-mideast-violence-may-thaw-ice-us-gingerly-discusses-taking-more.html?scp=1&sq=perlez,%20Mitchell%20Report%20on%20Mideast%20Violence%20May%20Thaw%20the%20Ice&st=cse (accessed December 20, 2011).

23. "The Tenet Plan: Israeli-Palestinian Ceasefire and Security Plan, Proposed by CIA Director George Tenet; June 13, 2001," http://www.yale.edu/lawweb/avalon/mideast/mid023.htm (accessed August 4, 2008); also see "George Tenet's Palestinian-Israeli Security Implementation Work Plan," June 11, 2001, www.ajtransparency.com/failes/87.pdf (accessed January 27, 2011).

24. James Bennet, "U.S. Envoy Meets Arafat and Asks for End of Violence," *New York Times,* November 29, 2001, http://www.nytimes.com/2001/11/29/world/us-envoy-meets-arafat-and-asks-for-end-to-violence.html (accessed December 20, 2011).

25. Avi Machlis, "Israeli Bus Blast Casts Shadow on Peace Process," *Financial Times,* November 30, 2001.

26. "Zinni: 'Vicious and Evil Terrorist Attacks,'" *CNN World,* December 1, 2001, http://articles.cnn.com/2001-12-01/world/zinni.statement_1_palestinian-authority-top-palestinian-officials-israelis?_s=PM:WORLD (accessed January 28, 2011).

27. Ari Fleischer, "Press Briefing by Ari Fleischer," December 12, 2001, http://georgewbush-whitehouse.archives.gov/news/releases/2001/12/20011212-8.html (accessed January 28, 2011).

28. Ari Fleischer, "Press Briefing," December 3, 2001, http://georgewbush-whitehouse.archives.gov/news/releases/2001/12/20011203-3.html (accessed January 28, 2011).

29. Tracy Wilkinson, "Israel Pounds Palestinian Authority," *Los Angeles Times*, December 14, 2001, http://articles.latimes.com/2001/dec/14/news/mn-14759 (accessed December 20, 2011).

30. Frum, *The Right Man*, 256; Woodward, *Bush at War*, 297; and Glenn Kessler, "Bush Sticks to the Broad Strokes," *Washington Post*, June 3, 2003, http://www.washingtonpost.com/ac2/wp-dyn/A5423-2003Jun2?language=printer (accessed December 20, 2011).

31. Mary Curtius, "Hamas Takes Responsibility for Attack," *Los Angeles Times*, January 10, 2002, http://articles.latimes.com/2002/jan/10/news/mn-21695 (accessed December 20, 2011).

32. Colin Powell, "Interview on Middle East Broadcasting Centre by Hisham Melham," January 9, 2002, http://2001-2009.state.gov/secretary/former/powell/remarks/2002/7148.htm (accessed January 29, 2011).

33. See Kessler, *The Confidante*, 123–24.

34. Ibid., 124.

35. See "UN Security Council Resolution 1397," March 12, 2002, http://www.state.gov/p.nea/rt/11124.htm (accessed August 6, 2008).

36. See "Mideast Turmoil: In Powell's Words, a Plea to Both Sides," *New York Times*, March 30, 2002, http://www.nytimes.com/2002/03/30/world/mideast-turmoil-in-powell-s-words-a-plea-to-both-sides.html?scp=1&sq=march%2030,%202002,%20colin%20powell&st=cse (accessed December 20, 2011).

37. Woodward, *Bush at War*, 34.

38. On evangelical Christian support for Israel, see David Firestone, "Evangelical Christians and Jews Unite for Israel," *New York Times*, June 9, 2002, http://www.nytimes.com/2002/06/09/us/evangelical-christians-and-jews-unite-for-israel.html?scp=1&sq=firestone%2C+Evangelical+Christians+and+Jews+Unite+for+Israel&st=nyt (accessed December 20, 2011).

39. "Israel True to Values, Ashcroft Says," *Washington Post*, April 3, 2003, A8.

40. See Juliet Eilperin, "Mideast Rises on DeLay's Agenda," *Washington Post*, October 16, 2003, A7.

41. George W. Bush, "President Discusses Missile Tests in Pakistan and Middle East," May 26, 2002, http://georgewbush-whitehouse.archives.gov/news/releases/2002/05/20020526-4.html (accessed December 19, 2011).

42. George W. Bush, "President Bush Calls for New Palestinian Leadership," June 24, 2002, http://georgewbush-whitehouse.archives.gov/news/releases/2002/06/ (accessed December 19, 2011).

43. "A Performance-Based Roadmap to a Permanent Two-State Solution to the Israeli-Palestinian Conflict," Israel Ministry of Foreign Affairs, April 30, 2003, http://www.state.gov/r/pa/prs/ps/2003/20062.htm (accessed April 20, 2012).

44. Daniel Dombey, "Scowcroft Lambasts Bush's Unilateralism," *Agonist*, October 14, 2002, http://agonist.org/story/2004/10/14/223144/74 (accessed August 6, 2008). See also Jeffrey Goldberg, "Letter from Washington:

Breaking Ranks," *New Yorker,* October 31, 2005, http://www.newyorker.com/ archive/2005/10/31/051031fa_fact2 (accessed August 6, 2008).

45. See "Text of George W. Bush's Letter to Ariel Sharon," April 14, 2002, www.ajtransparency.com/files/180.pdf (accessed January 27, 2011).

46. George W. Bush, "President's Statement on Palestinian Elections," January 9, 2005, http://georgewbush-whitehouse.archives.gov/news/releases/2005/01/ 20050109.html (accessed December 19, 2011).

47. George W. Bush, "State of the Union Address," February 2, 2005, http:// georgewbush-whitehouse.archives.gov/news/releases/2005/02/20050202–11 .html (accessed December 19, 2011).

48. United Nations Security Council Resolution 672, October 12, 1990, http:// daccess-dds-ny.un.org/doc/RESOLUTION/GEN/NR0/575/22/IMG/NR057522 .pdf?OpenElement (accessed June 24, 2010).

49. Meeting, President Bush with President Hafez Assad of Syria, November 23, 1990, OA/ID#CF01584-028, 1998-0099-F, National Security Council: Richard N. Haass Files.

50. Baker, *The Politics of Diplomacy,* 412.

51. Letter, William R. Brew to Albert Mokhiber, February 14, 1991, ID #301104, 2003-0261-F, White House Office of Records Management: General, Bush Presidential Records, George Bush Presidential Library, Texas A&M University, College Station.

52. See *Beyond the Gulf War: Peace Process Choices,* February 21, 1991, OA/ ID#CF01584-003, 1998-0099-F, National Security Council: Richard N. Haass Files.

53. "Address before a Joint Session of Congress on the Cessation of the Persian Gulf Conflict," March 6, 1991, http://bushlibrary.tamu.edu/research/ public_papers.php?id=2767&year=1991&month=3 (accessed July 14, 2008).

54. Memo, James Baker to George Bush, March 11, 1991, OA/ID#CF00946, 1999-0578-F, National Security Council: Robert M. Gates, Bush Presidential Records, George Bush Presidential Library.

55. Memo, James Baker to George Bush, March 13, 1991, OA/ID# CF00946, 1999-0578-F, National Security Council: Robert M. Gates, Bush Presidential Records, George Bush Presidential Library.

56. Memo, James Baker to George Bush, March 14, 1991, OA/ID#CF00946, 1999-0578-F, National Security Council: Robert M. Gates, Bush Presidential Records, George Bush Presidential Library.

57. See memo, Richard Haass to Brent Scowcroft, March 29, 1991, OA/ ID#CF00946, 1999-0578-F, National Security Council: Robert M. Gates, Bush Presidential Records, George Bush Presidential Library.

58. Letters, President Bush to President Assad, King Fahd, King Hussein, President Mubarak, Prime Minister Shamir, April 16, 1991, ID#229879, 1998-0497-F, White House Office of Records Management: Subject File—C.F., Bush

Presidential Records, George Bush Presidential Library, Texas A&M University, College Station.

59. See letter, Secretary of State Baker to American Embassy, Tel Aviv, April 1991, OA/ID#CF1503, 1998-0497-F, National Security Council: Richard N. Haass Files; and letter, Secretary of State Baker to Foreign Minister Bessmertnykh, April 1991, OA/ID#CF01503, 1998-0497-F, National Security Council: Richard N. Haass Files.

60. Letter, Re: Letter to Prime Minister Shamir from the President, May 31, 1991, OA/ID#CF01503, 1998-0497-F, National Security Council: Richard N. Haass Files.

61. See, for example, letter, William R. Brew (Director, Office of Israel and Arab-Israeli Affairs) to Dr. Perry Brickman (Atlanta Jewish Federation), June 1991, Document #2411929, 2003-0261-F, White House Office of Records Management: General Subject File, Bush Presidential Records, George Bush Presidential Library, Texas A&M University, College Station; Israel—Loan Guarantees [2], August 1991, OA/ID#CF01395, 2003-0261-F, National Security Council: Edmund J. Hull Files; and Israel—Loan Guarantees [3], August 1991, OA/ID#CF01395, 2003-0261-F, National Security Council: Edmund J. Hull Files.

62. Israel, OA/ID#07247, 2003-0261-F, White House Office of Legislative Affairs: James Renne Files, Bush Presidential Records, George Bush Presidential Library, Texas A&M University, College Station.

63. Letter, Re: Letter from President Assad to the President, May 31, 1991, OA/ID#CF01503, 1998-0487-F, National Security Council: Richard N. Haass Files.

64. See letter, Re: Letter to King Fahd from the President, May 31, 1991, OA/ID#CF01503, 1998-0497-F, National Security Council: Richard N. Haass Files; letter, Re: Letter to King Hussein from the President, May 31, 1991, OA/ID#CF01503, 1998-0497-F, National Security Council: Richard N. Haass Files; and letter, Re: Letter to President Mubarak from the President, May 31, 1991, OA/ID#CF01503, 1998-0497-F, National Security Council: Richard N. Haass Files.

65. Re: Talking points for Jordan, September 18, 1991, OA/ID#CF01393, 1998-0497-F, National Security Council: Edmund J. Hull Files.

66. See George H. W. Bush, "Remarks at the Opening Session at the Middle East Peace Conference in Madrid, Spain," October 30, 1991, http://bushlibrary.tamu.edu/research/public_papers.php?id=3566&year=1991&month=10 (accessed August 30, 2010).

67. "Meeting Notes on Minister Mohammad Dahlan's (MD) Visit to Washington, D.C.," April 2005, www.ajtransparency.com/files/319/pdf (accessed January 27, 2011).

68. George W. Bush, "President Welcomes Palestinian President Abbas to the White House," May 26, 2005, http://georgewbush-whitehouse.archives.gov/news/releases/2005/05/20050526.html (accessed December 19, 2011).

69. Scott Wilson and Glenn Kessler, "U.S. Funds Enter Fray in Palestinian Elections," *Washington Post,* January 22, 2006, http://www.washingtonpost.com/wp-dyn/content/article/2006/01/21/AR2006012101431.html (accessed January 18, 2011).

70. George W. Bush, "Press Conference of the President," January 27, 2006, http://georgewbush-whitehouse.archives.gov/news/releases/2006/01/20060126.html (accessed December 19, 2011).

71. Neve Gordon, "Kadima's Political Vision Actually Puts the Peace Process into Reverse," *History News Network,* n.d., http://hnn.us/node/23423 (accessed June 2, 2011).

72. Kessler, *The Confidante,* 208.

73. United Nations Security Council Resolution 1559, September 2, 2004, http://daccess-dds-ny.un.org/doc/UNDOC/GEN/N04/498/92/PDF/N0449892.pdf?OpenElement (accessed June 9, 2011).

74. George W. Bush, "President Discusses War on Terror," March 8, 2005, http://georgewbush-whitehouse.archives.gov/news/releases/2005/03/20050308-3.html (accessed December 19, 2011).

75. See "President Bush and German Chancellor Merkel Participate in Press Availability," July 13, 2006, http://georgewbush-whitehouse.archives.gov/news/releases/2006/07/20060713-4.html (accessed June 9, 2011).

76. Richard Wolffe, "Backstage at the Crisis," *Newsweek,* July 31, 2006, http://www.democraticunderground.com/discuss/duboard.php?az=view_all&address=103x224053 (accessed June 9, 2011).

77. Kessler, *The Confidante,* 217.

78. See Condoleezza Rice, "Special Briefing on Travel to the Middle East and Europe," July 21, 2006, http://2001–2009.state.gov/secretary/rm/2006/69331.htm (accessed June 8, 2011); and Condoleezza Rice, "Secretary of State Condoleezza Rice with Israeli Foreign Minister Livni in Jerusalem," July 24, 2006, http://2001–2009.state.gov/secretary/rm/2006/69409.htm (accessed June 9, 2011).

79. Helene Cooper and Jad Mouawad, "In First Stop, Rice Confers with Leaders of Lebanon," *New York Times,* July 25, 2006, http://www.nytimes.com/2006/07/25/world/middleeast/25rice.html (accessed June 9, 2011).

80. Kessler, *The Confidante,* 219.

81. See Anthony Shadid, "Inside Hezbollah, Big Miscalculations," *Washington Post,* October 8, 2006, http://www.washingtonpost.com/wp-dyn/content/article/2006/10/07/AR2006100701054.html (accessed June 10, 2011).

82. Kessler, *The Confidante,* 227.

83. "Overview of America's National Security Strategy," in *The National Security Strategy,* March 2006, http://georgewbush-whitehouse.archives.gov/nsc/nss/2006/sectionI.html (accessed June 20, 2011).

84. United Nations Security Council Resolution 1701, August 11, 2006,

http://daccess-dds-ny.un.org/doc/UNDOC/GEN/N06/465/03/PDF/N0646503
.pdf?OpenElement) (accessed June 20, 2011).
85. See Mohammad Bazzi, "Turning Rubble into Rhetoric," *Newsday,* September 3, 2006, A36.
86. See Chris Marsden, "US Vice President Cheney Endorses Israel's Assassination Policy," *World Socialist Web Site,* August 10, 2001, http://www.wsws.org/articles/2001/aug2001/isr-a10.shtml (accessed June 20, 2011); and Nathan Guttman, "Cheney Raises Storm with Remarks on Assassination," *Haaretz.com,* August 5, 2001, http://www.haaretz.com/print-edition/news/cheney-raises-storm-with-remarks-on-assassinations-1.66146 (accessed June 20, 2011).
87. George W. Bush, "President Bush Attends Annapolis Conference," November 27, 2007, http://georgewbush-whitehouse.archives.gov/news/releases/2007/11/20071127-2.html (accessed December 19, 2011).

## 6. Comparing the Bush Presidencies

1. John Quincy Adams, quoted in Joseph Blunt, *The American Annual Register for the Years 1827-8-9* (New York: E. and G. W. Blunt, 1830), 269, 274, http://www.archive.org/stream/p1americanannua129blunuoft#page/n5/mode/2up (accessed December 26, 2011).
2. Haass, *War of Necessity, War of Choice.*
3. Quoted in Shepard Forman, "Multilateralism as a Matter of Fact: U.S. Leadership and the Management of the International Public Sector," in *Multilateralism and U.S. Foreign Policy: Ambivalent Engagement,* ed. Stewart Patrick and Shepard Forman (Boulder, CO: Lynne Rienner, 2002), 439.
4. "Should the U.S. Use Military Force against Iran if It Does Not Dismantle Its Nuclear Program?" *ProCon.org: 2008 Election,* n.d., http://2008election.procon.org/view.resource.php?resourceID=1681 (accessed July 6, 2011).
5. Ibid.
6. Ibid.
7. Greg Kitsock, "Three Presidents Get My Vote," *Washington Post,* September 10, 2008, http://www.washingtonpost.com/wp-dyn/content/article/2008/09/09/AR2008090900036.html (accessed July 7, 2011).
8. Mary Ann Akers, "Which '08 Candidate Is Winning the Beer Vote?" *Washington Post,* January 3, 2008, http://voices.washingtonpost.com/sleuth/2008/01/which_08_candidate_is_winning.html (accessed July 7, 2011).

# Selected Bibliography

## George Bush Presidential Library, Texas A&M University, College Station

Many sources from the George Bush Presidential Library and Museum are available on the Internet at http://bushlibrary.tamu.edu/research/research.php. An exhaustive list of these sources, including speeches, is not included here.

National Security Council: Edmund J. Hull Files, Bush Presidential Records.
National Security Council: Nancy Bearg Dyke Files, Bush Presidential Records.
National Security Council: PRS Files, Bush Presidential Records.
National Security Council: Richard N. Haass Files, Bush Presidential Records.
National Security Council: Robert M. Gates Files, Bush Presidential Records.
National Security Council: Subject Files, Bush Presidential Records.
*Public Papers of the Presidents of the United States: George H. W. Bush.* Vol. 2. Washington, DC: Government Printing Office, 1990. http://bushlibrary. tamu.edu/research/public_papers.php?id=2124&year=1990&month=8 (accessed April 20, 2012).
White House Office of Legislative Affairs: James Renne Files, Bush Presidential Records.
White House Office of Media Affairs: Subject Files, Bush Presidential Records.
White House Office of Records Management: Alphabetical File, Bush Presidential Records.
White House Office of Records Management: Category—Palestine, Islamic Republic of, Bush Presidential Records.
White House Office of Records Management: General, Bush Presidential Records.
White House Office of Records Management: General Subject File, Bush Presidential Records.
White House Office of Records Management: Subject File—C.F., Bush Presidential Records.

## Other Sources

Again, this bibliography is not all inclusive. It excludes numerous articles from newspapers, Internet sites, and magazines, including, among others, the *New*

*York Times,* the *Washington Post, USA Today,* the *Baltimore Sun, Newsday, CNN. com,* the *Christian Science Monitor,* the *Los Angeles Times, Time, Newsweek,* the *New Yorker, BBC News,* the *Guardian,* and the *Financial Times.*

Aikman, David. *A Man of Faith: The Spiritual Journey of George W. Bush.* New York: Thomas Nelson, 2004.

Allison, Graham, and Philip Zelikow. *Essence of Decision: Explaining the Cuban Missile Crisis.* 2nd ed. New York: Longman, 1999.

Bacevich, Andrew J. *American Empire: The Realities and Consequences of American Diplomacy.* Cambridge, MA: Harvard University Press, 2004.

———. *The New American Militarism: How Americans Are Seduced by War.* New York: Oxford University Press, 2005.

Baker, James A., III, with Thomas DeFrank. *The Politics of Diplomacy: Revolution, War and Peace, 1989–1992.* New York: G. P. Putnam's Sons, 1995.

Baker, James A., III, with Steve Fiffner. *"Work Hard, Study . . . and Keep out of Politics!" Adventures and Lessons from an Unexpected Public Life.* New York: G. P. Putnam's Sons, 2006.

Barber, James David. *The Presidential Character: Predictive Performance in the White House.* 4th ed. Englewood Cliffs, NJ: Prentice Hall, 1992.

Bartlett, Bruce. *Impostor: How George W. Bush Bankrupted America and Betrayed the Reagan Legacy.* New York: Doubleday, 2006.

Berman, Paul, Max Boot, William F. Buckley Jr., Eliot A. Cohen, Niall Ferguson, and Aaron L. Friedberg. "Defending and Advancing Freedom: A Symposium." *Commentary* 120, no. 4 (2005): 21–68.

Beschloss, Michael R., and Strobe Talbott. *At the Highest Levels: The Inside Story of the End of the Cold War.* Boston: Little, Brown, 1993.

Biddle, Stephen. "Seeing Baghdad, Thinking Saigon." *Foreign Affairs* 85, no. 2 (2006): 2–14.

Bin Laden, Osama. "Bin Laden's Fatwa." *Online Newshour,* August 1996. http://www.pbs.org/newshour/terrorism/international/fatwa_1996.htm (accessed March 11, 2009).

Blair, Tony. *A Journey: My Political Life.* New York: Knopf, 2010.

Blix, Hans. "Blix's Feb. 14 Report to the UN." *CBS News,* February 14, 2003. http://www.cbsnews.com/stories/2003/02/14/iraq/main540681.shtml (accessed July 4, 2008).

———. "War in Iraq: Transcript of Blix's Remarks." *CNN.com/US,* January 27, 2003. http://www.cnn.com/2002/US/01/27/sprj.irq.transcript.blix/index.html (accessed July 1, 2008).

Blunt, Joseph. *The American Annual Register for the Years 1827-8-9.* New York: E. and G. W. Blunt, 1830. http://www.archive.org/streamp1americanannua129blunuoft#page/n5/mode/2up (accessed December 26, 2011).

Bolton, John R. "The International Aspects of Terrorism and Weapons of Mass

Destruction," November 1, 2002. http://www.nti.org/e_research/official_docs/dos/bolton_rogue.pdf (accessed June 25, 2008).

———. "The New Strategic Framework: A Response to 21st Century Threats," July 2002. http://www.nti.org/e_research/official_docs/dos/792JB.DOS.pdf (accessed June 25, 2008).

Bresheeth, Haim, and Nira Yuval-Davis, eds. *The Gulf War and the New World Order.* London: Zed Books, 1991.

Brookhiser, Richard. "The Mind of George W. Bush." *Atlantic Monthly,* April 2003. http://www.theatlantic.comdoc/200304/brookhiser (accessed April 2, 2008).

Brzezinksi, Zbigniew. *Second Chance: Three Presidents and the Crisis of American Superpower.* New York: Basic Books, 2007.

Buchanan, Patrick J. *Where the Right Went Wrong: How Neoconservatives Subverted the Reagan Revolution and Hijacked the Bush Presidency.* New York: Thomas Dunne Books, 2004.

Bull, Hedley. *The Anarchical Society: A Study of Order in World Politics.* New York: Columbia University Press, 1977.

Bush, George. *All the Best, George Bush: My Life in Letters and Other Writings.* New York: Scribner, 1999.

Bush, George, with Victor Gold. *Looking Forward: An Autobiography.* New York: Bantam Books, 1987.

Bush, George, and Brent Scowcroft. *A World Transformed.* New York: Random House, 1998.

Bush, George W. *A Charge to Keep.* New York: William Morrow, 1999.

———. *Decision Points.* New York: Crown, 2010.

———. "George W. Bush: 'America Reshaped Our Approach to the Middle East.'" *Middle East Quarterly,* Spring 2009. http://www.meforum.org/2137/george-w-bush-america-reshaped-approach-middle-east (accessed August 25, 2009).

———. "President Bush's Letter on the Regulation of Carbon Dioxide." *FYI: The AIP Bulletin of Science Policy News,* March 15, 2002. http://www.aip.org/fyi/2001/029.htm (accessed June 11, 2009).

Bush, George W., with Jay Nordinger. *We Will Prevail: President George W. Bush on War, Terrorism and Freedom.* New York: Continuum, 2003.

Callahan, Patrick. *Logics of American Foreign Policy: Theories of America's World Role.* New York: Pearson Longman, 2004.

Cheney, Richard B. Interview with Bob Schieffer. *Face the Nation,* March 16, 2003. http://www.cbsnews.com/stories/2003/03/17/ftn/main544228.shtml (accessed June 10, 2010).

———. Interview. NBC, *Meet the Press,* March 16, 2003. http://www.mtholyoke.edu/acad/intrel/bush/cheneymeetthepress.htm (accessed June 10, 2010).

———. "Transcript of Interview with Vice President Cheney on *Meet the Press,*" September 8, 2002. http://mtholyoke.edu/acad/intrel/bush/meet.htm (accessed June 29, 2008).

"The Choice 2000." *Frontline.* http://www.pbs.org/wgbh/pages/frontline/shows/choice2000 (accessed January 20, 2011).

Clarke, Richard A. *Against All Enemies: Inside America's War on Terror.* New York: Free Press, 2004.

Cordesman, Anthony H. *The Iraq War: Strategy, Tactics, and Military Lessons.* Washington, DC: Center for Strategic and International Studies, 2003.

Crabb, Cecil V., and Kevin V. Mulcahy. "George Bush's Management Style and Operation Desert Storm." *Presidential Studies Quarterly* 25, no. 2 (1995): 251–65.

Daalder, Ivo H., and James M. Lindsay. *America Unbound: The Bush Revolution in Foreign Policy.* Washington, DC: Brookings Institution Press, 2003.

Dean, John W. "An Early Assessment by Leading Presidential Scholars of George W. Bush's Presidency: Part One." *FindLaw,* November 7, 2003. http://writ.news.findlaw.com/scripts/printer_friendly.pl?page=/dean/20031107.html (accessed March 22, 2009).

——. "Predicting Presidential Performance: Is George W. Bush Active/Negative Like Nixon, LBJ, Hoover and Wilson?" *FindLaw,* May 21, 2004. http://writ.news.findlaw.com/scripts/printer_friendly.pl?page=/dean/20040521.html (accessed March 17, 2009).

"'Decision Points': Former President George W. Bush Reflects on the Most Important Decisions of His Presidential and Personal Life." *MSNBC,* November 8, 2010. http://www.msnbc.msn.com/id/40076644/ns/politics-decision_points/ (accessed May 24, 2011).

DeFronzo, James. *The Iraq War: Origins and Consequences.* Boulder, CO: Westview, 2010.

Diamond, Larry. *Squandered Victory: The American Occupation and the Bungled Effort to Bring Democracy to Iraq.* New York: Times Books, 2005.

Doyle, Michael W. "Kant, Liberal Legacies, and Foreign Policy." *Philosophy and Public Affairs* 12, nos. 3–4 (1983): 205–35.

——. "Liberalism and World Politics." *American Political Science Review* 80, no. 4 (1986): 1151–69.

Draper, Robert. *Dead Certain: The Presidency of George W. Bush.* New York: Free Press, 2007.

Duffy, Michael, and Dan Goodgame. *Marching in Place: The Status Quo Presidency of George Bush.* New York: Simon and Schuster, 1992.

Edwards, George C. *Governing by Campaigning: The Politics of the Bush Presidency.* New York: Longman, 2006.

——. *On Deaf Ears: The Limits of the Bully Pulpit.* New Haven, CT: Yale University Press, 2003.

Ehrenberg, John, J. Patrice McSherry, Jose Ramon Sanchez, and Caroleen Marji Sayej, eds. *The Iraq Papers.* New York: Oxford University Press, 2010.

Eisendrath, Craig R., and Melvin A. Goodman. *Bush League Diplomacy: How the Neoconservatives Are Putting the World at Risk*. New York: Prometheus Books, 2004.

Engel, Jeffrey A. "A Better World . . . but Don't Get Carried Away: The Foreign Policy of George H. W. Bush Twenty Years On." *Diplomatic History* 34, no. 1 (2010): 25–46.

Fawn, Rick, and Raymond Hinnebusch, eds. *The Iraq War: Causes and Consequences*. Boulder, CO: Lynne Rienner, 2006.

Feith, Douglas J. *War and Decision: Inside the Pentagon at the Dawn of the War on Terrorism*. New York: Harper, 2008.

Feldman, Leslie D., and Rosanna Perotti, eds. *Honor and Loyalty: Inside the Politics of the George H. W. Bush White House*. Westport, CT: Greenwood, 2002.

Ford, Gerald R. *A Time to Heal: The Autobiography of Gerald R. Ford*. New York: Harper and Row, 1979.

Frank, Justin A. *Bush on the Couch: Inside the Mind of the President*. New York: Harper, 2007.

Friedman, Alan. *Spider's Web: The Secret History of How the White House Illegally Armed Iraq*. New York: Bantam, 1993.

Frum, David. *The Right Man: The Surprise Presidency of George W. Bush*. New York: Random House, 2003.

Galbraith, Peter. *The End of Iraq: How American Incompetence Created a War without End*. New York: Simon and Schuster, 2006.

Gates, Robert M. *From the Shadows: The Ultimate Insider's Story of Five Presidents and How They Won the Cold War*. New York: Simon and Schuster, 1996.

Gellman, Barton. *Angler: The Cheney Vice Presidency*. New York: Penguin, 2008.

George, Alexander L. *Bridging the Gap: Theory and Practice in Foreign Policy*. Washington, DC: United States Institute of Peace, 1993.

———. *Presidential Decisionmaking in Foreign Policy: The Effective Use of Information and Advice*. Boulder, CO: Westview, 1980.

George, Alexander L., and Andrew Bennett. *Case Studies and Theory Development in the Social Sciences*. Cambridge, MA: MIT, 2005.

"George Bush: A Sense of Duty." Arts and Entertainment Network's *Biography* series. First broadcast November 1996.

Gilpin, Robert. *War and Change in World Politics*. New York: Cambridge University Press, 1981.

Gorbachev, Mikhail. *Memoirs*. New York: Doubleday, 1995.

Gordon, Michael R., and Bernard E. Trainor. *Cobra II: The Inside Story of the Invasion and Occupation of Iraq*. New York: Pantheon Books, 2006.

———. *The General's War: The Inside Story of the Conflict in the Gulf*. Boston: Little, Brown, 1995.

Graubard, Stephen R. *Mr. Bush's War: Adventures in the Politics of Illusion*. New York: Hill and Wang, 1992.

Green, Fitzhugh. *George Bush: An Intimate Portrait*. New York: Hippocrene Books, 1989.

Greene, John Robert. *The Presidency of George Bush*. Lawrence: University Press of Kansas, 2000.

Gregg, Gary L., II, and Mark J. Rozell, eds. *Considering the Bush Presidency*. New York: Oxford University Press, 2004.

Haass, Richard N. *The Opportunity: America's Moment to Alter History's Course*. New York: Public Affairs, 2005.

———. *War of Necessity, War of Choice: A Memoir of Two Iraq Wars*. New York: Simon and Schuster, 2009.

Halchin, L. Elaine. "The Coalition Provisional Authority (CPA): Origin, Characteristics, and Institutional Authorities." *CRS Report for Congress*, April 29, 2004. http://fpc.state.gov/documents/organization/32338.pdf (accessed August 20, 2010).

Halle, Louis J. *The Cold War as History*. New York: Harper and Row, 1967.

Hayes, Stephen F. *Cheney: The Untold Story of America's Most Powerful and Controversial Vice President*. New York: HarperCollins, 2007.

Hess, Gary R. *Presidential Decisions for War: Korea, Vietnam, and the Persian Gulf*. Baltimore: Johns Hopkins University Press, 2001.

Hughes, Karen. *Ten Minutes from Normal*. New York: Viking, 2004.

Hybel, Alex Roberto, and Justin Matthew Kaufman. *The Bush Administrations and Saddam Hussein: Deciding on Conflict*. New York: Palgrave Macmillan, 2006.

Ikenberry, G. John. "Rethinking the Origins of American Hegemony." *Political Science Quarterly* 104, no. 3 (1989): 375–400.

Indyk, Martin. *Innocent Abroad: An Intimate Account of American Peace Diplomacy in the Middle East*. New York: Simon and Schuster, 2009.

*Inside the Obama White House: Brian Williams Reports*. NBC. First broadcast June 2 and 3, 2009.

"The Invasion of Iraq: Operation Iraqi Freedom." *Frontline*, February 26, 2004. http://www.pbs.org/wgbh/pages/frontline/shows/invasion/cron (accessed March 10, 2005).

Isikoff, Michael, and David Corn. *Hubris: The Inside Story of Spin, Scandal, and the Selling of the Iraq War*. New York: Crown, 2006.

Jervis, Robert. "The Remaking of a Unipolar World." *Washington Quarterly* 29, no. 3 (2006–7): 7–19.

Kagan, Robert, and William Kristol. "Toward a Neo-Reaganite Foreign Policy." *Foreign Affairs* 75, no. 4 (1996): 18–32.

Kaufman, Robert G. *In Defense of the Bush Doctrine*. Lexington: University Press of Kentucky, 2007.

Kegley, Charles W., Jr. "The Bush Administration and the Future of American Foreign Policy: Pragmatism or Procrastination?" *Presidential Studies Quarterly* 19, no. 4 (1989): 717–31.

Kennan, George F. *American Diplomacy, 1900–1950*. Chicago: University of Chicago Press, 1951.

Keohane, Robert O., and Joseph S. Nye. *Power and Interdependence.* 3rd ed. New York: Longman, 2001.

Kessler, Glenn. *The Confidante: Condoleezza Rice and the Creation of the Bush Legacy.* New York: St. Martin's, 2007.

King, Nicholas. *George Bush: A Biography.* New York: Dodd, Mead, 1980.

Kirkendall, Richard S., ed. *The Truman Period as a Research Field: A Reappraisal, 1972.* Columbia: University of Missouri Press, 1974.

Kissinger, Henry. *American Foreign Policy: Three Essays.* New York: Norton, 1969.

———. *The Necessity for Choice: Prospects for American Foreign Policy.* New York: Harper Brothers, 1960.

———. *Nuclear Weapons and Foreign Policy.* Garden City, NY: Doubleday, 1957.

Kristol, Irving. *Reflections of a Neoconservative: Looking Back, Looking Ahead.* New York: Basic Books, 1983.

Kurtzer, Daniel C., and Scott B. Lasensky, with William B. Quandt, Steven L. Spiegel, and Shibley I. Telhami. *Negotiating Arab-Israeli Peace: American Leadership in the Middle East.* Washington, DC: United States Institute of Peace, 2008.

Levantrosser, William, and Rosanna Perotti, eds. *A Noble Calling: Character and the George H. W. Bush Presidency.* Westport, CT: Praeger, 2004.

Mann, James. *Rise of the Vulcans.* New York: Penguin, 2004.

Mansfield, Stephen. *The Faith of George W. Bush.* New York: Jeremy P. Tarcher/Penguin, 2003.

Mayer, Jane. *The Dark Side: The Inside Story of How the War on Terror Turned into a War on American Ideals.* New York: Doubleday, 2008.

Mazarr, Michael J., Don M. Snider, and James A. Blackwell Jr. *Desert Storm—The Gulf War and What We Learned.* Boulder, CO: Westview, 1993.

McAdams, Dan P. *George W. Bush and the Redemptive Dream: A Psychological Portrait.* New York: Oxford University Press, 2011.

McClellan, Scott. *What Happened: Inside the Bush White House and Washington's Culture of Deception.* New York: Public Affairs, 2008.

Mearsheimer, John. *The Tragedy of Great Power Politics.* New York: Norton, 2001.

Miller, Aaron David. *The Much Too Promised Land: America's Elusive Search for Arab-Israeli Peace.* New York: Bantam Books, 2008.

Minutaglio, Bill. *First Son: George W. Bush and the Bush Family Dynasty.* New York: Times Books, 1999.

Mitchell, Elizabeth. *W.: The Revenge of the Bush Dynasty.* New York: Hyperion, 2000.

Moens, Alexander. *The Foreign Policy of George W. Bush: Values, Strategy, and Loyalty.* Burlington, VT: Ashgate, 2004.

Muravchik, Joshua, and Stephen M. Walt. "The Neocons vs. the Realists." *National Interest,* September–October 2008. http://www.nationalinterest.org/PrinterFriendly.aspx?id=19672 (accessed October 30, 2009).

Neustadt, Richard E. *Presidential Power and the Modern Presidents: The Politics of Leadership from Roosevelt to Reagan.* New York: Free Press, 1990.

Owens, John E., and John W. Dumbrell, eds. *America's "War on Terrorism": New Dimensions in U.S. Government and National Security.* Plymouth, UK: Lexington Books, 2008.

Parmet, Herbert S. *George Bush: The Life of a Lone Star Yankee.* New York: Scribner, 1997.

Patrick, Stewart, and Shepard Forman, eds. *Multilateralism and U.S. Foreign Policy: Ambivalent Engagement.* Boulder, CO: Lynne Rienner, 2002.

Peleg, Ilan. *The Legacy of George W. Bush's Foreign Policy: Moving Beyond Neoconservatism.* Boulder, CO: Westview, 2009.

Pelletiere, Stephen. *America's Oil Wars.* Westport, CT: Praeger, 2004.

Phillips, David L. *Losing Iraq: Inside the Postwar Reconstruction Fiasco.* New York: Basic Books, 2005.

Polk, William R. *Understanding Iraq.* New York: Harper Perennial, 2005.

Pollack, Kenneth M. *The Threatening Storm: The Case for Invading Iraq.* New York: Random House, 2002.

Powell, Colin, with Joseph E. Persico. *My American Journey.* New York: Random House, 1995.

"The Presidents: George H. W. Bush." *American Experience.* http://www.pbs.org/wgbh/amex/presidents/video/ghw_bush_19.html#v27 (accessed June 28, 2011).

*Project for the New American Century.* http://www.newamericancentury.org/.

Purdum, Todd S. *A Time of Our Choosing: America's War in Iraq.* New York: Times Books, 2003.

Quandt, William B. *Peace Process: American Diplomacy and the Arab-Israeli Conflict since 1967.* 3rd ed. Washington, DC: Brookings Institution Press, 2005.

Rai, Milan. *War Plan Iraq: Ten Reasons against War on Iraq.* New York: Verso, 2002.

Record, Jeffrey. *Dark Victory: America's Second War against Iraq.* Annapolis, MD: Naval Institute Press, 2004.

Rice, Condoleezza. "Rice on Iraq, War and Politics." *Online News Hour,* September 25, 2002. http://www.pbs.org/newshour/bb/international/july-dec02/rice-9-25.html (accessed June 20, 2008).

Ricks, Thomas E. *Fiasco: The American Military Adventure in Iraq.* New York: Penguin, 2006.

Ross, Dennis. *The Missing Peace: The Inside Story of the Fight for Middle East Peace.* New York: Farrar, Straus and Giroux, 2004.

Rothkopf, David. *Running the World: The Inside Story of the National Security Council and the Architects of American Power.* New York: Public Affairs, 2005.

Rubenzer, Stephen J., and Thomas R. Faschingbauer. *Personality, Character, and*

*Leadership in the White House: Psychologists Assess the Presidents.* Washington, DC: Brassey's, 2004.

Rumsfeld, Donald. *Known and Unknown: A Memoir.* New York: Sentinel HC, 2011.

Sharansky, Natan. *A Case for Democracy: The Power of Freedom to Overcome Tyranny and Terror.* New York: Public Affairs, 2004.

Shellum, Brian. *A Chronology of Defense Intelligence in the Gulf War: A Research Aid for Analysts.* Washington, DC: Defense Intelligence Agency History Office, 1997.

Shogan, Robert. *The Riddle of Power: Presidential Leadership from Truman to Bush.* London: Dutton, 1991.

Shweder, Richard A. "George W. Bush and the Missionary Position." *Daedulus* 133, no. 3 (2004): 26–36.

Sifry, Micah L., and Christopher Cerf, eds. *The Gulf War Reader: History, Documents, Opinions.* New York: Times Books, 1991.

———. *The Iraq War Reader: History, Documents, Opinions.* New York: Simon and Schuster, 2003.

Simonton, Dean Keith. "Presidential IQ, Openness, Intellectual Brilliance, and Leadership: Estimates and Correlations for 42 U.S. Chief Executives." *Political Psychology* 27, no. 4 (2006): 511–26.

Singer, Peter. *The President of Good and Evil: The Ethics of George W. Bush.* New York: Dutton, 2004.

Smith, Colonel Daniel, USA (Ret.). "Preemption vs. Prevention: A Short Primer on the Bush War Doctrine." *Friends Committee on National Legislation,* April 16, 2003. http://www.fcnl.org/issues/int/sup/iraq_bush-war-doctrin .htm (accessed June 14, 2008).

Smith, Michael Joseph. *Realist Thought from Weber to Kissinger.* Baton Rouge: Louisiana State University Press, 1986.

Snyder, Jack. "One World, Rival Theories." *Foreign Policy* 145 (November–December 2004): 52–62.

Strasser, Steven, ed. *The 9/11 Investigations.* New York: Public Affairs, 2004.

Suedfeld, Peter, and Dana C. Leighton. "Early Communications in the War against Terrorism: An Integrative Complexity Analysis." *Political Psychology* 23, no. 3 (2002): 585–99.

Suskind, Ron. *The Price of Loyalty: George W. Bush, the White House, and the Education of Paul O'Neill.* New York: Simon and Schuster, 2004.

Tenet, George. *At the Center of the Storm: My Years at the CIA.* New York: HarperCollins, 2007.

Thatcher, Margaret. *The Downing Street Years.* New York: HarperCollins, 1993.

———. *Statecraft: Strategies for a Changing World.* London: HarperCollins, 2002.

Thiessen, Marc A., ed. *A Charge Kept: The Record of the Bush Presidency, 2001– 2009.* New York: Morgan James, 2009.

Waltz, Kenneth N. *Theory of International Politics*. New York: McGraw-Hill, 1979.

Washington Institute for Near East Policy. *Building for Peace: An American Strategy for the Middle East*, 1988. http://www.washingtoninstitute.org/templateC04.php?CID=9 (accessed July 15, 2008).

Weisberg, Jacob. *The Bush Tragedy*. New York: Random House, 2008.

Woodward, Bob. *Bush at War*. New York: Simon and Schuster, 2002.

———. *The Commanders*. New York: Simon and Schuster, 1991.

———. *Plan of Attack*. New York: Simon and Schuster, 2004.

———. *State of Denial: Bush at War, Part III*. New York: Simon and Schuster, 2006.

———. *The War Within: A Secret White House History, 2006–2008*. New York: Simon and Schuster, 2008.

Zelikow, Philip, and Condoleezza Rice. *Germany Unified and Europe Transformed: A Study in Statecraft*. Cambridge, MA: Harvard University Press, 1995.

## GOVERNMENT DOCUMENTS

Again, I have not included all documents below. In some cases, as with *The National Security Archive, The Palestine* Papers, United Nations Security Council resolutions, and the George W. Bush White House, State Department, and Defense Department archives, I list only the Internet homepage for the site. The documents used throughout the book may be obtained from there.

*Authorization for the Use of Military Force against Iraq Resolution*. S.J. Res. 2. Joint Resolution. 102nd Cong., 1st sess. January 12, 1991. The Library of Congress. http://thomas.loc.gov/cgi-bin/query/D?c102:1:./temp/~c10288xHeE (accessed June 4, 2008).

*Authorization for the Use of Military Force against Iraq Resolution of 2002*. Public Law 107-243, 102nd Cong., 1st sess., October 16, 2002. http://c-span.org/resources/pdf/hjres114.pdf (accessed June 26, 2008).

Baker, James A., III, Lee H. Hamilton, Lawrence S. Eagleburger, Vernon E. Jordan Jr., Edwin Meese III, Sandra Day O'Connor, Leon E. Panetta, William J. Perry, Charles S. Robb, and Alan K. Simpson. *The Iraq Study Group Report: The Way Forward—A New Approach*. New York: Vintage Books, 2006.

*Coalition Provisional Authority Order Number 1: De-Ba'athification of Iraqi Society*, May 16, 2003. http://www.iraqcoalition.org/regulations/20030516_CPAORD_1_DeBa_athification_of_Iraqi_Society_.pdf (accessed June 16, 2010).

*Coalition Provisional Authority Order Number 2: Dissolution of Entities*, May 23, 2003. http://www.iraqcoalition.org/regulations/20030823_CPAORD_2_Dissolution_of_Entities_with_Annex_A.pdf (accessed June 16, 2010).

"Declaration of Howard Teicher." United States District Court, Southern

District of Florida, January 31, 1995. http://naderlibrary.com/nader
.declhowardteicher.htm (accessed April 29, 2008).

DOD/OUSDP Memorandum. "Read Ahead for Secretary Rumsfeld RC Meeting,
Tuesday April 16, 2002: 'Necessity for Full Range of Training for Iraqi Oppo-
sition,'" April 12, 2002. http://www.waranddecision.com/doclib/20080420_
Readaheadontrainingopp.pdf (accessed April 22, 2011).

*Foreign Assistance Legislation for FY92–FY93.* HR Committee on Foreign Affairs.
102nd Cong., 1st sess., February 6–7, 1991.

*Iraq Liberation Act of 1998.* HR 4655, 105th Cong., 2nd sess. The Library of Congress.
http://thomas.loc.gov/cgi-bin/query/z?c105:H.R.4655.ENR (accessed June
4, 2008).

*Iraq Policy Documents.* http://merln.ndu.edu/MERLN/PFIraq/policyFileIraq
.html.

"The Iraq War—Part I: The U.S. Prepares for Conflict." The National Security Archive, n.d. George Washington University. http://www.gwu.edu/~nsarchiv/
NSAEBB/NSAEBB326/index.htm (accessed January 10, 2011).

"The Iraq War—Part II: Was There Even a Decision?" The National Security Archive, n.d. George Washington University. http://www.gwu.edu/~nsarchiv/
NSAEBB/NSAEBB328/index.htm (accessed January 10, 2011).

"The Iraq War—Part III: Shaping the Debate." The National Security Archive, n.d.
George Washington University. http://www.gwu.edu/~nsarchiv/NSAEBB/
NSAEBB330/index.htm (accessed January 10, 2011).

Kean, Thomas H., and Lee H. Hamilton. *The 9/11 Report: The National Commission on Terrorist Attacks upon the United States.* New York: St. Martin's, 2004.

*The Palestine Papers.* Al Jazeera Transparency Unit. http://transparency.aljazeera
.net/en/project/palestine-papers (accessed January 10, 2011).

"A Performance-Based Roadmap to a Permanent Two-State Solution to the Israeli-
Palestinian Conflict." Israel Ministry of Foreign Affairs, April 30, 2003. http://
www.state.gov/r/pa/prs/ps/2003/20062.htm (accessed April 20, 2012).

Rumsfeld, Donald H. "Prepared Testimony by the U.S. Secretary of Defense
Donald H. Rumsfeld." Senate Armed Services Committee Hearings on
Iraq, September 19, 2002. http://www.globalsecurity.org/military/library/
congress/2002_hr/rumsfeld919.pdf (accessed June 20, 2008).

"Sharm el-Sheikh Fact-Finding Committee: The Mitchell Plan, April 30, 2001."
http://www.yale.edu/lawweb/avalon/mideast/mitchell_plan.htm (accessed
August 3, 2008).

Sharp, Jeremy M. "Iraq: A Compilation of Legislation Enacted and Resolutions
Adopted by Congress, 1990–2003." *CRS Report for Congress,* March 27, 2003.
http://www.fpc.state.gov/documents/organization/19131.pdf (accessed July
4, 2009).

"Special Document—The Shamir Four-Point Plan." *Journal of Palestine Studies*
20, no. 4 (1991): 149–50.

"The Tenet Plan: Israeli-Palestinian Ceasefire and Security Plan, Proposed by CIA Director George Tenet; June 13, 2001." http://www.yale.edu/lawweb/avalon/mideast/mid023.htm (accessed August 4, 2008).

United Nations Security Council. http://www.un.org/Docs/sc/ (accessed December 20, 2011).

United States Department of Defense Secretary of Defense Speech Archive. http://www.defense.gov/speeches/SecDefArchive.aspx (accessed December 20, 2011).

United States State Department Archive. http://2001–2009.state.gov/ (accessed December 20, 2011).

The White House. President George W. Bush. http://georgewbush-whitehouse.archives.gov/ (accessed December 20, 2011).

# Index